Table of Contents

PRACTICE
MAKES
PERFECT

SPANISH VERB TENSES

Dorothy Devney Richmond

Printed on recyclable paper

PASSPORT BOOKS
a division of *NTC Publishing Group*
Lincolnwood, Illinois USA

To Martin

About the Author

Dorothy Devney Richmond is a private Spanish instructor and also teaches Spanish at the University of St. Thomas in St. Paul, Minnesota.

Ms. Devney Richmond holds degrees in Linguistics, Philosophy, and Educational Administration. She has studied and lived in Colombia and has traveled widely throughout South America.

In addition to *Practice Makes Perfect: Spanish Verb Tenses,* Ms. Devney Richmond has published, also through Passport Books, *Guide to Spanish Suffixes* (1992). She has also written *No-Fail Spanish,* a beginning work-text for adults, and two books for children studying Spanish: *Mi Primer Libro de Español* and *Mi Segundo Libro de Español.*

Acknowledgments

The contributions of several extraordinary people are to be found throughout this book, and I want each one to know that I am grateful for his or her talent, wisdom, and friendship. My first thanks go to Gilmore T. Schjeldahl, a former private student, whose interest in language construction turned many of our Spanish classes into Linguistics seminars. It was during these classes that the idea for this book arose and the original outline was laid. Lola Lorenzo, a native of Madrid who worked with me on another book, proofread and improved greatly the first manuscript. Lola also contributed to the list of Verbs That Take a Preposition. Joe Thurston, a true technological wizard who has helped me with many projects, took on the computer aspects of writing this book, and in the process forestalled a major memory crisis. His talents and humor once again proved invaluable. Curt Roy, who has studied with me privately for several years, and who since the beginning showed a distinct taste for linguistic analysis, worked through nearly every inch of this book and was delightfully candid in letting me know what made sense and what did not. I am confident that Curt has done a great service to users of this book. Two of my students from the University of St. Thomas, Mary Monn and Karen Muller, graciously and carefully worked through several chapters, each offering helpful comments and suggestions from the serious student's perspective. Carlos Badessich, Associate Professor of Spanish at the University of St. Thomas, answered countless *preguntas,* going well beyond the usual standards of academic generosity. Susana Blanco Iglesias proofread the final manuscript. Susana's intelligence and wit turned this long and arduous job into several highly productive and enjoyable sessions. I was fortunate to work with Tim Rogus, Senior Foreign Language Editor for NTC Publishing Group. Tim's ideas and suggestions were no less than inspired, and the result is a book of far greater scope and clarity than the one originally submitted. Elizabeth Millán, Foreign Language Editor for NTC, then took on the task of turning the final manuscript into the text you now have. This is a monumental job that requires artistry and grace combined with meticulous attention to detail and academics. Elizabeth came through in all areas. I reserve for myself sole responsibility for any errors. The contributions of these highly talented people turned the work involved in preparing this book into a marvelous journey. I am honored to know and be associated with each of them.

Dorothy Devney Richmond

Introduction

More than any other aspect of learning a foreign language, verbs challenge the learner. *Practice Makes Perfect: Spanish Verb Tenses* is a systematic, logical approach to the study of Spanish verbs, including their tenses, moods, and special uses. This information is provided in a workbook format, with clear explanations of each use of a verb. Each section contains exercises which relate directly to material most recently covered and which also bring in previously covered material for constant review. Some of the exercises are open-ended and require readers to supply the information that relates to them. One example of this kind of exercise is the True-False questionnaire that accompanies many of the units.

Spanish Verb Tenses takes you far beyond the rote memorization so commonly associated with studying verbs and tenses and enables you to grasp fully the importance as well as the subtleties the verb plays in every sentence we utter, write, read, or think.

The verb is the engine of the sentence. Without a verb, the sentence technically and figuratively goes nowhere. Thus, a careful, systematic study of verbs in any language is crucial to communication in any form.

Yet this careful study of the verbs need not be the drudge work so commonly associated with verbs, namely, memorizing a zillion conjugations. If you think of working with verbs as creating a scaffolding for the language, which is really what verbs provide, the task at hand can seem far more meaningful and less daunting.

You may have already seen several Spanish verb books, and may be wondering what, if anything, another verb book on the market could add. What sets *Spanish Verb Tenses* apart from other Spanish verb books is its scope and intent to teach the full picture with regard to verbs.

Most books devoted to Spanish verbs provide you with conjugations and little else. At times exercises are provided, but the emphasis nearly always is on the mechanical aspect of conjugating the verb, rendering these books more verb dictionaries than actual teaching or reviewing texts. And while correctly conjugating a verb is an extremely important aspect of speaking and writing well, it is still pure mechanics unless you understand the implications of one use of a verb over another and why you choose this particular use.

Practice Makes Perfect: Spanish Verb Tenses offers you not only hundreds of verbs with their particular conjugations, but also lets you know both when and *why* a particular verb can be used: You are given social, philosophical, and linguistic reasons and applications for the use of verbs.

The Spanish word for *tense,* in the grammatical sense, is *tiempo,* which is also the Spanish word for *time.* The philosophical and psychological aspects of time, so central to working with the tenses, unfortunately often are overlooked. To take something so rich as language, the vehicle of thought, and pare it down to its technical particulars, is to take something that is very beautiful and diminish it.

My experience with students of Spanish has taught me that the degree of difficulty of the task before them is not a determinant either of interest or success. What I have learned is that a step-by-step, logical approach, which includes clear explanations and reasons for learning Spanish well, intrigues the learner. Interest, not ease, is the greatest guarantor of success.

There are three main parts to this book:

Part I–The Present Tense: The twelve units in this part cover verb usage from basic conjugation of regular verbs, formation of questions, detailed information and work on the challenging verbs *ser* and *estar* (the verbs *to be*), use of the personal *a,* reflexive verbs, a host of irregular verbs along with their uses and nuances, and the present progressive mood.

Part II—The Past, Future, and Conditional Tenses: This part covers the six most basic indicative tenses (after the present): preterite; imperfect; future; conditional; present perfect; and past perfect. Their uses, conjugations, and various applications are discussed, and ample exercises are included.

Part III—The Imperative, Subjunctive, and Compound Tenses, and the Passive Voice: This final section of the text begins with the imperative (command form), which sets up nicely the next chapter, the present subjunctive. These are followed by the imperfect subjunctive; future perfect; conditional perfect; present perfect subjunctive; pluperfect subjunctive, and, finally, the passive voice, which covers all tenses in this special use.

Following the text are two appendices: Conjugation charts for all the tenses except for the present, and a very helpful list of verbs that require a preposition before another word. Also included in this book are contextual glossaries, Spanish-English and English-Spanish.

Spanish Verb Tenses will be helpful to motivated high-school and college students and adults, who are either starting fresh or returning to study Spanish. It is an excellent companion to any Spanish language basic text and is a superb review workbook. *Spanish Verb Tenses* is also a sound reference source for both teachers and students of Spanish.

It is my sincere wish that this book will help those studying Spanish, at any level, to achieve their goals of speaking, writing, and reading this beautiful language with greater competence, confidence, and enjoyment.

Dorothy Devney Richmond

PART I

The Present Tense

The Present Tense

The **present tense** is used to report what is happening and what is true *now*. The **present tense** can be pin-point specific or cover vast amounts of time. Whether the action referred to is true only at this very moment or its truth sweeps over eons, the key is that at its core it still must be true *now*, at this very moment. Consider four kinds of "present" below:

The specific *present*—"right now":

> It *is* 10:32:44 P.M.

> At this very moment I *see* a shooting star.

> I now *pronounce* you husband and wife.

The broader, yet enclosed *present*:

> I *work out* at the gym four times a week.

> Every Friday Mitch *brings* doughnuts to the office.

> We *go* to our cabin three or four times a year.

The progressive *present*:

> I *am eating* a doughnut.

> You *are studying*.

> He *is reading* a book.

The general, ongoing *present*:

> Nearly all countries *have* some form of organized government.

> The President of the United States *lives* in Washington, D.C.

> The Pope *is* the head of the Catholic Church.

Some Basic Terminology for Verbs

infinitive: The verb in its pure form; the idea of the verb. In English, all infinitives include the word "to": to sing; to eat; to live, etc. In Spanish, all infinitives end in either *-ar, -er,* or *-ir: cantar* (*to sing*); *comer* (*to eat*); *vivir* (*to live*). The infinitive is like a hand grenade before you pull the pin: no real action, but a lot of potential.

conjugation: Changing the verb from its infinitive form (where there is no action) so that it agrees with a subject (actor) and thus has a referent in reality: from "to sing" (infinitive—no action) to "Mary sings." In this sentence, "sings" is a conjugated verb. When you conjugate a verb, you pull the pin from the hand grenade and release its action.

verb base (stem or root): All infinitives end in either *-ar, -er,* or *-ir.* When you drop these, you are left with the verb base. The verb base of *cantar* is *cant-;* the base of *comer* is *com-,* and the base of *vivir* is *viv-.*

verb ending: What you will add to the verb base in order to conjugate the verb.

subject: The actor(s) in the sentence. *Mary* sings. *We* eat. *I* live.

regular verb: A verb is regular if its verb base remains intact, and regular *-ar, -er,* or *-ir* endings are attached to it.

irregular verb: A verb is irregular if its verb base does not remain intact, and/or it does not take a regular *-ar, -er,* or *-ir* ending.

Subject Pronouns

In English there are seven subject pronouns: I; you; he; she; it; we; they. In Spanish one has the same set of pronouns to choose from; however, the selection is greater due to gender ("we," "they," and the second person, plural form of "you" have masculine and feminine forms) as well as the broader use of the word "you" (there are four words for "you" in Spanish).

For the most part, the word "it" is an understood subject and thus there is no specific word for "it" in this context. The subject pronouns are as follows:

Singular	Plural
yo (I)	**nosotros** (we—masc./masc. & fem.) **nosotras** (we—fem. only)
tú (you—familiar)	**vosotros** (you—familiar; masc./masc. & fem.) **vosotras** (you—familiar; fem.)
él (he) **ella** (she) **usted** (you—formal)	**ellos** (they—masc./masc. & fem.) **ellas** (they—fem. only) **ustedes** (you—formal)

It is important to note that the familiar plural **vosotros** form is used primarily in Peninsular Spanish (i.e., in Spain), while throughout Latin America **ustedes** is used in both formal and familiar situations. In the exercises in this text, notation will be made letting you know which form to use: *pl. fam.* means "plural familiar" and *pl. form.* means "plural formal." Unless noted, *you* should be translated by the singular, familiar *tú.*

Conjugation of Regular Verbs

Conjugation of Regular *-ar* Verbs

All English verbs in their infinitive form are preceded by the word "to": to speak, to work, to study, etc. All Spanish verbs in their infinitive form end either in *-ar, -er,* or *-ir.* In this section we are going to deal with regular *-ar* verbs.

The term *conjugation,* in grammatical study, refers to the change the verb makes in order to accommodate the subject of the sentence. In English not a lot of conjugation goes on: I *speak;* you *speak;* he *speaks;* she *speaks;* we *speak;* they *speak.* Only the third person, singular, makes the change in most English verbs (present tense), taking on the letter "s."

When conjugating regular *-ar* verbs, there are six different verb endings that correspond to the six boxes in the Subject Pronoun chart.

Simple Sentence Construction

The minimum you need to create a sentence are a subject (someone or something doing something) and a verb (that which is being done). The following recipe is all you need in order to create simple sentences in Spanish:

Subject Pronoun + Verb Base + Verb Ending

1. Subject pronouns are listed on the previous page.

2. The verb base (or stem) is attained by stripping the infinitive of its *-ar* ending.

   example: to sing = **cantar:** remove the *-ar,* and you have **cant,** the verb base.

3. The ending is what you attach directly to the verb base. The six *-ar* endings are listed below and correspond to the Subject Pronoun chart.

Regular -ar Endings			
yo	o	nosotros nosotras	**amos** **amos**
tú	as	vosotros vosotras	**áis** **áis**
él ella usted	a a a	ellos ellas ustedes	**an** **an** **an**

Note: The abbreviation for **usted** is **Ud.**, and for **ustedes** it is **Uds.** Both are commonly used in writing and always are capitalized.

You are now ready to create simple sentences.

Following the recipe, **Subject + Verb Base + Verb Ending,** you first need to select a subject. We will use **yo** (I). Next, choose a verb. We will use **hablar** (to speak). Take off the **-ar,** and you have the verb base, *habl-.* Finally, select the ending that goes with your subject: As we are using **yo,** that ending must be **o.**

Subject + Verb Base + Verb Ending

yo   habl   o   = yo hablo (I speak)

This is all you need to do in order to conjugate a verb and to create a simple sentence. Below is the completely conjugated verb **hablar:**

yo hablo (I speak)

nosotros hablamos (we speak—masc./masc. & fem.)
nosotras hablamos (we speak—fem.)

tú hablas (you speak)

vosotros habláis (you all speak—masc./masc. & fem.)
vosotras habláis (you all speak—fem.)

él habla (he speaks)
ella habla (she speaks)
Ud. habla (you speak)

ellos hablan (they speak—masc./masc. & fem.)
ellas hablan (they speak—fem.)
Uds. hablan (you all speak)

Listed below are several regular -ar verbs. This list is followed by exercises in which you can practice conjugating the verbs and creating simple sentences.

amar	to love	**hablar**	to speak, talk
andar	to walk	**llegar**	to arrive
bailar	to dance	**llevar**	to wear, carry
buscar	to look for, search for	**mirar**	to watch, look at
cantar	to sing	**pagar**	to pay (for)
comprar	to buy	**practicar**	to practice
entrar (en)	to enter (into)	**preparar**	to prepare
escuchar	to listen (to)	**tocar**	to touch, play (an instrument)
esperar	to hope, wait (for)	**tomar**	to take
estudiar	to study	**trabajar**	to work

Note: Some Spanish verbs inherently contain prepositions that we must add to the English equivalent, e.g., **escuchar** (to listen *to*): **yo *escucho* la radio** = I *listen to* the radio.

ejercicio | **1-1-1**

Traduce las siguientes frases:

1. I sing. _____

2. You sing. _____

3. He sings. _____

4. We sing. _____

5. They (*m.*) sing. _____

6. I pay. _____

7. I pay for the house. _____

8. You pay. _____

9. They (*f.*) pay. _____

10. She studies. _____

11. He studies. _____

12. I study. _____

13. We study. _____

14. You walk. _____

15. We walk. _____

16. I work. _____

17. He works. _____

18. They work. _____

19. We work. _____

20. He dances. _____

21. I love. _____

22. You love. _____

23. She loves. _____

24. We love. _____

25. They love. _____

26. I practice. _____

27. He practices. _____

28. They enter. _____

29. I watch the house. _____

30. I look at the garden. _____

31. They watch the car. _____

32. She listens. _____

33. They (*f.*) listen. _____

34. I listen. _____

35. He buys the car. _____

36. I buy the dog. _____

37. You buy the house. _____

38. I speak with Miguel. _____

39. She pays for the books. _____

40. We study Spanish. _____

¿Cuál es verdadero o falso para ti?

(Which is true or false for you?) Escribe la respuesta—una V o una F—en el espacio en blanco.

_____ 1. Yo hablo inglés.

_____ 2. Yo trabajo en un banco.

_____ 3. Yo estudio español en la escuela.

_____ 4. Yo canto muy bien.

_____ 5. Yo bailo muy bien.

_____ 6. Yo toco el piano.

_____ 7. Yo compro la ropa en Sears.

_____ 8. Yo miro la televisión en el dormitorio.

_____ 9. Yo preparo café en la mañana.

_____ 10. Mi amigo/a habla español.

_____ 11. Mi amigo/a trabaja en una tienda.

_____ 12. Mi amigo/a toca la guitarra.

Making a sentence negative: To make an affirmative sentence negative, simply add *no* directly before the verb.

examples:

Yo no hablo portugués.
I don't speak Portuguese.

Tú no escuchas la radio.
You don't listen to the radio.

Él no canta con el coro.
He doesn't sing with the choir.

Nosotros no trabajamos aquí.
We don't work here.

Vosotros no estudiáis francés.
You (pl. fam.) don't study French.

Ellos no esperan el autobús.
They don't wait for the bus.

¿Cuál es verdadero o falso para ti?

_____ 1. Yo no estudio italiano.

_____ 2. Yo no toco el trombón.

_____ 3. Yo no ando a la escuela.

_____ 4. Yo no llevo uniforme a la escuela.

_____ 5. Yo no hablo con mis amigos por teléfono.

_____ 6. Yo no canto en la iglesia.

_____ 7. Mis amigos y yo no estudiamos español.

_____ 8. Mis amigos y yo no miramos la televisión.

_____ 9. Mi mejor (*best*) amigo/a no trabaja en un restaurante.

_____ 10. Mi mejor amigo/a no toca el violín.

Conjugation of Regular *-er* Verbs

To conjugate regular *-er* verbs, you will follow the same rules set out in the previous section on the conjugation of regular *-ar* verbs. The only difference is in the endings, which are shown at the top of the next page.

Regular *-er* Endings			
yo	**o**	nosotros nosotras	**emos** **emos**
tú	**es**	vosotros vosotras	**éis** **éis**
él ella usted	**e** **e** **e**	ellos ellas ustedes	**en** **en** **en**

Below is the conjugated verb **comer** (to eat):

yo como   **nosotros comemos**
                                         nosotras comemos

tú comes   **vosotros coméis**
                                         vosotras coméis

él come   **ellos comen**
ella come   **ellas comen**
usted come   **ustedes comen**

Listed below are several regular *-er* verbs, followed by exercises which use them.

aprender	to learn	**deber**	to owe
beber	to drink	**leer**	to read
comer	to eat	**meter (en)**	to put (into)
cometer (un error)	to make (a mistake)	**poseer**	to possess, own
comprender	to understand	**romper**	to break
correr	to run	**temer**	to fear, dread
creer	to believe	**vender**	to sell

ejercicio   1-1-2

1. I learn. _____

2. I drink. _____

3. He drinks. _____

4. You eat. _____

5. We eat. _____

6. I understand. _____

7. I don't understand. _____

8. They understand. _____

9. You understand. _____

10. You don't understand. _____

11. I run. _____

12. You run. _____

13. She runs. _____

14. They don't run. _____

15. We run. _____

16. I believe. _____

17. I don't believe. _____

18. He believes. _____

19. We owe. _____

20. I read. _____

21. You read. _____

22. You don't read. _____

23. He reads. _____

24. She reads. _____

25. We read. _____

26. I make a mistake. _____

27. I put. _____

28. You put. _____

29. He puts. _____

30. We put. _____

31. They (*m.*) put. _____

32. They (*f.*) put. _____

33. We break. _____

34. They (*f.*) break. _____

35. I break. _____

36. You sell. _____

37. We sell. _____

38. I don't sell. _____

39. She doesn't sell. _____

40. We learn. _____

¿Cuál es verdadero o falso para ti?

*Note that when the subject is understood via the verb conjugation, for example, **Como** = I eat, the subject pronoun is not necessary.*

_____ 1. Como mucho en McDonald's.

_____ 2. Bebo leche cada día.

_____ 3. No comprendo francés.

_____ 4. Leo los libros de Agatha Christie.

_____ 5. Aprendo mucho en mi clase de español.

_____ 6. Sears vende ropa.

_____ 7. La biblioteca vende libros.

_____ 8. Corro en el maratón.

_____ 9. A veces (*at times*) cometo errores.

_____ 10. Normalmente, el gato bebe leche.

_____ 11. Creo en fantasmas.

_____ 12. Muchas personas en los Estados Unidos comprenden español.

Conjugation of Regular *-ir* Verbs

This is the final set of regular verbs. To conjugate regular *-ir* verbs, follow the same rules of conjugation as set forth in Unit 1 (page 5). Note that the endings, which are listed below, are the same as those for *-er* verbs except in the ***nosotros*** and ***vosotros*** boxes.

Regular *-ir* Endings			
yo	o	nosotros nosotras	**imos** **imos**
tú	es	vosotros vosotras	**ís** **ís**
él ella usted	e e e	ellos ellas ustedes	**en** **en** **en**

Below is the conjugated verb **vivir** (to live):

yo vivo	**nosotros vivimos** **nosotras vivimos**
tú vives	**vosotros vivís** **vosotras vivís**
él vive **ella vive** **usted vive**	**ellos viven** **ellas viven** **ustedes viven**

Listed below are several regular *-ir* verbs, followed by exercises using them.

abrir	to open	**escribir**	to write
admitir	to admit	**existir**	to exist
asistir (a)	to attend	**permitir**	to permit
cubrir	to cover	**recibir**	to receive
decidir	to decide	**subir**	to climb, go up
describir	to describe	**sufrir**	to suffer
descubrir	to discover	**unir**	to unite
discutir	to discuss	**vivir**	to live

ejercicio   1-1-3

1. I open the windows. _____

2. She suffers a lot. _____

3. We live in the United States. _____

4. You write a lot of letters. _____

5. The child admits everything (*todo*). _____

6. John climbs the staircase (*la escalera*). _____

7. I discover a cat in the house. _____

8. Many people suffer. _____

9. We decide. _____

10. Unicorns (*los unicornios*) don't exist. _____

11. You (*pl. form.*) write well. _____

12. Mary describes the spiders (*las arañas*). _____

13. We write many letters. _____

14. They don't attend school. _____

15. Mary and John discuss the book. _____

16. You unite the two parts (*las partes*). _____

17. The boys describe everything. _____

18. You (*pl. fam.*) cover the tables. _____

19. John doesn't attend the meeting (*la reunión*). _____

20. I receive gifts (*regalos*) for my birthday. _____

¿Cuál es verdadero o falso para ti?

_____ 1. Vivo en un apartamento.

_____ 2. Escribo mucho en mi clase de español.

_____ 3. Stephen King escribe libros de horror.

_____ 4. Recibo regalos en diciembre.

_____ 5. El Presidente de los Estados Unidos vive en Washington, D.C.

_____ 6. Asisto a la universidad.

_____ 7. Los fantasmas no existen.

_____ 8. Normalmente, no abro las ventanas de la casa en enero.

_____ 9. Discuto mis problemas con mis amigos.

_____ 10. Sufro mucho en mi clase de español.

_____ 11. Muchas oficinas no permiten fumar (*smoking*).

_____ 12. El jefe (*boss*) le describe el trabajo al empleado.

Asking Questions

Now that you can conjugate verbs and form sentences, the next step is forming questions.

Asking Simple Questions: A simple question is one which elicits either a "yes" or a "no" for an answer. In Spanish, this involves placing the conjugated verb in front of the subject.

Tú hablas español (You speak Spanish) becomes **¿Hablas tú español?** (Do you speak Spanish?)

In English, we often precede a formed sentence with the auxiliary verb *do* or *does* to create a question. In this context, the words *do* and *does* **do not exist** in Spanish.

¿Vives tú en España?
Do you live in Spain?

¿Trabajáis en el banco?
Do you (pl. fam.) work in the bank?

¿Come él aquí con frecuencia?
Does he eat here often?

¿Leen ellos el periódico cada día?
Do they read the newspaper every day?

ejercicio   1-1-4

(Remember that when the subject pronoun is understood, you may omit it.)

1. Do you speak English? _____

2. Do you understand? _____

3. Do you (*pl. fam.*) study a lot? _____

4. Does he sing well? _____

5. Does she sell clothing? _____

6. Does he work here? _____

7. Do they live there? _____

8. Do unicorns exist? _____

9. Does she write books? _____

10. Does he make many mistakes? _____

11. Do you read in the library? _____

12. Does she understand? _____

Asking Complex Questions: Complex questions are those requesting more than a simple "yes" or "no." The asker wants specific information or an explanation.

To form complex questions, you will precede a simple question (as formed above) with one of the following interrogatives. Note the accent marks:

¿Quién? ¿Quiénes?	Who? (*always* takes the 3rd person, singular or plural verb)
¿Qué?	What?
¿Cuándo?	When?
¿Dónde?	Where?
¿Por qué?	Why?
¿Cómo?	How?

examples:

¿Quién trabaja aquí?
Who works here?

¿Qué comes tú?
What are you eating?

¿Cuándo estudias?
When do you study?

¿Dónde viven ellos?
Where do they live?

¿Por qué existimos?
Why do we exist?

¿Cómo decido yo?
How do I decide?

ejercicio   1-1-5

1. Where do you live? _____

2. Where do you work? _____

3. When do you study? _____

4. When do you write? _____

5. Who understands? _____

6. Who doesn't sing? _____

7. Why does he dance? _____

8. Why do we work? _____

9. What are you preparing? _____

10. What are you (*pl. form.*) watching? _____

11. How do they sell so much (*tanto*)? _____

12. How does she read so much? _____

> **Asking Limiting Questions:**   The person asking a limiting question wants to know *Which?* or *How much?* or *How many?* of the noun in question. In other words, the asker wants a limit placed on that noun. *How many **books** do you read? I read **ten books.***

> To form limiting questions, use one of the interrogatives listed below: **¿Cuál?** (or **¿Cuáles?**) generally will be followed by a verb with the English word "one" or "ones" understood. **¿Cuánto?** (or **¿Cuántos?**) generally will be followed by a noun, and finally the appropriate conjugated verb. Study the examples below.

¿Cuál?	Which? (sing.)
¿Cuáles?	Which? (pl.)
¿Cuánto? (masc.); ¿Cuánta? (fem.)	How much?
¿Cuántos? (masc.); ¿Cuántas? (fem.)	How many?

examples:

¿Cuál prefieres?*   **¿Cuáles prefieres?**
Which (one) do you prefer?   *Which (ones) do you prefer?*

¿Cuánto pan come él?   **¿Cuántos libros** lees?
How much bread does he eat?   *How many books do you read?*

¿Cuánta leche bebe usted?   **¿Cuántas ciudades** visitan ustedes?
How much milk do you drink?   *How many cities do you visit?*

ejercicio   1-1-6

1. Which [one] functions (*funcionar*)? _____

2. Which [one] needs (*necesitar*) water? _____

3. Which [ones] function? _____

4. Which [ones] need water? _____

5. How much money do you (*form.*) pay? _____

6. How much Spanish do we learn? _____

7. How many cars do you buy? _____

8. How many books do you sell? _____

9. How much water does he drink? _____

---

*The verb *preferir* is irregular (it is discussed in Unit 8, Stem-Changing Verbs, page 52). It is used here because this is a very common use of this verb.

10. How much truth (*la verdad*) does he possess? _____

11. How many people live in Mexico? _____

12. How many windows do they open? _____

traducción   **1-1-7**

Marcos lives in Montana. His mother works in a school where she teaches music and Phys. Ed. In the morning she plays the piano, sings, and practices with the band. In the afternoon, her students and she run and walk a lot, and at times they dance. His father works in a bakery. He prepares and sells bread. He enters (into) the bakery very early in the morning, puts the bread into the oven, and waits. While he waits he reads the newspaper, watches television, listens to the radio, or studies Spanish (he writes and speaks very well). He admits that sometimes he takes a nap, but he does not admit when he makes a mistake. He receives many compliments. Many people in Montana buy and eat the bread from the bakery.

vocabulario

bakery	**la panadería**	oven	**el horno**
band	**la banda**	people	**las personas**
bread	**el pan**	Phys. Ed.	**educación física**
compliment	**el cumplido**	sometimes	**a veces**
early	**temprano**	student	**el estudiante**
morning	**la mañana**	(to) take a nap	**echar una siesta**
music	**música**	(to) teach	**enseñar**
newspaper	**el periódico**	very	**muy**

_____

_____

_____

_____

_____

_____

_____

Ser and *Estar*

Of all the verbs in the Spanish language, **ser** and **estar** present perhaps the greatest hurdles for the native English speaker. However, because they are two of the most crucial verbs in the language, they deserve the attention they require for their mastery.

To begin, **ser** and **estar** are irregular verbs. This means that they do not follow the nice, tidy conjugations you learned in the preceding unit. Thus you must commit to memory their various forms.

The hurdles referred to, however, have not so much to do with memorizing their forms as learning when to use which verb: **ser** and **estar** both mean "to be." In English, we have only one verb "to be," which, when conjugated, translates to: I *am*, you *are*, he *is*, she *is*, we *are*, they *are*. In Spanish both **ser** and **estar** translate to these same meanings, but contain within them more exact implications. Thus, in learning to work with **ser** and **estar**, you are, in effect, being asked to separate into categories various ways of *being*.

The simplest, but by no means all-inclusive, dichotomy to be made of these verbs is to say that **ser** is used in *enduring* situations, while **estar** is used in situations that are *short-term*, or which involve *location* or the result of some action. Thus, if you want to say, "I *am* a human being," you will use the verb **ser**, but if you want to say, "I *am* kneeling," "I *am* in the library," or "The window *is* open," you will use the verb **estar**.

Below are the conjugations of **ser** and **estar**, followed by a more complete discussion of when you will use these verbs.

ser *(to be)*	
yo soy (I am)	**nosotros somos** (we are—m./m. & f.) **nosotras somos** (we are—f.)
tú eres (you are)	**vosotros sois** (you all are—m./m. & f.) **vosotras sois** (you all are—f.)
él es (he is) **ella es** (she is) **usted es** (you are)	**ellos son** (they are—m./m. & f.) **ellas son** (they are—f.) **ustedes son** (you all are)

estar *(to be)*	
yo estoy (I am)	**nosotros estamos** (we are—m./m. & f.) **nosotras estamos** (we are—f.)
tú estás (you are)	**vosotros estáis** (you all are—m./m. & f.) **vosotras estáis** (you all are—f.)
él está (he is) **ella está** (she is) **usted está** (you are)	**ellos están** (they are—m./m. & f.) **ellas están** (they are—f.) **ustedes están** (you all are)

Situations in which *ser* is used

Origin: One's origin is an unchangeable fact, one of the few truly permanent aspects of one's life. It does not matter where you live now: If you were born in Minnesota, you *always* will be from Minnesota. Thus, you would say:

Yo **soy** de Minnesota. I *am* from Minnesota.

¿De dónde **eres** tú? Where *are* you from?

Yuri **es** de Rusia. Yuri *is* from Russia.

Relationships: There are two types of relationships one can have with others: familial and selected.

Familial: These are blood relationships (parents, siblings, cousins, etc.), and even though these relationships may sometimes be volatile, they do endure. Thus, one says:

Ellos **son** mis padres. They *are* my parents.

Vosotros **sois** mis hermanos. You *are* my brothers.

Ella **es** mi hermana. She *is* my sister.

Selected: Friends, enemies, spouses, employers, etc., achieve relationships with us by selection. And while the status of these relationships does change from time to time, a person generally operates under the assumption that a friend today will be a friend tomorrow, till death do us part. Thus, one says:

Tú **eres** mi amigo. You *are* my friend.

Él **es** mi esposo. He *is* my husband.

Somos vecinos. *We are* neighbors.

Physical attributes: Aspects of one's body are not to be taken lightly: They go everywhere with a person—they are not changed by location or how one feels. Even though hair color goes from brunette to gray, and beauty sometimes fades, these changes generally do not take place overnight; rather, they are considered enduring.

Yo **soy** alto/a. I *am* tall.

Rizitos de Oro **es** rubia. Goldilocks *is* blonde.

Ellos **son** delgados. They *are* slim.

Personality characteristics: Like physical attributes, personalities do change from time to time; however, people tend to behave and react to life pretty much the same one day to the next (do not confuse one's personality with his or her moods which can and do change quickly, and thus are covered under *estar*).

> Ella **es** amable. She *is* nice.

> Ustedes **son** cómicos. You all *are* funny.

> **Eres** cortés. *You are* polite.

Possession: What is yours is yours and nobody can take it from you. Even as you write your will, the house and all its priceless knickknacks are still yours. Just because you can't take them with you doesn't mean they aren't yours until you go!

> La casa **es** mía. The house *is* mine.

> El cristal **es** mío. The crystal *is* mine.

> Nada aquí **es** tuyo. Nothing here *is* yours.

Profession: It is true that most people change jobs, and even careers, many times in their lives. However, one generally does not accept a job offer only to turn around and write his or her letter of resignation. When one is employed, even part-time, the employee takes on the aspects of that position, as though it were an added personality characteristic.

> Perry Mason **es** abogado. Perry Mason *is* a lawyer.

> Kate Moss y Fabio **son** modelos. Kate Moss and Fabio *are* models.

> Ustedes **son** estudiantes. All of you *are* students.

Identification: When identifying anything, whether animal, vegetable, or mineral, you will use *ser*. Some linguistic philosophers will tell you (if you ask) that, independent of the object, names (or identifying words) are meaningless. In other words, the name *is* the object, and thus endures as long as does its referent.

> Ésta **es** una frase. This *is* a sentence.

> El señor Ed **es** un caballo. Mr. Ed *is* a horse.

> Éstos **son** calcetines. These *are* socks.

Date and time: However fleeting time may seem (and therefore short-term—*estar* territory), it still must be argued that now is now. In other words, though it may appear odd to regard the statement, "It is June 11," as enduring, realize that the unstated subject is "Today," as in "Today *is* June 11." Thus, giving the date is actually a form of identification. Similarly, with time, "It is 10:30" has as its unstated subject *now*.

> Hoy **es** el veintiséis de septiembre. Today *is* September 26.

> Mañana **es** sábado. Tomorrow *is* Saturday.

> ¿Qué hora **es?** What time *is* it?

> **Son** las tres de la mañana. It's 3:00 a.m.

Nationality: This is similar to origin, in that your place of birth never can be denied. However, the United States being the great melting pot that it is, we differ from persons in many other countries because here one's origin and nationality often differ. Thus, one could say, "Yo *soy* de los Estados Unidos," indicating *origin,* and, in the same breath, "Yo *soy* francés," indicating *nationality.* Note that nationalities are not capitalized in Spanish.

Gabriel García Márquez **es** colombiano. Gabriel García Márquez *is* Colombian.

La Princesa Diana **es** inglesa. Princess Diana *is* English.

Dudley Doright **es** canadiense. Dudley Doright *is* Canadian.

Natural color: This is a bit tricky, because color can take either *ser* or *estar*, depending on the changeability of the color. Obviously, grass is green, the sky is blue, and snow is white—in the abstract. However, there are times when the grass is not green, say, after a drought, and who has never seen gray skies or yellow snow? (At these times you would use *estar*.) So remember, when an object is referred to in its natural color, you will use *ser*.

La leche **es** blanca. Milk *is* white.

Mi casa **es** marrón. My house *is* brown.

La bandera de Japón **es** roja y blanca. Japan's flag *is* red and white.

¿Cuál es verdadero o falso para ti?

_____ 1. Soy estudiante.

_____ 2. Mi casa es blanca.

_____ 3. Mi jefe (*boss*) y yo somos amigos.

_____ 4. Mi mejor (*best*) amigo es mecánico.

_____ 5. Oprah Winfrey es inteligente.

_____ 6. El clima de Hawai es tropical.

_____ 7. Los colores rojo y azul son mis favoritos.

_____ 8. Las hamburguesas son muy populares en los Estados Unidos.

_____ 9. Beethoven es famoso por su música.

_____ 10. Shakespeare es famoso por sus pinturas.

_____ 11. Soy arquitecto.

_____ 12. No soy profesor de inglés.

ejercicio	1-2-1

These sentences take the verb **ser** *only.*

1. I am from the United States. _____

2. You are my friend. _____

3. He is handsome. _____

4. She is very interesting. _____

5. They are astronauts (*astronautas*) from another planet (*el planeta*). _____

_____

6. You (*pl. fam.*) are American. _____

7. Today is Monday. _____

8. My socks are white. _____

9. Elizabeth Taylor is an actress. _____

10. He is tall. _____ She is tall. _____

11. They are handsome men. _____

12. Where are you all (*pl. fam.*) from? _____

13. We are from Panama. _____

14. What time is it? _____

   It is ten o'clock. _____

15. Who are you? _____ Who are they? _____

16. They are not my friends. _____

17. Fido is my dog and Fufu is your cat. _____

18. Hamburgers and French fries are very popular in the United States. _____

_____

19. What is this? _____ It is a shoe. _____

20. What is this? _____ It is a flower. _____

Situations in which *estar* is used

Location: The location of *anything* takes *estar*. Whether it is short-term (I *am* in the shower) or permanent (Paris *is* in France), if it's location you're dealing with, your verb is *estar* (not *ser*).

   Yo **estoy** en el comedor. I *am* in the dining room.

   ¿Dónde **estás** tú? Where *are* you?

   ¿Dónde **está** Londres? Where *is* London?

Mood: One's mood could be termed a short-term personality characteristic. Our moods describe how we feel at any given moment. In our discussion of *ser*, we learned that personality characteristics tend to be pervasive and enduring. But your moods, like your emotional status, ride the roller coaster of life: One day you're happy, the next day you're sad—it all depends on the ever-changing circumstances of your life.

   Yo **estoy** feliz. I *am* happy.

   Ellos **están** tristes. They *are* sad.

   Vosotros **estáis** enojados. You (*pl. fam.*) *are* angry.

   Ella **está** de buen/mal humor. She *is* in a good/bad mood.

Physical condition: Like your moods, how you feel physically also changes from day to day: one day hale and hearty, the next day sick as a dog.

>Ella **está** bien. She *is* fine.
>
>**Estamos** enfermos. *We are* sick.
>
>Ellos **están** cansados. They *are* tired.

Result of action: This refers to what you are doing. If you have just sat down, it means that you are seated. Soon you will be standing and, if you are studying this in church, you may be kneeling any minute now. Even being dead, which is about as enduring as it gets, takes *estar*, for it is the result of having lived.

>**Estoy** sentado/a. I *am* seated.
>
>**Estás** de pie. *You are* standing.
>
>Ella **está** de rodillas. She *is* kneeling.
>
>La mosca **está** muerta. The fly *is* dead.
>
>Estos televisores **están** dañados. These television sets *are* broken.

Unnatural color or condition: When you are very sick, your face may turn green; however, unless you are from another planet, this color is unnatural (and unattractive) to you. Meat that has sat around far too long takes on an unsavory shade of gray; bananas turn black; and old newspapers turn yellow. In a nutshell, in describing things that aren't as they were originally intended, you will use *estar*.

>El cielo **está** gris. The sky *is* gray.
>
>Esta nieve **está** amarilla. This snow *is* yellow.
>
>Las manos **están** sucias. Her hands *are* dirty.
>
>Él **está** feo con esos pantalones. He *is* ugly in those pants.

Going from the general to the particular: If you like coffee as I do, then you would agree that "El café *es* la bebida de los dioses" (Coffee *is* the drink of the gods), and you would use *ser* to express this absolute truth. This does not mean, however, that every individual cup of coffee in the world is wonderful. So, when referring to a *specific* cup of coffee, or plate of spaghetti or order of fries, you will use *estar*.

>Este café **está** muy bueno. This coffee *is* very good.
>
>Este café **está** malísimo. This coffee *is* horrible.
>
>Estas papas fritas **están** riquísimas. These French fries *are* delicious.

¿Verdadero o falso?

_____ 1. Estoy en mi casa.

_____ 2. Estoy interesado/a en español.

_____ 3. Mi mejor amigo/a probablemente está en casa.

_____ 4. México está en Norteamérica.

_____ 5. Madrid y Sevilla están en España.

_____ 6. Mi mejor amigo/a y yo estamos enfermos/as.

_____ 7. Estoy sentado/a.

_____ 8. A veces, una persona está de rodillas en la iglesia.

_____ 9. No estoy de pie.

_____ 10. Cristóbal Colón está muerto.

_____ 11. Cuando miro la televisión por muchas horas, estoy aburrido/a.

_____ 12. Normalmente, mis amigos y yo estamos de buen humor.

ejercicio   1-2-2

*These sentences take the verb **estar** only.*

1. I am with John. _____ I am not with John. _____

2. She is with Marcos. _____ She is not with Marcos. _____

3. I am fine. _____ I am not happy. _____

4. Where are you? _____ Where is Felipe? _____

5. John is mad. _____ They are mad. _____

6. Jane is standing but we are sitting. _____

7. I am sad because you are not here. _____

8. Jane is anxious because we are not ready. _____

9. He is kneeling because we are in the church. _____

10. The chairs are not in the kitchen. _____

11. Many boys are in the house. _____

12. Why are you (*pl. fam.*) here? _____

13. Argentina is in South America. _____

14. Are the dogs in the living room? _____

15. The tomatoes are green. _____

16. This chicken (*el pollo*) is very good! _____

17. John is depressed (*deprimido*). _____

18. Why aren't you happy? _____

19. She is embarrassed (*avergonzada*). _____

20. They are in a bad mood because the television is broken and therefore (*por eso*) they are bored.

_____

ejercicio   **1-2-3**

*Fill in the blanks below with the appropriate use of **ser** or **estar**.*

1. Yo _____ enfermo/a.

2. Yo _____ alto/a.

3. Tú _____ en la escuela.

4. Ellos _____ americanos.

5. Juan _____ feliz.

6. Tú _____ una persona amable.

7. Nosotros _____ tristes.

8. Este pescado _____ delicioso.

9. Vosotras _____ bonitas.

10. ¿Cómo _____ tú?

11. ¿Dónde _____ Juan?

12. ¿De dónde _____ tú?

13. Martín _____ médico.

14. Mis plumas _____ rojas.

15. Ustedes _____ con Paco y José.

16. Ellas _____ amigas de Felipe.

17. Tú _____ bajo/a.

18. Nosotros _____ bajos.

19. St. Paul _____ en Minnesota.

20. ¿Quién _____ el Presidente de los Estados Unidos?

21. La banana _____ negra.

22. Mi coche no _____ en el garaje.

23. ¿Qué hora _____ ?

_____ las dos y media de la tarde.

24. Vosotros _____ cansados.

25. Yo _____ de buen humor.

traducción   **1-2-4**

When I am happy I sing, but today I am in a bad mood. My cat is sick, my television is broken, and this morning my coffee is terrible. Today is Monday. I work in a bookstore. Two people are in the store now, a man and a woman. The man is tall and he is looking for books that don't exist. Why is he here? The woman is short and very thin. She buys the newspaper here every day. Sometimes she reads five or six magazines beforehand. She always wears sunglasses and a big hat. She is very mysterious. I believe that she is a spy. Who is she and why is she here?

vocabulario

(to) be in a bad mood	**estar de mal humor**	newspaper	**el periódico**
beforehand	**antes**	sometimes	**a veces**
bookstore	**la librería**	spy	**el/la espía**
every day	**cada día**	sunglasses	**las gafas de sol**
hat	**el sombrero**	this morning	**esta mañana**
here	**aquí**	today	**hoy**
(to) look for	**buscar**	very	**muy**
man	**el hombre**	woman	**la mujer**

Hay

The word *hay* is among the hardest-working words in the Spanish language. It is used to acknowledge the existence of a thing or things. And tiny as it is, it means all of the following:

1. There is . . . .

2. There are . . . .

3. Is there . . . ?

4. Are there . . . ?

examples:

Hay una mosca en mi sopa. *There is* a fly in my soup.

Hay cincuenta y dos naipes en una baraja. *There are* 52 cards in a deck.

¿Hay un médico en la casa? *Is there* a doctor in the house?

¿Cuántos peces **hay** en el océano? How many fish *are there* in the ocean?

No hay gasolina en el coche. *There isn't any* gas in the car.

¿Verdadero o falso?

_____ 1. Hay cincuenta estados en los Estados Unidos.

_____ 2. Hay muchos libros en la biblioteca.

_____ 3. Hay cinco baños en mi casa.

_____ 4. No hay ventanas en mi cocina.

_____ 5. En mi clase de español hay más de quince estudiantes.

_____ 6. Hay muchas tiendas en el Mega Mall en Minnesota.

_____ 7. Hay muchas estrellas (*stars*) de cine en Hollywood.

_____ 8. No hay leche en mi refrigerador ahora.

_____ 9. Hay ocho océanos distintos en el mundo.

_____10. Hay más personas en México que en la República Dominicana.

_____11. No hay azúcar en una Coca-Cola de dieta.

_____12. Hay un televisor en mi dormitorio.

ejercicio   **1-3-1**

1. There is a dog in the car. _____

2. There are three forks (*tenedores*) on the table. _____

3. Is there a bathroom in this building (*edificio*)? _____

4. Are there chairs (*sillas*) in the living room? _____

5. There isn't any water in the glass (*el vaso*). _____

Describe your house or apartment, using *hay* (*Hay dos baños; Hay tres ventanas en la cocina*, etc.).

Write your description below.

_____

_____

_____

_____

_____

_____

_____

_____

_____

_____

Tener

The verb *tener* (to have) is important in Spanish, not only because it is such a basic and often-used verb, but because of its many uses: (1) it can show possession; (2) it is used to show age; (3) it is used in several idiomatic expressions; and (4) it can show obligation. In this section we will consider all four of these uses. First, however, its conjugation (*tener* is an irregular verb):

tengo	**tenemos**
tienes	**tenéis**
tiene	**tienen**

Possession: The simplest and most common use of *tener* is to show possession.

Tengo un perro.
I have a dog.

Tenemos cinco dólares.
We have five dollars.

Tienes un hermano.
You have one brother.

Tenéis una casa bonita.
You (pl. fam.) have a pretty house.

Juan **tiene** un gato.
John *has* a cat.

Ellos **tienen** los tenedores.
They *have* the forks.

¿Verdadero o falso?

_____ 1. Tengo un animal doméstico.

_____ 2. El helado tiene muchas calorías.

_____ 3. Mi casa tiene tres dormitorios.

_____ 4. El café tiene cafeína.

_____ 5. Mi familia tiene una casa de vacaciones.

_____ 6. Los Estados Unidos tiene frontera con Canadá.

_____ 7. En mi clase de español, tenemos mucha tarea.

_____ 8. Muchas personas tienen más de un teléfono en la casa.

_____ 9. No tengo coche.

_____ 10. La tienda Sears tiene muchos departamentos.

ejercicio 1-4-1

1. I have ten dollars. _____

2. You have my books. _____

3. She has a diamond (*el diamante*). _____

4. He has the knives (*el cuchillo*) and the spoons (*la cuchara*). _____

_____

5. We have a new house. _____

6. All of you (*fam. pl.*) have many friends. _____

7. They have several cousins. _____

8. I don't have the money. _____

9. Who has my keys (*la llave*)? _____

10. Why do you have a bird (*el pájaro*) in your car? _____

_____

Age: In English, we use the verb *to be* to show age: I *am* twenty-nine years old. In Spanish, however, one *has* years: ***Tengo*** veintinueve años.

When asking the age of someone (or something), you literally will ask how many years (or months, days, etc.) he, she, or it has:

¿Cuántos años **tienes** tú? How old are you?

¿Cuántos años **tiene** Juan? How old is Juan?

¿Cuántos años **tiene** el coche? How old is the car?

¿Cuántos años **tienen** ellos? How old are they?

ejercicio 1-4-2

1. I am (*state how old you are*). _____

2. You are fifteen years old. _____

3. Mary is forty years old. _____

4. My car is four years old. _____

5. How old are you? _____

6. How old is the President? _____

7. Those boys are fifteen years old. _____

8. Her cat is eight years old. _____

9. Our house is one hundred years old. _____

10. How old are they? _____

Idiomatic expressions: There are several phrases in Spanish that use *tener* where in English we use the verb *to be*. For example, instead of *being hungry* (an adjective), one *has hunger* (a noun). Below is a list of the most common of these idiomatic expressions. Note (by **mucho** or **mucha**) which nouns are masculine and which are feminine.

tener (mucha) hambre	to be (very) hungry
tener (mucha) sed	to be (very) thirsty
tener (mucho) frío	to be (very) cold
tener (mucho) calor	to be (very) warm
tener (mucho) miedo	to be (very) afraid
tener (mucha) suerte	to be (very) lucky
tener (mucha) prisa	to be in a (big) hurry
tener (mucho) sueño	to be (very) sleepy, tired
tener razón	to be right
no tener razón	to be wrong

ejercicio   1-4-3

1. I am hungry. _____

2. You're thirsty. _____

3. He's cold. _____

4. We're lucky. _____

5. They're in a hurry. _____

6. I am very hungry. _____

7. You're very thirsty. _____

8. He's warm. _____

9. I'm very lucky. _____

10. You (*pl. fam.*) are in a big hurry. _____

_____   _____

ejercicio   1-4-4

How do you, or others, feel in the following situations?

1. Tú no comes nada hoy. _____

2. Juan compra una Coca-Cola. _____

3. Juanita gana un millón de dólares. _____

4. Es enero y tú no tienes un suéter. _____

5. Jorge cree que dos y dos son cinco. _____

6. María corre al autobús. _____

7. Es julio y tú estás en Puerto Rico. _____

8. Un monstruo está en tu armario. _____

9. Tú crees que seis menos cuatro son dos. _____

10. Es muy tarde y Ana y Margarita están bostezando (*yawning*). _____

> **Obligation:**   In order to show obligation, you will use the following recipe:
>
> **tener (conjugated) + que + infinitive**
>
> *examples:*
>
> **Tengo que practicar** el piano.   **¿Tenemos que comer** esta carne?
> *I have to practice* the piano.   *Do we have to eat* this meat?
>
> **Tienes que estudiar.**   **Tenéis que limpiar** la casa.
> *You have to study.*   *You (pl. fam.) have to clean* the house.
>
> **Juan tiene que estudiar.**   **Ellos tienen que bailar.**
> *John has to study.*   *They have to dance.*

ejercicio   1-4-5

1. I have to read this book. _____

2. You have to watch this program. _____

3. Fred and Ginger have to dance. _____

4. He has to open the store every morning. _____

5. We have to decide now. _____

6. You (*pl. fam.*) have to write thank-you letters (letters of thanks). _____

7. They have to sell their car. _____

8. I don't have to eat this soup. _____

9. You have to take the medicine. _____

10. We have to buy wine for the party. _____

¡Te toca a ti! (*It's your turn!*)

List five things that you have to do tomorrow:

1. _____

2. _____

3. _____

4. _____

5. _____

traducción	I-4-6

My name is Paco and today is my birthday. I am seven years old. All my friends are in my house because every year I have a big party. They are hungry and thirsty. I am hungry and thirsty, too. We have cake, ice cream, and milk. But first they have to sing "Happy Birthday." Afterwards we eat. Later I open my presents because there are many presents for me.

vocabulario

afterwards	**después**	first	**primero**
all	**todos**	great big (before a noun)	**gran**
also	**también**	Happy Birthday	**Feliz Cumpleaños**
because	**porque**	ice cream	**el helado**
birthday	**el cumpleaños**	later	**luego**
cake	**la torta**	party	**la fiesta**
every	**cada**	present	**el regalo**

_____

_____

_____

_____

_____

The Personal *a*

When the direct object of the verb is a specific person (or persons), you must place an *a* directly before the mention of that person (or persons). This is known as the personal *a*. The direct object is that noun which is affected directly by the verb, and it usually follows the verb immediately in both English and Spanish.

examples:

Yo amo **a** Lucy.　　　　　Miramos **a** Jorge.
I love Lucy.　　　　　　　We watch George.

Buscas **a** mi hermano.　　Esperáis **a** vuestro maestro.
You look for my brother.　You wait for your teacher.

Él ve **a** Susana.　　　　　Ellos aman **a** sus padres.
He sees Susan.　　　　　　They love their parents.

The personal *a* is unique to Spanish and, as you can see in the examples given above, it does not translate. Adding the personal *a* can be seen as a sign of respect, an acknowledgment that the person is more important than his or her car:

Veo a Juan.　　　　　　**Veo el coche de Juan.**
I see John.　　　　　　　I see John's car.

A few notes:

1. You will *not* use the personal *a* with the verbs **ser** (to be), **tener** (to have), or **hay** (there is; there are):

   Juan **es** colombiano.　　**Tengo** dos hermanos.
   John is Colombian.　　　I have two brothers.

   Hay un chico en la casa.
   There is a boy in the house.

2. You will *not* use the personal *a* when the direct object is an *unspecified* person:

   Necesito una secretaria　**Busco** un amigo leal.
   bilingüe.　　　　　　　　I'm looking for a loyal
   I need a bilingual secretary.　friend.

3. You will use the personal *a* with your pets and/or other animals with whom you have a personal relationship. You will *not* use the personal *a* with strays, nesting birds, alley cats, squirrels in your back yard, insects, cockroaches, and any other animals with whom you do not wish to form an allegiance.

Amo **a** mi preciosa gata,
Princesa.
I love my darling cat, Princess.

Odio las termitas.
I hate termites.

4. In a complex question that requires the personal *a*, place the *a* before the interrogative:

¿**A** quién amas?
Whom do you love?

¿**A** quién miras?
Whom are you watching?

5. When there is a series of direct objects that are people (and/or pets), each will require a personal *a*:

Veo **a** Juan, **a** María, **a** Miguel, **a** Margarita y **a** Fido.

6. When the personal *a* precedes the definite article **el,** these contract to form **al:**

Veo **al** chico.
I see the boy.

Ella ama **al** hombre.
She loves the man.

Escuchamos **al** Presidente.
We listen to the President.

ejercicio   1-5-1

*Insert the personal **a** when needed in the following sentences:*

1. Yo veo _____ Marta.

2. Yo veo _____ la casa blanca.

3. Huck Finn quiere _____ Becky Thatcher.

4. Marco tiene _____ una hermana.

5. Busco _____ mi primo.

6. Busco _____ mis zapatos.

7. Juana es _____ la presidenta del club.

8. Comprendo _____ Marcos.

9. Hay _____ cinco personas en mi familia.

10. Mateo ama _____ su familia.

ejercicio   1-5-2

*(Each of the following sentences requires a personal **a**.)*

1. Romeo loves Juliet. _____

2. I see John. _____

3. I don't believe Mary. _____

4. We listen to Jorge. _____

5. You look for Andrés. _____

6. They discover a thief (*el ladrón*) in the house. _____

7. Whom do you love? _____

8. Do you see the girl? _____

9. Do you believe the President? _____

10. We're waiting for Sylvia. _____

11. I watch Felipe and Teresa. _____

12. Timmy loves Lassie. _____

A Dozen Highly Useful Irregular Verbs

Below are twelve commonly used irregular verbs, along with their conjugations. It is very important to know these verbs and how to use them. In this section, we will look at their most basic uses, as well as special features of certain verbs.

dar (to give)			**poder** (to be able to)		
doy	das	da	puedo	puedes	puede
damos	dais	dan	podemos	podéis	pueden

decir (to say, tell)			**poner** (to put)		
digo	dices	dice	pongo	pones	pone
decimos	decís	dicen	ponemos	ponéis	ponen

hacer (to make, do)			**querer** (to want)		
hago	haces	hace	quiero	quieres	quiere
hacemos	hacéis	hacen	queremos	queréis	quieren

ir (to go)			**salir** (to leave)		
voy	vas	va	salgo	sales	sale
vamos	vais	van	salimos	salís	salen

jugar (to play)			**venir** (to come)		
juego	juegas	juega	vengo	vienes	viene
jugamos	jugáis	juegan	venimos	venís	viene

oír (to hear)			**ver** (to see)		
oigo	oyes	oye	veo	ves	ve
oímos	oís	oyen	vemos	veis	ven

ejercicio   1-6-1

1. I give. _____
2. I say. _____
3. They hear. _____
4. He hears. _____
5. You make. _____
6. I play. _____
7. I make. _____
8. You (*pl. fam.*) see. _____
9. We give. _____
10. She goes. _____
11. They come. _____
12. He says. _____

13. You put. _____
14. I put. _____
15. We see. _____
16. I see. _____
17. They want. _____
18. You play. _____
19. I leave. _____
20. You say. _____
21. I hear. _____
22. He wants. _____
23. I go. _____
24. They play. _____

¡Te toca a ti!

Responde a estas preguntas con frases completas:

1. ¿Qué quieres para tu cumpleaños? _____

2. Normalmente, ¿dónde pones tu dinero? _____

3. Típicamente, ¿a qué hora vienes a la escuela? _____

4. Desde (*from*) la ventana de tu sala, ¿qué ves? _____

5. ¿Qué le das a tu mejor amigo/a para su cumpleaños este año? _____

6. ¿Qué dices cuando estás enojado/a? _____

7. Más o menos, ¿cuántas veces vas al cine cada año? _____

8. Usualmente, ¿adónde vas después de las clases? _____

9. Generalmente, ¿a qué hora sales de casa por la mañana? _____

10. ¿Qué haces cuando alguien te dice una mentira? _____

Querer, poder, and *deber:* **Phrases with two verbs**

As you learned in the section on *tener que,* when two verbs are next to each other and operate together to form a single idea, the first verb is conjugated and the second verb remains in its infinitive form.

You know that *deber* means "to owe." Directly preceding another verb, however, *deber* means "ought," as in "I *ought* to study." The verb *deber* is regular. You also know *querer* means "to want," and *poder* means "to be able to."

Debo salir de la oficina.
I should leave the office.

Podemos ver la luz.
We can see the light.

¿Puedes nadar bien?
Can you swim well?

¿Queréis cenar ahora?
Do you want to eat dinner now?

Ella quiere ser lingüista.
She wants to be a linguist.

Ellos no deben decirnos nada.
They shouldn't tell us anything.

ejercicio   I-6-2

Responde a las preguntas:

1. ¿Qué puedes hacer muy bien?

   a) _____

   b) _____

   c) _____

2. ¿Qué es lo que no puedes hacer?

   a) _____

   b) _____

   c) _____

3. ¿Qué quieres hacer mañana?

   a) _____

   b) _____

   c) _____

4. ¿Qué debes hacer cada día?

   a) _____

b)_____

c)_____

5. ¿Qué es lo que no debes hacer en la casa? _____

6. ¿Qué puede hacer Barbra Streisand? _____

7. ¿Qué puede hacer Isaac Stern? _____

8. ¿Qué puede hacer Kirby Puckett? _____

9. ¿Qué puede hacer Julia Child? _____

10. ¿Qué puede hacer Stephen King? _____

11. ¿Qué pucdc haccr un pez? _____

12. ¿Qué puede hacer Mikhail Baryshnikov? _____

Hacer and *estar*: **Their use in describing the weather**

One specific and important use of the verbs *hacer* and *estar* is in talking about the weather. Both *hacer* and *estar* will operate only in the third person singular in this context, as the subject is the nebulous "it." Note below that it will always be **hace** + *noun* and **está** + *adjective*. You cannot mix and match these expressions because they won't make sense if you do. In other words, memorize the following expressions.

idioms with *hacer*		expressions with *estar*	
hace (mucho) frío	it is (vcry) cold	**está nublado**	it is cloudy
hace (mucho) calor	it is (very) warm	**está lloviendo**	it is raining
hace (mucho) sol	it is (very) sunny	**está nevando**	it is snowing
hace (mucho) viento	it is (very) windy	**está lloviznando**	it is drizzling
hace fresco	it is cool	**está lluvioso**	it is rainy, wet
hace (muy) buen tiempo	it is (very) nice out	**cstá húmedo**	it is humid
hace (muy) mal tiempo	it is (very) bad out	**está seco**	it is dry

ejercicio   1-6-3

Responde a las siguientes preguntas:

1. ¿Qué tiempo hace hoy? _____

2. ¿Qué tiempo hace en diciembre? _____

3. ¿Qué tiempo hace en abril? _____

4. ¿Qué tiempo hace en julio?_____

5. Normalmente, ¿qué tiempo hace en tu cumpleaños? _____

Jugar: **To play a game**

The verb *jugar* means "to play (a game); to gamble." Its conjugations are: **juego; juegas; juega; jugamos; jugáis; juegan.** Be careful to not confuse *jugar* with *tocar,* which means "to play (a musical instrument)." Below are listed several games one can play. Note the inclusion of the word *a* and the appropriate definite article before the name of the game. Speakers in many Spanish-speaking countries, however, also use this verb without the inclusion of *a* (*juego béisbol*).

jugar al ajedrez	to play chess
jugar al baloncesto	to play basketball
jugar al béisbol	to play baseball
jugar al billar	to play billiards, pool
jugar a las damas	to play checkers
jugar al fútbol	to play soccer
jugar al fútbol americano	to play football
jugar al golf	to play golf
jugar al hockey	to play hockey
jugar a un juego	to play a game
jugar a los naipes	to play cards
jugar al tenis	to play tennis
jugar al voleibol	to play volleyball

ejercicio   1-6-4

Even though some of the following players are from the past, answer the questions in the present tense:

1. ¿Qué juega Babe Ruth? _____

2. ¿Qué juega Wayne Gretzky? _____

3. ¿Qué juega Minnesota Fats? _____

4. ¿Qué juega Pelé? _____

5. ¿Qué juegan Bobby Fischer y Boris Spasky? _____

6. ¿Qué juegan Chris Evert y Billie Jean King? _____

7. ¿Qué juega Arnold Palmer? _____

8. ¿Qué juegan Kareem Abdul Jabar y Larry Bird? _____

9. ¿Qué juega Joe Namath? _____

10. ¿Qué juegan los niños en una tabla roja y negra? _____

Ir + a + infinitive: Expression of future action

When you know the verb *ir* (to go) in the present tense, you also can speak of the future, as in what you are "going to do," or what "is going to happen." To do this, follow these three easy steps:

ir (conjugated) + a + infinitive

examples:

Voy a cantar.
I am going to sing.

¿Qué vas a hacer mañana?
What are you going to do tomorrow?

Va a llover.
It's going to rain.

Vamos a comprar una lámpara.
We are going to buy a lamp.

¿Cuándo vais a salir del cuarto?
When are you going to leave the room?

Ellos no van a estar aquí.
They aren't going to be here.

ejercicio	1-6-5

1. I'm going to practice. _____

2. You're going to work. _____

3. She is going to watch television. _____

4. We're going to sell the car. _____

5. They're going to drink the milk. _____

6. I'm not going to do anything. _____

7. What are you going to do? _____

8. Are you going to study or watch TV? _____

9. We are not going to buy candy. _____

10. When are you (*pl.fam.*) going to play? _____

Some phrases of future time:

mañana	tomorrow	**la semana que viene**	next week
esta tarde	this afternoon	**el mes que viene**	next month
esta noche	tonight	**el año que viene**	next year

¡Te toca a ti!
Responde a estas preguntas:

1. ¿Qué vas a hacer esta noche? _____

2. ¿Qué ropa vas a llevar mañana? _____

3. ¿Qué vas a comer esta tarde? _____

4. ¿Vas a tener una fiesta la semana que viene? _____

5. En tu opinión, ¿quién va a ser el próximo Presidente de los Estados Unidos? _____

_____

6. ¿Dónde vas a vivir el año que viene? _____

7. ¿Adónde vas a ir el verano que viene? _____

8. ¿Cuándo vas a ver a tu mejor amigo/a? _____

¿Verdadero, falso o probable?

_____ 1. Voy a leer una revista esta noche.

_____ 2. Mi mejor amigo/a va a darme un regalo para mi cumpleaños.

_____ 3. Hace frío hoy.

_____ 4. Voy a comprar un coche el año que viene.

_____ 5. Hace calor, hace sol y hace buen tiempo hoy.

_____ 6. No voy a comer nada hoy.

_____ 7. Voy a votar en las elecciones este noviembre.

_____ 8. Mi familia y yo vamos a vivir en otro estado el año que viene.

_____ 9. Mi mejor amigo/a va a vender su casa este mes.

_____ 10. Nunca voy a cometer otro error.

_____ 11. No voy a salir de la casa mañana.

_____ 12. Nadie va a venir a mi casa esta noche.

traducción   1-6-6

Tomorrow is my best friend's birthday. I'm going to have a party for him. I can invite many people because my house is big. I have lots of parties and I always do the same thing. I go to the bakery and I buy a cake. I tell the baker that I want lots of flowers and my friend's name on the cake. I put the cake on the table in the dining room where everyone can see it—I hear that a dramatic centerpiece is important. The guests come to my house at seven o'clock. We talk and eat and drink—sometimes we dance or we play a game—and then we give gifts to the guest of honor. It's going to be a wonderful party.

vocabulario

always	**siempre**	flowers	**las flores**
baker	**el panadero**	gift	**el regalo**
bakery	**la panadería**	guest	**el invitado**
because	**porque**	honor	**el honor**
best	**mejor**	(to) invite	**invitar**
cake	**la torta**	name	**el nombre**
centerpiece	**el centro de mesa**	(the) same thing	**lo mismo**
dining room	**el comedor**	sometimes	**a veces**
dramatic	**dramático**	then	**entonces**
everyone	**todos**	wonderful	**maravilloso**

Saber and *Conocer*

Just as we learned that *ser* and *estar* on the surface mean the same thing, namely, "to be," the verbs *saber* and *conocer* both mean "to know." On closer inspection, however, these two verbs perform two very different functions: *Saber* means "to know information," while *conocer* means "to know, or be familiar with, a person, place, or thing."

Saber

First we will consider *saber*, and its various uses. Essentially, *saber* means "to know facts and information." It implies full knowledge (while *conocer* implies familiarity).

saber *(to know information)*	
sé	sabemos
sabes	sabéis
sabe	saben

Note that *saber* is irregular only in the *yo* form.

> **Saber: To know information.** When dealing with facts and information, you will use *saber*.
>
> **Sé** tu dirección. *I know* your address.
>
> **Él no sabe** dónde trabajo. *He doesn't know* where I work.
>
> **Sabemos** el número de teléfono. *We know* the telephone number.

ejercicio   **1-7-1**

1. I know your name. _____

2. You know the answer. _____

3. She knows where you live. _____

4. We don't know why he is angry. _____

5. Do you know who has the money? _____

6. They don't know anything about me. _____

7. Does he know where María is? _____

8. You (*pl. fam.*) know a lot. _____

> ***Saber que . . . : To know that . . . .***   In English we have the option of saying either "I know *that* he's here somewhere," or simply, "I know he's here somewhere." In Spanish, we do not have that option and must include the relative pronoun *que* (that) which **always** will be followed by a complete sentence.
>
> **Sé que** su nombre es Juan. *I know that his name is John.*
>
> **¿Sabes que** ella está embarazada? *Do you know that she is pregnant?*
>
> **Ellos no saben que** los vemos. *They don't know that we see them.*

---

ejercicio   **1-7-2**

1. I know that John is tall. _____

2. You know that I'm hungry. _____

3. She knows that you're thirsty. _____

4. Do you know that I'm twenty-nine years old? _____

5. We know that he is in a hurry. _____

6. They don't know that I'm here. _____

7. Do you (*pl. fam.*) know that there are snakes (*culebras*) in the garden (*el jardín*)? _____

_____

8. He doesn't know that you're in the garden. _____

> ***Saber* + infinitive: To know *how* to do something.**   To say that you know *how* to do something in Spanish, you simply add the infinitive immediately after the conjugated *saber*. Do **not** add *cómo* (how).
>
> **Sé** leer. *I know how to read.*
>
> **No sé** cocinar. *I don't know how to cook.*
>
> **Él sabe** escribir bien. *He knows how to write well.*
>
> **Sabemos** esquiar. *We know how to ski.*

ejercicio	1-7-3

1. I know how to sing. _____

2. You know how to speak Spanish. _____

3. She knows how to cook very well. _____

4. He doesn't know how to speak French. _____

5. Fred and Ginger know how to dance. _____

6. You (*pl. fam.*) know how to play the piano. _____

7. Do you know how to ski? _____

8. Who knows how to open this door? _____

traducción	1-7-4

John is my mechanic. He knows a lot about cars, and I am happy because I don't know anything about cars. No, it's not completely true. I know where the gas tank is and I know how to fill it. I know how to drive and I know that I can't park in front of a fire station. John knows that he has to know about cars and about people, because many people know very little about cars.

vocabulario			

(to) drive	**conducir**	(to) know about	**saber de**
(to) fill	**llenar**	mechanic	**el mecánico**
fire station	**la estación de bomberos**	(to) park	**aparcar**
gas tank	**el tanque de gasolina**	people (in general)	**la gente**
in front of	**enfrente de**	true	**cierto**

_____

_____

_____

_____

Conocer

If you are *familiar* with a person, a place, or a thing, you will need the verb *conocer*. The key word here is *familiarity*, for one can never know another person, place, or thing completely.

conocer *(to be familiar with)*	
conozco	conocemos
conoces	conocéis
conoce	conocen

Note that, as with *saber*, the verb *conocer* is irregular only in the *yo* form.

Conocer + a: To know a person.   When talking about knowing another person (or someone's pet animal—not a stray), the conjugated *conocer* will be followed by the personal *a* except when you use an object pronoun.

Conozco a Felipe.
I know Phillip.

Tú conoces a María.
You know Mary.

María conoce a Eduardo.
Mary knows Edward.

Lo **conocemos.**
We know him.

La **conocéis.**
You know her.

María y Jorge lo **conocen.**
Mary and George know him.

ejercicio	1-7-5

1. I know Antonia. _____

2. You know Isabel. _____

3. He knows his father-in-law. _____

4. We know you. _____

5. You (*pl. fam.*) know Juan. _____

6. She knows Juana and Paco. _____

7. Do you know my cats Fifi and Fufu? _____

8. He doesn't know me. _____

9. I know her. _____

10. You know her. _____

11. He knows him. _____

12. You know us. _____

13. You all (*pl. fam.*) know him. _____

14. She knows them. _____

15. Yes, I know them. _____

16. Nobody knows me here. _____

Conocer **+ location: To know a place.**   To visit is to become familiar. Whether you know a location inside-out (like your hometown) or hardly at all (where you went on a sixth-grade field trip), you will use *conocer.* To indicate how well you know a place, you use *muy bien* (very well) or *muy poco* (hardly at all).

Conozco Puerto Rico. *I know/am familiar with/have been to* Puerto Rico.

La actriz conoce muy bien Hollywood. *The actress knows* Hollywood *very well.*

Las arañas conocen bien mi sótano. *Spiders know* my basement *well.*

Él conoce muy poco Las Vegas. *He is slightly familiar with* Las Vegas.

ejercicio	1-7-6

1. I (don't) know Chicago. _____

2. The President knows Washington, D.C., well. _____

3. The mayor knows the city well. _____

4. Dorothy knows Oz. _____

5. They don't know/haven't been to Paris. _____

6. Have you been to/Do you know Ireland? _____

7. George knows the jungle (*la selva*). _____

8. The bird knows its tree (*el árbol*). _____

Conocer **+ noun: To know, be well versed in an area.**   Virtually everybody has at least one area of talent, whether it be cooking, politics, or changing a tire. Perhaps you have read all of Shakespeare's plays or Agatha Christie's mysteries. Whatever your area(s) of expertise, you *know* that field, and to say so you will use *conocer.*

Mi mecánico conoce bien los motores alemanes. *My mechanic knows* German engines well.

El fotógrafo conoce las cámaras japonesas. *The photographer knows* Japanese cameras.

Juanito conoce los libros del Dr. Seuss. *Johnny knows* Dr. Seuss's books.

ejercicio   I-7-7

1. The doctor knows the body well. _____

2. The priest knows the Bible well. _____

3. The hairdresser knows his clients' hair. _____

4. Bo knows basketball. _____

5. The manicurist knows her clients' fingernails. _____

6. The cook knows the food of Mexico. _____

7. The architect knows the architecture of Chicago. _____

8. The farmer knows the land. _____

traducción   I-7-8

I don't know why, but I believe that I know you. Do you know my cousin, Enrique? Yes? Well, then you know that his wife knows how to speak Russian—but she can't read it. She has lots of wonderful parties because she knows everybody and because she knows how to cook like a professional chef. I know that you want to meet (know) her. I'm going to arrange the introduction.

vocabulario

(to) arrange	**arreglar**	Russian	**ruso**
chef (*f.*)	**la cocinera**	well	**pues**
introduction	**la presentación**	wife	**la esposa**
(to) meet	**conocer**	wonderful	**maravilloso**

_____

_____

_____

_____

_____

Unit 8

Stem-Changing Verbs

Earlier, we discussed the two parts of the infinitive: (1) the **ending** (-*ar*, -*er*, or -*ir*) and (2) the **base** (what is left when the ending is removed). Another word for the base is the **stem,** and with regular verbs, the stem (or base) always remains the same.

The verbs covered in this unit have changes that take place in *both* the stem and the conjugation ending. There are three kinds of stem-changing verbs, and we will consider each separately.

1. *o* **changes to** *ue:* The first group of stem-changing verbs involves changing the stem's *o* to *ue* in all forms but *nosotros* and *vosotros*. Their endings for conjugation remain regular. Note the examples:

contar *(to count)*	**mover** *(to move)*	**dormir** *(to sleep)*
cuento contamos	**muevo** movemos	**duermo** dormimos
cuentas contáis	**mueves** movéis	**duermes** dormís
cuenta cuentan	**mueve mueven**	**duerme duermen**

One of the features of stem-changing verbs is that the change takes place in the first, second, and third person singular, and the third person plural. If you were to draw a line around these changed verbs, you would come up with something resembling a boot. This shape is often referred to as the "boot of irregularity."

Listed below are several *o* → *ue* verbs:

almorzar	to eat lunch	**mostrar**	to show
aprobar	to approve	**mover**	to move (an object)
colgar	to hang (up)	**probar**	to prove, test, sample, taste
contar	to count	**recordar**	to remember
costar	to cost	**resolver**	to solve
devolver	to return (an object)	**rogar**	to beg, pray
dormir	to sleep	**sonar**	to sound, ring
encontrar	to find	**soñar (con)**	to dream (about)
envolver	to wrap (up)	**tostar**	to toast
morder	to bite	**volver**	to return
morir	to die	**volar**	to fly

¿Cuál es verdadero o falso para ti?

_____ 1. Yo duermo en el dormitorio.

_____ 2. Yo cuento mi dinero cada día.

_____ 3. El héroe Superhombre vuela.

_____ 4. Cada mañana tuesto el pan.

_____ 5. Normalmente, sueño cuando duermo.

_____ 6. Típicamente, almuerzo en casa.

_____ 7. A veces mis amigos y yo almorzamos en un restaurante.

_____ 8. Mis amigos me muestran sus casas.

_____ 9. A veces encuentro dinero en el sofá.

_____ 10. El oro cuesta más que la plata.

_____ 11. Después de hablar por teléfono, cuelgo.

_____ 12. Después de leer un libro de la biblioteca, lo devuelvo.

ejercicio   1-8-1

1. I eat lunch. _____

2. You eat lunch. _____

3. The dog bites. _____

4. We approve. _____

5. You (*pl. fam.*) beg. _____

6. They count the money. _____

7. You show the house. _____

8. She sleeps. _____

9. We solve the problem. _____

_____

10. She wraps the gift. _____

_____

11. I hang up the telephone. _____

_____

12. You return the shirt. _____

_____

13. He dies. _____

14. The telephone rings. _____

_____

15. I find the money. _____

_____

16. We return. _____

17. Dumbo flies. _____

18. Jane toasts the bread. _____

_____

19. We pray for peace. _____

20. He dreams about a tiger. _____

_____

21. I don't remember anything. _____

22. The book costs ten dollars. _____

_____

23. You move the chairs. _____

_____

24. I taste the coffee. _____

_____

2. *e* changes to *ie*:   The second group of stem-changing verbs involves changing the stem's *e* to *ie* in all forms except *nosotros* and *vosotros*.

cerrar *(to close)*		**perder** *(to lose)*		**hervir** *(to boil)*	
cierro	cerramos	**pierdo**	perdemos	**hiervo**	hervimos
cierras	cerráis	**pierdes**	perdéis	**hierves**	hervís
cierra	**cierran**	**pierde**	**pierden**	**hierve**	**hierven**

Listed below are several *e* → *ie* stem-changing verbs. Note that a few have both an *o* and an *e* in the stem. You can be sure that these are *e* → *ie* stem-changing verbs (and **not** *o* → *ue*) because you will always change the vowel prior to the ending: comenzar; confesar; consentir; convertir.

acertar	to guess, get right	**encender**	to light, kindle
advertir	to advise, warn	**entender**	to understand
cerrar	to close, shut	**fregar**	to scrub, wash dishes
comenzar	to begin	**hervir**	to boil
confesar	to confess	**mentir**	to lie, tell a lie
consentir	to consent	**negar**	to deny
convertir	to convert	**pensar (en)**	to think (about)
defender	to defend	**perder**	to lose
empezar	to begin	**preferir**	to prefer

querer	to want, wish	sugerir	to suggest
referir	to refer	temblar	to tremble
sentir	to feel sorry, regret	tropezar (con)	to stumble, bump into

¿Cuál es verdadero o falso?

_____ 1. Yo pierdo muchas cosas en mi casa.

_____ 2. Entiendo español.

_____ 3. Mi clase de español comienza a las diez de la mañana.

_____ 4. Pinocho miente mucho.

_____ 5. Para preparar el café, una persona hierve el agua.

_____ 6. Cerramos la boca para hablar.

_____ 7. Un abogado defiende a sus clientes.

_____ 8. Cierro las ventanas cuando hace frío.

_____ 9. Pienso mucho en mi familia.

_____ 10. Mis amigos piensan en mí.

_____ 11. Cada noche friego los platos.

_____ 12. Entre el café y el té, yo prefiero el café.

ejercicio   1-8-2

1. I close the door. _____

2. You guess. _____

3. He washes (scrubs) the dishes. _____

4. We advise you. _____

5. They deny everything. _____

6. He regrets it a lot. _____

7. You (*pl. fam.*) begin. _____

8. She defends me. _____

9. You boil the water. _____

10. They lie to me. _____

11. You (*pl. fam.*) consent. _____

12. She suggests. _____

13. We tremble. _____

14. I prefer water. _____

15. He wants a dog. _____

16. Do you understand? _____

17. He loses the magazine. _____

18. She bumps into the sofa. _____

19. They confess. _____

20. The program begins. _____

21. I think about the war. _____

22. You light the candle. _____

23. We convert the money to dollars. _____

24. I refer the case to the professor. _____

3. *e* changes to *i*: The third, and final, group of stem-changing verbs involves changing the *e* in the stem to an *i* (except with *nosotros* and *vosotros*). This type is found **only** in *-ir* verbs.

seguir *(to follow)*		**repetir** *(to repeat)*	
sigo	seguimos	**repito**	repetimos
sigues	seguís	**repites**	repetís
sigue	**siguen**	**repite**	**repiten**

Below are listed several *e* → *i* verbs. Of the three stem-changing verb groups, this is the smallest.

bendecir	to bless	**gemir**	to groan, moan
colegir	to deduce	**impedir**	to impede, hinder
competir	to compete	**maldecir**	to curse
conseguir	to obtain, get	**medir**	to be long, measure
corregir	to correct	**pedir**	to request, ask for
decir	to say, tell	**reír**	to laugh
despedir	to fire	**repetir**	to repeat
elegir	to elect	**seguir**	to follow, continue
freír	to fry	**servir**	to serve

¿Cuál es verdadero o falso?

_____ 1. En un restaurante bueno, el mesero nos sirve la comida.

_____ 2. Muchos atletas compiten en las olimpiadas.

_____ 3. Frío huevos cada mañana para el desayuno.

_____ 4. Cada cuatro años, elegimos al Presidente.

_____ 5. Un metro mide cien centímetros.

_____ 6. Pinocho siempre dice la verdad.

_____ 7. Un profesor corrige muchos exámenes.

_____ 8. El Papa en el Vaticano bendice a la gente con frecuencia.

_____ 9. Esta semana pido un aumento a mi jefe.

_____ 10. Cuando quiero información del mundo, consigo un periódico.

_____ 11. Cuando compro un aparato nuevo, siempre sigo las instrucciones antes de usarlo.

_____ 12. Muchas veces los padres repiten las instrucciones a los niños.

ejercicio   I-8-3

1. I compete. _____

2. You correct the test. _____

3. He asks for help. _____

4. She laughs a lot. _____

5. He gets a job. _____

6. We elect the winner. _____

7. We fry the potatoes. _____

8. You (_pl. fam._) tell the truth. _____

9. You fire the employee. _____

10. We request more money. _____

11. She groans. _____

12. He impedes the progress. _____

13. They tell us the truth. _____

14. I follow you. _____

15. You (*pl. fam.*) serve us. _____

16. Who says this? _____

17. She is five feet tall. _____

18. They curse. _____

19. He deduces the truth from the facts. _____

20. You compete against him. _____

21. They laugh a lot because they are happy. _____

22. All of you (*pl. form.*) repeat the lesson. _____

23. The priest blesses you. _____

24. What are you asking for? _____

traducción   I-8-4

Hi. I'm Oswald. I sell houses. It's hard, but somebody has to do it. Houses cost a lot these days, and therefore I usually show each client more or less twenty houses. We often return to the first house and the client tells me that he wants to buy it. I tremble with rage (sometimes I curse or groan) because I think of all the time that I waste, but then I think about my commission and I understand why I sell houses. I'm not lying to you when I confess (to you) that I want to sell houses forever.

vocabulario

client	**el cliente**	somebody	**alguien**
commission	**la comisión**	these days	**estos días**
forever	**para siempre**	time	**el tiempo**
rage	**la rabia**	(to) waste, lose	**perder (e → ie)**

_____

_____

_____

_____

Noteworthy Infinitives

As you know by now, many verbs are irregular in Spanish. However, many of these irregular verbs fall into categories and you can recognize them by their infinitives. In this unit we will break them down.

Verbs ending with -*cer* preceded by a vowel: The following verbs all end in -*cer*. On closer inspection, however, you will notice that the -*cer* is preceded by a vowel. All such verbs are irregular only in the *yo* form, where a z precedes the c. All other conjugated forms are regular in the present tense.

conocer *(to know a person)*		**parecer** *(to seem)*	
conozco	conocemos	**parezco**	parecemos
conocemos	conocéis	pareces	parecéis
conoce	conocen	parece	parecen

Below is a list of commonly used verbs in this category, along with their respective *yo* forms.

agradecer	to be thankful	*yo agradezco*
aparecer	to appear	*yo aparezco*
conocer	to know a person	*yo conozco*
crecer	to grow	*yo crezco*
desaparecer	to disappear	*yo desaparezco*
establecer	to establish	*yo establezco*
merecer	to deserve, merit	*yo merezco*
nacer	to be born	*yo nazco*
obedecer	to obey	*yo obedezco*
ofrecer	to offer	*yo ofrezco*
parecer	to seem	*yo parezco*
pertenecer	to belong	*yo pertenezco*
placer	to please, gratify	*yo plazco*
reconocer	to recognize	*yo reconozco*
yacer	to lie down	*yo yazco*

ejercicio   1-9-1

1. Yo (conocer) _____ a Juan.

2. Yo (pertenecer) _____ a un club.

3. Yo no (reconocer) _____ a nadie aquí.

4. Yo (ofrecer) _____ cien dólares al ganador.

5. Yo (merecer) _____ un aumento (*raise*).

6. Este programa me (parecer) _____ absurdo.

7. Estos libros me (pertenecer) _____ .

8. Cada día muchos bebés (nacer) _____ en el mundo.

9. Si un bebé no come bien, no (crecer) _____ bien.

10. A veces un fantasma (aparecer) _____ en los sueños de los supersticiosos.

Verbs ending with -*ucir*:   Verbs that end with -*ucir* are similar to verbs ending with -*cer* in that a *z* is inserted in the *yo* form. As with the preceding, -*cer* verbs, all other forms are regular.

producir (*to produce*)		**traducir** (*to translate*)	
produzco	producimos	**traduzco**	traducimos
produces	producís	traduces	traducís
produce	producen	traduce	traducen

Verbs in this category:

conducir	to conduct, drive	*yo conduzco*
deducir	to deduce	*yo deduzco*
deslucir	to tarnish, spoil	*yo desluzco*
inducir	to induce, persuade	*yo induzco*
introducir	to insert, introduce	*yo introduzco*
lucir	to light up, display	*yo luzco*
producir	to produce	*yo produzco*
reducir	to reduce	*yo reduzco*
traducir	to translate	*yo traduzco*

ejercicio	I-9-2

Responde a las siguientes preguntas con frases completas:

1. ¿Conduces un coche automático o de marchas (*stick shift*)? _____

_____

2. ¿Produces mucho trabajo? _____

3. ¿Traduces muchas frases en este libro? _____

4. ¿Qué produce el panadero? _____

5. ¿Introduces una moneda en el teléfono público? _____

_____

6. ¿Normalmente, reducen los impuestos los políticos? _____

_____

Verbs ending with *-cer* or *-cir* preceded by a consonant: When a verb ending with *-cer* or *-cir* is preceded by a consonant, the *yo* form will have the *c* replaced by *z*. All other forms are regular.

ejercer (*to exert, exercise*)		zurcir (*to mend*)	
ejerzo	ejercemos	**zurzo**	zurcimos
ejerces	ejercéis	zurces	zurcís
ejerce	ejercen	zurce	zurcen

Verbs in this category:

convencer	to convince, persuade	*yo convenzo*
ejercer	to exert, exercise	*yo ejerzo*
esparcir	to scatter, spread	*yo esparzo*
vencer	to conquer, defeat	*yo venzo*
zurcir	to mend, darn	*yo zurzo*

ejercicio	I-9-3

1. I scatter seeds (*semillas*) in the garden. _____

2. I conquer the enemy (*el enemigo*). _____

3. I darn the socks (*los calcetines*). _____

4. I exert a lot of energy (*la energía*) on my studies. _____

_____

5. The warriors (*los guerreros*) conquer their enemies. _____

_____

Verbs ending in *-ger* or *-gir*: The *g* is soft (sounds like *h*) in the infinitive, and that same sound must be retained in its conjugated form. Since a *g* before an *o* in Spanish is hard (as in *go*), the *g* in the *yo* form will change to *j* in order to keep it soft. All other forms are regular.

coger (*to catch, seize, grab*)		**corregir [e → i]** (*to correct*)	
cojo	cogemos	**corrijo**	corregimos
coges	cogéis	corriges	corregís
coge	cogen	corrige	corrigen

Verbs in this category:

coger	to catch, seize, grab	*yo cojo*
colegir (*e → i*)	to deduce	*yo colijo*
corregir (*e → i*)	to correct	*yo corrijo*
dirigir	to direct	*yo dirijo*
elegir (*e → i*)	to elect, choose	*yo elijo*
escoger	to select	*yo escojo*
exigir	to demand, require	*yo exijo*
fingir	to pretend	*yo finjo*
proteger	to protect	*yo protejo*
recoger	to pick up, gather	*yo recojo*
sumergir	to submerge, immerse	*yo sumerjo*
surgir	to surge, spurt	*yo surjo*

ejercicio   1-9-4

1. I protect my family. _____

2. I correct my problems. _____

3. The teacher (*el maestro*) corrects many papers (*trabajos*). _____

_____

4. Sometimes I pretend to be happy when I am sad. _____

_____

5. I select my friends with a lot of care (*el cuidado*). _____

_____

6. Every four years we elect a new leader (*el líder*). _____

_____

7. I pick up my socks from the floor (*el suelo*). _____

8. I catch a taxi for the airport (*el aeropuerto*). _____

9. I demand a lot from my employees (*empleados*). _____

10. I submerge the sweater in cold water. _____

> **Verbs ending in -*aer*:** When an infinitive ends in -*aer*, its *yo* form will end with -*aigo*. All other forms will be regular.

caer *(to fall)*		**traer** *(to bring)*	
caigo	caemos	**traigo**	traemos
caes	caéis	traes	traéis
cae	cacn	trae	traen

Verbs in this category:

atraer	to attract	*yo atraigo*
caer	to fall	*yo caigo*
contraer	to contract	*yo contraigo*
raer	to scrape, rub off	*yo raigo*
retraer	to bring back	*yo retraigo*
sustraer	to remove, subtract	*yo sustraigo*
traer	to bring	*yo traigo*

ejercicio   **1-9-5**

Fill in the blanks with the appropriate form of the verb:

1. Usualmente yo (traer) _____ algo a una fiesta.

2. El pintor (raer) _____ la vieja pintura del lienzo (*canvas*).

3. El azúcar (atraer) _____ a las moscas.

4. Juan (contraer) _____ matrimonio con María el próximo mes.

5. Los estudiantes de matemáticas (sustraer) _____ la cantidad mínima de la cantidad máxima.

Verbs ending in -*uir* (not preceded by a *g*): In the previous categories, we saw verbs which, when conjugated, became irregular only in the *yo* form. The following group of infinitives produces irregular conjugations in all the singular forms, as well as the third person plural. In each of these forms a *y* is added to the stem.

huir *(to flee, run away)*		**destruir** *(to destroy)*	
huyo	huimos	**destruyo**	destruimos
huyes	huís	**destruyes**	destruís
huye	**huyen**	**destruye**	**destruyen**

Verbs in this category (along with the *yo* form):

concluir	to conclude	*yo concluyo*
constituir	to constitute	*yo constituyo*
construir	to construct, build	*yo construyo*
contribuir	to contribute	*yo contribuyo*
destruir	to destroy	*yo destruyo*
fluir	to flow	*yo fluyo*
huir	to flee, run away	*yo huyo*
incluir	to include	*yo incluyo*
influir	to influence	*yo influyo*

ejercicio   **1-9-6**

Fill in the blanks with the appropriate form of the verb:

1. Yo (construir) _____ una casa de madera.

2. Yo nunca (contribuir) _____ dinero a un político.

3. El río (fluir) _____ al oeste.

4. El plato (huir) _____ con la cuchara (*spoon*).

5. Los libros de H. L. Mencken me (influir) _____ mucho.

6. La bomba (destruir) _____ el edificio.

7. Tú (concluir) _____ la reunión a las ocho de la noche.

8. El homicidio (constituir) _____ un crimen grave.

9. El novelista siempre (incluir) _____ varios personajes en los libros.

10. Las bibliotecas (contribuir) _____ mucho a la sociedad.

Verbs ending in -guir.   Earlier in this unit, we looked at verbs ending in -ger or -gir that had to retain the soft g. In this section, our job is to retain the hard g throughout the conjugations. In infinitives ending in -guir, the u is merely a hard sound marker; without it, the g would be soft. Because the infinitive has a hard g sound, so must its conjugations. And because g in front of o is a naturally hard sound, the u is no longer necessary. Thus, in the yo form, the u is dropped. All other forms are regular.

distinguir (to distinguish)		**seguir [e → i]** (to follow)	
distingo	distinguimos	**sigo**	seguimos
distingues	distinguís	sigues	seguís
distingue	distinguen	sigue	siguen

Verbs in this category:

conseguir (e → i)	to get, obtain	*yo consigo*
distinguir	to distinguish	*yo distingo*
erguir (e → i)	to erect, lift up	*yo irgo**
extinguir	to extinguish	*yo extingo*
perseguir (e → i)	to pursue, persecute	*yo persigo*
seguir (e → i)	to follow	*yo sigo*

*In **erguir**, the stressed e changes to i: **irgo; irgues; irgue; erguimos; erguís; irguen.**

---

ejercicio   **I-9-7**

Fill in the blanks with the appropriate verb form:

1. Yo (distinguir) _____ entre lo bueno y lo malo.

2. La policía (seguir) _____ al criminal.

3. Yo (extinguir) _____ las velas (*candles*).

4. Yo (conseguir) _____ trabajo en la compañía telefónica.

5. Los líderes (erguir) _____ un monumento a la libertad.

6. En el verano los mosquitos me (perseguir) _____ .

7. Naomi (conseguir) _____ toda su ropa por catálogo.

8. Mis clases de matemáticas e inglés (seguir) _____ a mi clase de español.

9. Muchas personas no (distinguir) _____ el rojo del verde.

10. Yo te (seguir) _____ a la fiesta.

11. Ustedes no (conseguir) _____ nada de esta oficina.

12. Los bomberos (*firefighters*) (extinguir) _____ el incendio.

Reflexive Verbs

A verb is reflexive when the subject (the performer of the action) and the object (the receiver of that action) are the same.

For example, the verb in the sentence *I see you* is not reflexive because *I* (the subject/actor) and *you* (the object/receiver) are not the same person. However, if I look in the mirror and see myself, the verb is reflexive because *I* (the subject) and *me* (the object) are the same person. Another way of looking at reflexive verbs is to say that the action doesn't go anywhere.

In English, the object of a reflexive verb is usually one of the following: myself; yourself; himself; herself; itself; ourselves; themselves. In Spanish, reflexive verbs require reflexive object pronouns, which are employed in the same manner as direct and indirect object pronouns:

If there is one verb in the clause, the object pronoun precedes the verb.

Me veo. I see *myself.*

If there are two verbs in the clause, the object either precedes the first verb *or* is attached directly to the second verb. Either is acceptable.

Me quiero ver. *or* Quiero ver**me**. I want to see *myself.*

Another important distinction is that in English, our use of the reflexive pronoun is quite restricted and generally involves the full being: I love *myself,* You know *yourself,* He hates *himself,* and so on.

In Spanish, however, this notion of being reflexive is far more expansive. As long as the action is going back to the actor, it is considered a reflexive verb. Thus, *I wash my hair, You take a bath,* and *We brush our teeth* are all examples of sentences that will require reflexive pronouns in Spanish.

These are the reflexive pronouns	
me	nos
te	os
se	se

examples:

bañarse *(to take a bath)*		sentarse *(to sit down)*	
me baño	nos bañamos	me siento	nos sentamos
te bañas	os bañáis	te sientas	os sentáis
se baña	se bañan	se sienta	se sientan

Note that *sentarse* is an *e* → *ie* stem-changing verb. It means literally to "seat oneself."

A few things to know before working with reflexive verbs

1. Many reflexive verbs are stem-changing (these are noted in the list at the end of this unit), and you will conjugate them just as you learned in the previous units.

2. Many involve the mentioning of a body part or parts (e.g., *cepillarse*—to brush). Generally speaking, use the definite article rather than the possessive adjective before the body part (because of the reflexive pronoun, it is obvious whose body is being discussed):

   Me cepillo **el** pelo. I brush *my* hair.

   Ella se cepilla **los** dientes. She brushes *her* teeth.

   Te lavas **el** pelo. You wash *your* hair.

3. Nearly all verbs in the language can be **either** reflexive or non-reflexive: I can scratch myself (reflexive) or I can scratch my cat (non-reflexive). Thus, the list below is far from exhaustive. However, there are certain actions that *usually* are reflexive due to the nature of the action (bathing, shaving, brushing teeth, etc.). For the most part, these are the verbs you will find below.

4. One unusual verb below is *irse* (to go away). This strays from the general description of the reflexive verb in that this is not a case where the subject and object are the same. Instead, the reflexive pronoun *intensifies* the action. One other exception is *comerse* (to gobble up) which does not mean "to eat oneself."

Some commonly used reflexive verbs:

acostarse (*o* → *ue*)	to go to bed
afeitarse	to shave oneself
bañarse	to bathe oneself
casarse (con alguien)	to get married; to marry (someone)
cepillarse	to brush oneself
despertarse (*e* → *ie*)	to wake up
desvestirse (*e* → *i*)	to undress oneself
dormirse (*o* → *ue*)	to fall asleep
ducharse	to take a shower
enfermarse	to get sick
enojarse	to get angry, mad
irse	to go away
lavarse	to wash oneself
levantarse	to stand up, get up

llamarse	to call oneself
mirarse	to look at oneself
peinarse	to comb one's hair
ponerse	to become
ponerse (la ropa)	to put on (clothing)
preocuparse (por)	to worry (about)
probarse ($o \rightarrow ue$)	to try on (clothing)
quitarse	to take off, remove (clothing)
secarse	to dry oneself
sentarse ($e \rightarrow ie$)	to sit down, seat oneself
sentirse ($e \rightarrow ie$)	to feel (emotionally, physically)
verse	to see oneself
vestirse ($e \rightarrow i$)	to get dressed

examples:

Me quito el sombrero.
I take off my hat.

Nos vestimos en la mañana.
We get dressed in the morning.

Te acuestas a las once.
You go to bed at eleven o'clock.

Os llamáis Brígida y Pancho.
Your names are Brigida and Pancho.

Romeo **se casa con** Julieta.
Romeo *marries* Juliet.

Ellas se ponen nerviosas.
They become/get nervous.

¿Cuál es verdadero o falso para ti?

_____ 1. Me acuesto a las diez de la noche.

_____ 2. Me despierto a las seis y media de la mañana.

_____ 3. Me lavo el pelo cada día.

_____ 4. Me ducho cada mañana.

_____ 5. Me siento enfermo/a ahora.

_____ 6. Me pongo feliz cuando recibo un regalo para mi cumpleaños.

_____ 7. Me preocupo mucho por el dinero.

_____ 8. Me cepillo los dientes tres veces cada día.

_____ 9. Me enfermo más en el invierno que en el verano.

_____ 10. Me llamo Juan.

_____ 11. Después de ducharme, me visto.

_____ 12. Antes de acostarme, me quito la ropa y me pongo el pijama.

ejercicio   **1-10-1**

1. I go to bed. _____

2. You wash your hair. _____

3. He shaves every morning. _____

4. She shaves her legs. _____

5. You (*pl. fam.*) wake up. _____

6. They sit down. _____

7. She goes away. _____

8. My name is Rex. _____

9. You take a shower. _____

10. We get dressed. _____

11. You (*pl. fam.*) fall asleep. _____

12. She takes a bath. _____

13. I worry about the future. _____

14. You (*pl. form.*) wake up. _____

15. I get undressed (*desnudarse*) at night. _____

16. Your name is Alicia. _____

17. He takes off his shirt. _____

18. You (*pl. form.*) see yourselves in the mirror. _____

19. I feel sick. _____

20. You comb your hair. _____

21. We brush our teeth. _____

22. She falls asleep. _____

23. Do you take a shower? _____

24. His name is Martin. _____

traducción   I-10-2

Every night Marta goes to bed at eleven-thirty. She falls asleep quickly and she never has nightmares. Every morning she wakes up at six-thirty, but she doesn't get up until seven o'clock. She enters the bathroom where she brushes her teeth and looks at herself in the mirror. Some days she takes a bath, but usually she takes a shower because it's faster and because Marta feels cleaner. After the shower (or bath), Marta combs her hair and dries her hair. She gets dressed, walks to the kitchen where she sits down, drinks coffee, and reads the newspaper for fifteen minutes. Then she goes (away) to work.

vocabulario

bathroom	**el baño**	nightmare	**la pesadilla**
clean	**limpio**	quickly	**rápidamente**
fast	**rápido**	shower	**la ducha**
(to) look at (oneself)	**mirar(se)**	then	**entonces**
mirror	**el espejo**	work	**el trabajo**

_____

_____

_____

_____

_____

_____

_____

_____

_____

_____

_____

On a separate piece of paper, describe your morning routine, using as many reflexive verbs as you can.

Gustar et al.

There are several verbs in Spanish (and in English as well) that are commonly used *only* in the third person singular or plural. The most common of these verbs is ***gustar*** (to be pleasing to).

While in English one will say, "I like the cat" ("I" being the subject and "the cat" being the object), in Spanish you will say, literally, "The cat pleases me" ("The cat" now being the subject and "I" the object).

The key to the verbs in this section is to remember that they nearly always operate in their third person singular and plural forms. The things being discussed have their effect on people: Frogs fascinate *me;* Noise bothers *you;* Recipes for chili interest *him.*

To work with these verbs, you will use the following recipe:

indirect object pronoun + 3rd person singular or plural verb + noun(s)

examples:

singular subject
Me gusta el gato. I like the cat. **No te gusta el libro.** You don't like the book. **Le gusta la casa.** He likes the house. **No nos gusta el perro.** We don't like the dog. **Os gusta la luz.** You like the light. **Les gusta la revista.** They like the magazine.
plural subject
Me gustan los gatos. I like the cats. **No te gustan los libros.** You don't like the books. **Le gustan las casas.** He likes the houses. **No nos gustan los perros.** We don't like the dogs. **Os gustan las luces.** You like the lights. **Les gustan las revistas.** They like the magazines.

When mentioning the name of a person (or persons), place the name (or pronoun) between the preposition *a* and the indirect pronoun. This adds clarity and/or emphasis.

A **Juan** le gusta bailar.
John likes to dance.

A **los chicos** les gusta hablar.
The boys like to talk.

A **ella** le encanta el café.
She loves coffee.

A **ellos** no les falta nada.
They don't need anything.

bastar	to be sufficient/enough to: to suffice
disgustar	to be repugnant to; to "hate"
doler (*o → ue*)	to be painful to; to hurt
encantar	to be enchanting to; to "love"
faltar	to be lacking to; to be missing to
fascinar	to be fascinating to
gustar	to be pleasing to; to "like"
importar	to be important to
interesar	to be interesting to
molestar	to bother
parecer	to seem; to appear to
sobrar	to be left over to; to be in surplus

¿Verdadero o falso?

_____ 1. Me interesa la historia de los Estados Unidos.

_____ 2. Me molestan las arañas.

_____ 3. Me importan mucho mis estudios.

_____ 4. Muchos programas en la televisión me parecen absurdos.

_____ 5. Me duelen los pies ahora.

_____ 6. Los libros de Stephen King me fascinan.

_____ 7. Me encanta la música de Rubén Blades.

_____ 8. Me falta un botón en mi camisa ahora.

_____ 9. No me interesan los políticos.

_____ 10. A veces me duele la espalda.

_____ 11. Ahora me duelen mucho los ojos.

_____ 12. Normalmente, me sobra dinero.

ejercicio   1-11-1

1. Truth is important to me. _____

2. I don't like spiders. _____

3. My stomach aches. _____

4. I have too many books. _____

5. She likes the fall. _____

6. It seems ridiculous to me. _____

7. I love your dress! _____

8. We have ten dollars left over. _____

9. Your attitude disgusts me (I hate your attitude). _____

10. I love ice cream. _____

11. You are missing a button. _____

12. These photos are fascinating to us. _____

13. The movie is interesting to them. _____

14. What is important to you? _____

15. His manners disgust me. _____

16. He seems egotistical to me. _____

¿Cuál es verdadero o falso para tu mejor amigo o amiga?

_____ 1. A él (A ella) le gusta ir al cine.

_____ 2. A él (A ella) le importa el dinero.

_____ 3. A él (A ella) le encantan los dramas de William Shakespeare.

_____ 4. A él (A ella) le duele la cabeza con frecuencia.

_____ 5. A él (A ella) le duelen los dientes a veces.

_____ 6. A él (A ella) le fascinan las teorías de Albert Einstein.

_____ 7. A él (A ella) le interesa cocinar.

_____ 8. A él (A ella) le molestan los mentirosos (*liars*).

¡Te toca a ti!

Responde a las siguientes preguntas con frases completas:

1. ¿Qué comida te gusta más? _____

2. ¿Qué tienda te encanta? _____

3. ¿Qué cosas te interesan mucho? _____

4. ¿Qué te interesa mucho? _____

5. ¿Te falta dinero para comprar un Porsche? _____

6. ¿Qué te molesta mucho? _____

7. ¿Qué estación del año te encanta? ¿Por qué? _____

_____

8. ¿Qué aspectos de otras personas te fascinan? _____

_____

¿Cuál es verdadero o falso para estos personajes de la literatura?

_____ 1. A Romeo le fascina Julieta.

_____ 2. A Huck Finn y Tom Sawyer les disgusta la escuela.

_____ 3. A Don Quijote le gusta quedarse en casa.

_____ 4. A Mary Poppins le encantan los niños.

_____ 5. A Caperucita Roja le molesta el lobo.

_____ 6. A Gulliver el mundo le parece muy pequeño.

_____ 7. A Rapunzel le sobra mucho pelo.

_____ 8. A Pinocho le encanta la verdad.

_____ 9. A la Mala Bruja del Oeste le faltan los zapatos de rubí.

_____ 10. A la Bella Durmiente le falta un beso del príncipe.

_____ 11. Al Rey Midas no le importa ni le interesa el oro.

_____ 12. A las malas hermanastras, les duelen los pies cuando se ponen los zapatos de la Cenicienta.

traducción   **1-11-2**

Today is the Fourth of July. Tonight we're going to have a party and tomorrow morning I'm going to sleep (until) very late because I don't have to work. I love the summer! It seems to me that June, July, and August are the best months of the year. I don't have to go to school. I go to bed late and I get up late. I eat when I'm hungry; I drink when I'm thirsty; and I fall asleep when I'm tired. Nothing bothers me in the summer. On the other hand, three months of sun and warmth are enough for me, and by the first of September I'm ready for the fall.

vocabulario

(to) be ready	**estar listo/a**	month	**el mes**
(the) best (*pl.*)	**los mejores**	on the other hand	**en cambio**
fall	**el otoño**	summer	**el verano**
(the) first	**el primero**	tomorrow morning	**mañana por la mañana**
late	**tarde**	warmth	**el calor**

The Present Progressive

The use of the present progressive is easy to spot in English. The time is in the present, and *-ing* is attached to the verb, e.g., I am *studying* (now). The addition of *-ing* to a verb indicates that the action is *in progress,* hence the label, present progressive.

Before we begin to work with this aspect of the present tense, it is important to note that you will use the present progressive *less* in Spanish than in English. In English, we use the present progressive very broadly, often to describe what is going on in our lives in general: I am *living* in New York; I am *working* in a bank; I am *taking* dance lessons.

In Spanish, however, the use of the present progressive is more restricted, and is used mostly to indicate what a person is doing *right now.* In other words, you will use the present progressive to describe what you are doing or what is happening at the time you report it. The rest of the time you will use the simple present tense: I *live* in New York; I *work* in a bank; I *take* dance lessons.

Formation of the Present Progressive

As in English, there are two parts to the present progressive: the auxiliary *to be* and the *present participle,* which is the verb with *-ing* attached. In Spanish, the auxiliary is *estar:* **estoy; estás; está; estamos; estáis; están.** The conjugated *estar* is then followed by the *present participle.*

> **Regularly formed present participles:** Nearly all present participles are formed regularly. To form these, do the following:
>
> > *-ar verbs:* **drop the -ar and add -ando** (*hablando; estudiando; trabajando; pensando*)
> >
> > *-er verbs:* **drop the -er and add -iendo** (*comiendo; bebiendo; vendiendo; poniendo*)
> >
> > *-ir verbs:* **drop the -ir and add -iendo** (*abriendo; sufriendo; escribiendo; viviendo*)

Note that *-er* verbs and *-ir* verbs share the same present participle ending. Also, except for *-ir* stem-changing verbs (see page 77), verb stems will not change: *pensando; volando; entendiendo; almorzando; volviendo,* etc.

examples:

Estoy **hablando.**
I am *speaking.*

Estás **comiendo.**
You are *eating.*

Él está **abriendo** la puerta.
He is *opening* the door.

Estamos **estudiando.**
We are *studying.*

Estáis **bebiendo** leche.
You are *drinking* milk.

Ellos están **escribiendo** una carta.
They are *writing* a letter.

In the course of an average day, which of the following things do you do? Put an X by those things.

_____ 1. Estoy trabajando.

_____ 2. Estoy estudiando español.

_____ 3. Estoy practicando el piano.

_____ 4. Estoy vendiendo ropa.

_____ 5. Estoy escribiendo una carta.

_____ 6. Estoy pensando en mi familia.

_____ 7. Estoy comprando comida.

_____ 8. Estoy cocinando.

_____ 9. Estoy contando el dinero

_____ 10. Estoy confesando un crimen.

_____ 11. Estoy moviendo los muebles (*furniture*) en la casa.

_____ 12. Estoy resolviendo mis problemas.

_____ 13. Estoy lavando los platos.

_____ 14. Estoy conduciendo (manejando) el coche.

_____ 15. No estoy haciendo nada.

ejercicio 1-12-1

1. I am buying a gift for Juan. _____

2. You are watching the television. _____

3. He is playing the piano. _____

4. We are eating pizza and drinking lemonade. _____

5. You (*pl. fam.*) are receiving many gifts. _____

6. You (*pl. form.*) are covering the furniture. _____

7. We are eating lunch. _____

8. I am thinking about my best friend. _____

9. What are you doing? _____

10. What is she eating? _____

Irregularly formed present participles: *-Er* and *-ir* verbs whose stem ends in a vowel (e.g., *leer* or *influir*) require a slight twist when forming the present participle. With these verbs, the participle ending will be **-yendo** (to avoid having three vowels in a row). Several of these verbs along with their respective present participles are listed below.

-er verbs			-ir verbs		
atraer	to attract	*atrayendo*	**construir**	to construct	*construyendo*
caer	to fall	*cayendo*	**contribuir**	to contribute	*contribuyendo*
contraer	to contract	*contrayendo*	**destruir**	to destroy	*destruyendo*
creer	to believe	*creyendo*	**fluir**	to flow	*fluyendo*
leer	to read	*leyendo*	**huir**	to flee	*huyendo*
poseer	to possess	*poseyendo*	**incluir**	to include	*incluyendo*
raer	to scrape	*rayendo*	**influir**	to influence	*influyendo*
releer	to reread	*releyendo*	**instituir**	to institute	*instituyendo*
retraer	to bring back	*retrayendo*	**ir**	to go	*yendo*
sustraer	to remove	*sustrayendo*	**oír**	to hear	*oyendo*
traer	to bring	*trayendo*	**sustituir**	to substitute	*sustituyendo*

Note that the present participle for the verb *ir* is *yendo*.

Think of one of your friends. Which of the following statements could you conceivably make about him or her in the course of an average day? Put an X by those things he or she might do.

_____ 1. Está leyendo el periódico.

_____ 2. Está contribuyendo dinero a la iglesia.

_____ 3. Está trayendo los libros a la escuela.

_____ 4. Está construyendo una casa.

_____ 5. Está huyendo de la policía.

_____ 6. Está releyendo un buen libro.

_____ 7. Está destruyendo una casa.

_____ 8. Está sustituyendo a un profesor en la escuela.

_____ 9. Está oyendo mucho ruido (*noise*).

_____ 10. Está influyendo mucho a otro/a amigo/a.

ejercicio   1-12-2

1. The river is flowing to the south. _____

2. The client is not believing the car salesman (*vendedor de coches*). _____

_____

3. We are not reading anything. _____

4. The President is influencing the people. _____

_____

5. Hatred (*el odio*) is destroying our society (*la sociedad*). _____

_____

6. Romeo is fleeing with Juliet. _____

7. She isn't hearing anything in the basement (*el sótano*). _____

_____

8. What are you reading? _____

9. Who is bringing wine to the party? _____

10. Why are you (*pl. form.*) constructing a house in the suburbs (*las afueras*)? _____

_____

Present participles for -*ir* stem-changing verbs: For -*ir* stem-changing verbs, do the following to form the present participle:

o → ue verbs become *o → u:*	**dormir → *durmiendo***	sleeping
	morir → *muriendo*	dying
e → ie verbs become *e → i:*	**advertir → *advirtiendo***	warning
	consentir → *consintiendo*	consenting
	hervir → *hirviendo*	boiling
	mentir → *mintiendo*	lying
	preferir → *prefiriendo*	preferring
	referir → *refiriendo*	referring
	sentir → *sintiendo*	regretting
	sugerir → *sugiriendo*	suggesting

e → i **verbs remain** *e → i:*

competir → *compitiendo*	competing
conseguir → *consiguiendo*	getting
decir → *diciendo*	saying; telling
medir → *midiendo*	measuring
pedir → *pidiendo*	requesting
reír → *riendo*	laughing
repetir → *repitiendo*	repeating
seguir → *siguiendo*	following
servir → *sirviendo*	serving

ejercicio   **1-12-3**

Fill in the blank with the appropriate present participle from the preceding list to make a meaningful sentence:

1. El gato está _____ en el sofá.

2. Pinocho está _____ a Gipetto.

3. Yo estoy _____ el agua para preparar el café.

4. La criada (*maid*) está _____ la cena.

5. Los niños se están _____ del payaso (*clown*).

6. Los Yanquis de Nueva York están _____ contra las Medias Blancas de Chicago.

7. El cómico está _____ bromas (*jokes*) al público.

8. Después de probar el insecticida, las cucarachas se están _____ .

9. La policía está _____ el carro del criminal.

10. El adolescente está _____ a sus padres las llaves del carro.

Object pronouns with the present progressive: When the verb in its present progressive form takes an object (or objects), the object(s) will be attached directly to the present participle. When there are two objects, remember the **RID** rule: **R**eflexive; **I**ndirect; **D**irect. This is the *only* order in which object pronouns can go. Note also the accents below, which are necessary to maintain the conjugated verb's original stress.

examples:

Estoy **mirándolo.**
I am *watching it.*

Estás **escribiéndole.**
You are *writing to him.*

Él está **duchándose.**
He is *taking a shower.*

Ella está **comprándoselo.**
She is *buying it for herself.*

Estamos **discutiéndolo.**
We are *discussing it.*

Estáis **cantándonos.**
You are *singing to us.*

Ellos están **cepillándose los dientes.**
They are *brushing their teeth.*

Ellos están **haciéndomelos.**
They are *making them for me.*

In the course of an average morning, which of the following do you do? Put an X before those things.

_____ 1. Estoy duchándome.

_____ 2. Estoy cepillándome los dientes.

_____ 3. Estoy acostándome.

_____ 4. Estoy bañándome.

_____ 5. Estoy lavándome el pelo.

_____ 6. Estoy quitándome la ropa.

_____ 7. Estoy durmiéndome.

_____ 8. Estoy contándoles un chiste a mis amigos.

_____ 9. Estoy viéndome en el espejo.

_____ 10. Estoy preocupándome por el peso.

_____ 11. Estoy sentándome para tomar café.

_____ 12. Estoy poniéndome la ropa.

ejercicio 1-12-4

1. I am studying it (*m.*). _____

2. You are singing it (*f.*) to us. _____

3. He is writing me a letter. _____

4. Are you writing to them? _____

5. Why are you (*pl. form.*) telling me this? _____

6. Why are you telling it (*m.*) to me? _____

7. They are sitting down. _____

8. We are reading it (*m.*). _____

9. She is lying to me. _____

10. What are you giving me? _____

11. They are following us. _____

12. What is she reading to you? _____

PART II

The Past, Future, and Conditional Tenses

The Preterite Tense

The **preterite tense** allows you to refer to specific past actions performed (1) at a fixed point in time, (2) a specific number of times, or (3) during an enclosed amount of time.

The key is the quantitative nature of the action. If the action is in the past and you can pin-point it as to when or how many times it occurred, you will use the preterite tense. It is as though there were a frame or box around the action. Consider the following sentences:

Fixed point in time:

> I *called* you *at 3:00*.
>
> He *bought* the car on *Tuesday afternoon*.
>
> We *saw* the movie *last night*.

Specific number of actions:

> I *called* you *five times*.
>
> They *ate ten sandwiches*.
>
> She *read* the book *twice*.

Enclosed amount of time:

> I *worked* for *eight hours*.
>
> The movie *lasted two and a half hours*.
>
> He *lived* there for *two years*.

In each of the preceding sentences, the action's time is specific, measured in some way, either by the clock, the calendar, or number of times the action occurred.

It is important to remember that while an obvious feature of the preterite tense is how it quantifies action, we do not always state the quantity of our actions. When the quantity is not stated, it is generally implied. Consider these sentences:

1. I *went* to John's party.

2. We *ate* at McDonald's.

3. The meeting *was* boring.

In the first two sentences, the implication is that the person performed the action *once*. In the third, the implication is that the *entire* meeting, from beginning to end, was boring.

A good test for determining if a sentence is in the preterite is to consider if it is reasonable to ask "For how long?" or "When?" the action took place.

For example, if someone tells you, "John called me," you can reasonably ask, "When?" and expect a specific answer. But if this person says, "John used to call me several times a day," you probably would be wasting your time if you asked *when*.

In other words, "John called me" is in the preterite, while "John used to call me several times a day" is not (this latter sentence is in the imperfect tense, which will be discussed in the next unit).

Regular Verbs in the Preterite

To form regular verbs in the preterite you do the following:

-ar verbs: drop the -ar and add the following endings:	
-é -amos -aste -asteis -ó -aron	*(I spoke, you spoke, etc.)* **yo hablé nosotros hablamos** **tú hablaste vosotros hablasteis** **él habló ellos hablaron**

Note that the *nosotros* form is identical in the preterite and the present tenses for *-ar* verbs.

examples:

Yo **hablé.**   **Hablamos** con Juan.
I *spoke.*   *We spoke* with John.

Tú **miraste** la película.   Vosotros **comprasteis** palomitas.
You *watched* the movie.   You *bought* popcorn.

Ella me **llamó** tres veces.   Ellos **contaron** el dinero.
She *called* me three times.   They *counted* the money.

-er and -ir verbs: drop the -er or -ir and add the following endings:		
-í -imos -iste -isteis -ió -ieron	*(I ate, you ate, etc.)* **yo comí nosotros comimos** **tú comiste vosotros comisteis** **él comió ellos comieron**	*(I opened, you opened, etc.)* **yo abrí nosotros abrimos** **tú abriste vosotros abristeis** **él abrió ellos abrieron**

Note: Most stem-changing verbs change only in the present tense (*not* in the preterite), e.g., *contar* (to count): *yo cuento* (I count); *yo conté* (I counted). The exceptions to this are *-ir* stem-changing verbs, and are discussed under **irregular verbs,** on page 88.

examples:

Escribí una carta.   **Comimos** pizza.
I *wrote* a letter.   *We ate* pizza.

Vendiste tu casa.
You sold your house.

Rompisteis las ventanas.
You broke the windows.

Ella **bebió** tres vasos de leche.
She *drank* three glasses of milk.

Ellos **abrieron** las cajas.
They *opened* the boxes.

Before working with the preterite, it is important to be familiar with the more common preterite "markers," or words and phrases that indicate specific time frames. Several are listed below.

ayer	yesterday	**la semana pasada**	last week
anoche	last night	**el mes (año) pasado**	last month (year)
esta mañana	this morning	**hace _____**	_____ ago
esta tarde	this afternoon	**ayer por la mañana/tarde**	yesterday morning/afternoon

Para ti, ¿cuál es verdadero o falso?

_____ 1. Hablé por teléfono ayer por la tarde.

_____ 2. Comí una ensalada anoche.

_____ 3. Abrí las ventanas en mi casa hace dos horas.

_____ 4. Miré la televisión anoche.

_____ 5. Bebí jugo de naranja esta mañana.

_____ 6. Asistí a la escuela la semana pasada.

_____ 7. Compré un coche el año pasado.

_____ 8. Vendí mi casa el mes pasado.

ejercicio   II-1-1

1. I bought a shirt yesterday. _____

2. You studied last night. _____

3. She worked for two hours. _____

4. We washed the dishes. _____

5. They sang five songs. _____

6. I ran to the corner. _____

7. You wrote a letter. _____

8. She opened the door. _____

9. We didn't open those windows. _____

10. They sold the car. _____

11. We danced the tango last night. _____

12. They spoke with the owner. _____

13. I took a shower this morning. _____

14. You washed your hair. _____

15. They went to bed at eleven-thirty. _____

¡Te toca a ti!

Responde, con frases completas, a las siguientes preguntas:

1. ¿Hablaste por teléfono anoche? _____

2. ¿Dónde te compraste la camisa? _____

3. ¿Qué comiste anoche? _____

4. ¿Qué recibiste para tu último cumpleaños? _____

5. ¿Escuchaste la radio hoy? _____

6. ¿Tomaste café ayer por la mañana? _____

7. ¿Bailaste el fin de semana pasado? _____

8. ¿Estudiaste español el año pasado? _____

Orthographic Changes in Regular Verbs

There are three standard orthographic (spelling) changes in Spanish which affect verbs in the preterite as well as in other tenses. In the preterite, these changes occur only in the first person singular *yo* form. They are as follows:

1. verbs ending in **-gar:** insert a **u** before the **e: yo llegué** (I arrived)

2. verbs ending in **-car:** the **c** changes to **qu** before the letter **e: yo practiqué** (I practiced)

3. verbs ending in **-zar:** the **z** changes to **c** before the letter **e: yo empecé** (I began)

The reason for the first two changes is phonetic: in order to retain the original hard **g** and **c** sounds, the letter **u** is inserted (the letters **g** and **c** are soft before the vowels **e** and **i**). In the last change it is because the letter **z** *never* directly precedes the letter **e** in Spanish (except in rare cases when **ze** are the first two letters of a word).

Some frequently used verbs in these categories, with the preterite *yo* form:

llegar	to arrive	*yo llegué*
jugar	to play (a game)	*yo jugué*

pagar	to pay (for)	*yo pagué*
regar	to water (a plant)	*yo regué*
segar	to mow (grass, etc.)	*yo segué*
tragar	to swallow	*yo tragué*
vagar	to wander	*yo vagué*
aparcar	to park	*yo aparqué*
buscar	to look for, search	*yo busqué*
clarificar	to clarify	*yo clarifiqué*
clasificar	to classify	*yo clasifiqué*
destacar	to stand out	*yo destaqué*
empacar	to pack	*yo empaqué*
justificar	to justify	*yo justifiqué*
practicar	to practice	*yo practiqué*
sacar	to take out, take a picture	*yo saqué*
tocar	to touch, play (an instrument)	*yo toqué*
autorizar	to authorize	*yo autoricé*
comenzar	to commence, begin	*yo comencé*
empezar	to begin	*yo empecé*
organizar	to organize	*yo organicé*
rezar	to pray	*yo recé*
simbolizar	to symbolize	*yo simbolicé*
trazar	to trace	*yo tracé*
tropezarse (con)	to bump (into)	*yo me tropecé*

Remember: Only verbs in the *yo* form are affected by these orthographic changes.

ejercicio II-1-2

1. I practiced the piano for an hour. _____

2. I arrived at two o'clock. _____

3. I organized the party. _____

4. I began to dance on the table. _____

5. I played the guitar for two hours at the reception. _____

6. I played tennis with the pro (*el jugador profesional*). _____

7. I took twenty pictures of my cat. _____

8. I authorized the purchase. _____

9. I classified the information. _____

10. I bumped into your house's step (*el peldaño*). _____

11. I parked the car in a prohibited space. _____

12. I never stood out in English for my pronunciation. _____

_____

13. I swallowed the medicine without thinking. _____

_____

14. I paid the gas bill. _____

15. I watered my friend Lola's plants. _____

Final note: While these three types of verbs do not exactly follow the regular pattern of forming the preterite tense, they are still considered regular verbs in the preterite because these changes occur at *all* times in *all* tenses.

Irregular Verbs in the Preterite

There are several irregular verbs in the preterite. While patterns do emerge and the endings are similar, it is important to understand the various types of conjugations.

The following eleven verbs all take this set of endings:

-e	-imos
-iste	-isteis
-o	-ieron

1. **andar** to walk — anduv- — anduve; anduviste; anduvo . . .
2. **estar** to be — estuv- — estuve; estuviste; estuvo . . .
3. **tener** to have — tuv- — tuve; tuviste; tuvo . . .
4. **caber** to fit — cup- — cupe; cupiste; cupo . . .
5. **haber** auxiliary, to have — hub- — hube; hubiste; hubo . . .
6. **poder** to be able to — pud- — pude; pudiste; pudo . . .
7. **poner** to put, place — pus- — puse; pusiste; puso . . .
8. **saber** to know — sup- — supe; supiste; supo . . .
9. **hacer** to make, do — hic- — hice; hiciste; hizo . . .
10. **querer** to want — quis- — quise; quisiste; quiso . . .
11. **venir** to come — vin- — vine; viniste; vino . . .

Note:

1. Verbs 1–3 take the letter *uv* in the new stem; 4–8 take a *u;* and 9–11 take an *i.*

2. The only exception above is the third person singular of *hacer,* which is *hizo.* (The *c* changes to *z* to avoid the *k* sound.)

3. There are no accent marks on these irregular endings.

4. For their full conjugations, consult the preterite verb chart in the appendix.

Para ti, ¿cuál es verdadero o falso?

_____ 1. Tuve una fiesta hace dos semanas.

_____ 2. Anduve a la escuela esta mañana.

_____ 3. Anoche no pude dormir.

_____ 4. No hice nada ayer.

_____ 5. Alguien vino a mi casa el fin de semana pasado.

_____ 6. Puse los zapatos en el armario anoche.

_____ 7. Estuve increíblemente enfermo/a ayer.

_____ 8. Anduve al cine esta semana.

ejercicio   11-1-3

1. I walked to the store. _____

2. He came to my party. _____

3. Last night I couldn't sleep. _____

4. They had an accident last Tuesday. _____

5. We made the beds this morning. _____

6. When did you know (find out) the answer? _____

7. You (*pl. fam.*) were here for no more than ten minutes. _____

_____

8. I put the clothes in the closet. _____

9. What did you do last night? _____

10. They had to work for ten hours yesterday. _____

11. I put on my shoes. _____

12. We were there for half an hour. _____

13. Who made these invitations? _____

14. She didn't come to the meeting because she had an accident. _____

_____

15. I was in the store for twenty minutes and then I came here. _____

_____

¡Te toca a ti!

¿Qué hiciste ayer? List ten things that you did yesterday:

1. _____

2. _____

3. _____

4. _____

5. _____

6. _____

7. _____

8. _____

9. _____

10. _____

Ser and ir: The preterite conjugations for *ser* and *ir* are identical. But don't worry, because the context will carry the desired meaning, and *ser* is used less often than *ir* in the preterite.

ser		ir	
(I was, you were, etc.)		*(I went, you went, etc.)*	
fui	fuimos	fui	fuimos
fuiste	fuisteis	fuiste	fuisteis
fue	fueron	fue	fueron

ejercicio   ll-1-4

1. I went to the game. _____

2. I was president of the club for one year. _____

3. He went to the store (in order) to buy eggs. _____

4. Why did you go away? _____

5. They didn't go yesterday because they went last week. _____

_____

6. We didn't go to the wedding. _____

7. Did you (*pl. fam.*) go to school today? _____

8. Who was the big winner yesterday? _____

9. The party was terrible. _____

10. The meeting was/went well. _____

11. Anita and Pepe were boyfriend/girlfriend (*novios*) for two years, but they never went to Venice.

_____

12. He was my best friend for ten years. _____

13. We went separately (*por separado*) to the same store. _____

_____

14. Where did you (*pl. form.*) go last night? _____

15. How was the party? _____ It was a disaster!

_____

Decir and ***traer:***   The verbs *decir* (to say, tell) and *traer* (to bring) are conjugated as follows:

decir		traer	
(I said/told, you said/told, etc.)		*(I brought, you brought, etc.)*	
dije	dijimos	traje	trajimos
dijiste	dijisteis	trajiste	trajisteis
dijo	dijeron	trajo	trajeron

Verbs related to, and conjugated in the same manner as *traer:*

atraer	to attract	(**atraje,** etc.)
distraer	to distract	(**distraje,** etc.)
retraer	to bring back, dissuade	(**retraje,** etc.)
sustraer	to remove, take away	(**sustraje,** etc.)

ejercicio   II-1-5

1. I told the children my name. _____

2. You told me a lie. _____

3. He brought wine to the party. _____

4. He said that he spoke with Carlos last week. _____

5. We said that we didn't eat the cookies. _____

6. The television distracted me. _____

7. What did you (*pl. form.*) say to Mary? _____

8. What did you tell her? _____

9. His manners attracted me. _____

10. What did he say when you told him that you wrote the letter? _____

    _____

11. I didn't tell them anything. _____

12. What did you bring us? _____

13. They didn't tell me the truth. _____

14. Did he tell you what he told me yesterday? _____

15. The sugar attracted the flies. _____

***Dar* and *ver*:**   The verbs *dar* and *ver* are very similar in their preterite conjugations and thus are easy to learn together. While *dar* is clearly irregular, *ver* is irregular only in that the accent marks on the first and third person singular are omitted. Their conjugations are as follows:

dar		ver	
(*I gave, you gave, etc.*)		(*I saw, you saw, etc.*)	
di	dimos	vi	vimos
diste	disteis	viste	visteis
dio	dieron	vio	vieron

ejercicio   II-1-6

1. I gave John a package yesterday. _____

2. I saw John yesterday. _____

3. She gave me a book. _____

4. She saw us at the movies. _____

5. What did you give him for his birthday? _____

6. Which (What) movie did you (*pl. fam.*) see last night? _____

_____

7. When they saw me, they gave me the money. _____

_____

8. You (*pl. form.*) didn't give us anything. _____

9. Did you see the cat that Miguel gave me? _____

10. I didn't see the present that they gave us. _____

traducción   II-1-7

I went to Puerto Rico last January. It was wonderful! A friend of mine is a travel agent, and when she offered me the opportunity to go to the Caribbean for a week of sun and fun—for very little money—I said to her, "When do we go?" The day that we left it snowed six inches here. When we arrived in San Juan, sun, heat, and sand greeted us. We took a taxi to our hotel, I took my bathing suit out of my suitcase and we went to the beach. The next day we went to El Yunque, the rain forest, where we walked for hours and saw many beautiful birds and trees. I couldn't believe it—it was so beautiful! The next day we went to Luquillo Beach and swam and read and relaxed. We did this every day until—alas!—we had to return to reality.

vocabulario

alas!	**¡ay!**	(to) offer	**ofrecer**
bathing suit	**el traje de baño**	rain forest	**la selva tropical**
beach	**la playa**	(to) relax	**relajarse**
bird	**el pájaro**	sand	**la arena**
fun	**la diversión**	(to) snow	**nevar**
inch	**la pulgada**	(to) take out	**sacar**
(the) next day	**al día siguiente**	travel agent	**el/la agente de viajes**

_____

_____

_____

_____

-Ir stem-changing verbs: As mentioned earlier, most stem-changing verbs change only in the present. However, *-ir* stem-changing verbs make small changes in the preterite. There are three kinds of *-ir* stem-changing verbs in the present tense, and they make the following changes in the preterite, but *only* in the third person singular and plural.

In *o → ue* verbs in the present, the *o* changes to *u* in the preterite:

dormir *(to sleep)*	
(I slept, you slept, etc.)	
dormí	dormimos
dormiste	dormisteis
durmió	**durmieron**

In *e → ie* verbs in the present, the *e* changes to *i* in the preterite:

mentir *(to lie)*	
(I lied, you lied, etc.)	
mentí	mentimos
mentiste	mentisteis
mintió	**mintieron**

In *e → i* verbs in the present, the *e* changes to *i* in the preterite:

pedir *(to request, ask for)*	
(I requested, you requested, etc.)	
pedí	pedimos
pediste	pedisteis
pidió	**pidieron**

Verbs in these categories:

o → ue verbs in the present:		*e → ie* verbs in the present:		*e → i* verbs in the present:	
dormir	to sleep	**advertir**	to advise, warn	**medir**	to measure, be long
morir	to die	**mentir**	to lie	**pedir**	to request, ask for
		preferir	to prefer	**repetir**	to repeat
		sentir(se)	to feel	**seguir**	to follow, continue
				servir	to serve

ejercicio II-1-8

1. She slept for ten hours. _____

2. They lied to me. _____

3. He requested more coffee. _____

4. The cockroaches died. _____

5. Our lawyer warned us of the danger (*el peligro*). _____

_____

6. At that moment she preferred not to say anything. _____

_____

7. Did they advise you of your rights? _____

8. Dorothy followed the yellow brick (*de ladrillos*) road. _____

_____

9. They repeated the question twice. _____

10. He asked for a raise. _____

Verbs that change i → y in the preterite: In those -*er* and -*ir* verbs in which a vowel immediately precedes the infinitive ending, the third person singular and plural change from *i* to *y*. In all other forms there is a written accent over the letter *i:*

creer (*to believe*)	
(*I believed, you believed, etc.*)	
creí	creímos
creíste	creísteis
creyó	**creyeron**

Verbs in this category:

		él	**ellos**
caer	to fall	**cayó**	**cayeron**
caer(se)	to fall down	**se cayó**	**se cayeron**
creer	to believe	**creyó**	**creyeron**
leer	to read	**leyó**	**leyeron**
oír	to hear	**oyó**	**oyeron**
poseer	to possess	**poseyó**	**poseyeron**
proveer	to provide	**proveyó**	**proveyeron**

exceptions:

1. The verb *traer* (and its compound verbs *atraer* and *distraer*): see page 91 for their conjugations.

2. Verbs ending in *-guir* (e.g., *seguir*): the *u* is not pronounced.

3. Verbs ending in *-uir* (e.g., *destruir*) make the change from *i* → *y*; however, the written accent over the *i* appears only in the first person singular form. See as follows:

destruir *(to destroy)*	
(I destroyed, you destroyed, etc.)	
destruí	destruimos
destruiste	destruisteis
destruyó	**destruyeron**

Verbs in this category:

		él	**ellos**
construir	to build, construct	**construyó**	**construyeron**
contribuir	to contribute	**contribuyó**	**contribuyeron**
destruir	to destroy	**destruyó**	**destruyeron**
fluir	to flow, run	**fluyó**	**fluyeron**
huir	to flee, run away	**huyó**	**huyeron**
incluir	to include	**incluyó**	**incluyeron**
influir	to influence	**influyó**	**influyeron**

ejercicio   II-1-9

1. John didn't hear me. _____

2. They read my book twice. _____

3. The trees fell down during the storm. _____

4. Romeo and Juliet ran away. _____

5. The caterers (*los abastecedores*) didn't provide enough bread. _____

_____

6. The thieves (*los ladrones*) destroyed our house. _____

7. Did you read my newspaper? _____

8. They contributed one hundred fifty dollars last year. _____

_____

9. The dish ran away with the spoon. _____

10. Humpty Dumpty fell down. _____

11. The tears flowed from my eyes. _____

12. The branch fell from the tree. _____

13. They fled from the scene of the crime. _____

14. They constructed an enormous house. _____

_____

15. Why didn't he include us? _____

Verbs ending in *-ucir:* All verbs ending with *-ucir* are conjugated like *producir.*

producir *(to produce)*	
(I produced, you produced, etc.)	
produje	**produjimos**
produjiste	**produjisteis**
produjo	**produjeron**

Verbs in this category:

		él	ellos
conducir	to drive, lead	**condujo**	**condujeron**
deducir	to deduce, infer	**dedujo**	**dedujeron**
inducir	to induce, lead	**indujo**	**indujeron**
introducir	to introduce	**introdujo**	**introdujeron**
producir	to produce	**produjo**	**produjeron**
reducir	to reduce, cut down	**redujo**	**redujeron**
traducir	to translate	**tradujo**	**tradujeron**

ejercicio   II-1-10

1. I produced a movie last year. _____

2. You translated the document well. _____

3. We drove to the theater. _____

4. The magician produced a rabbit from the hat. _____

_____

5. You (*pl. fam.*) drove twenty miles. _____

6. I translated this sentence from English to Spanish. _____

_____

7. We led the boys to the cafeteria. _____

8. They drove us to the wedding. _____

9. How many pages did you translate? _____

10. How far (*hasta dónde*) did you drive? _____

11. I deduced the answer. _____

12. The President didn't reduce taxes (*los impuestos*) last year. _____

_____

traducción   11-1-11

H. L. Mencken was a great writer. He was born in Baltimore in 1880, where he lived his entire life, and he died in 1956. He wrote many essays on politics and social issues, but his principal interest, I believe, was language, in particular, the English of the United States. One of his most famous books is *The American Language,* in which Mencken discussed the richness of the United States and how many other languages influenced this language. He also produced a series of autobiographies and diaries. He read all types of literature and possessed a strict personal ethic. He believed that a person should work hard, play hard, and above all, think.

vocabulario

(to be) born	**nacer**	language (particular)	**el idioma**
essay	**el ensayo**	politics	**la política**
ethic	**el credo**	richness	**la riqueza**
issue	**la cuestión**	type	**la clase**
language (general)	**el lenguaje**	writer	**el escritor**

_____

_____

_____

_____

_____

_____

Verbs that change meaning in the preterite: Because the preterite tense implies that an action occurred either at or over a specific period of time, certain verbs change meaning in this tense. Note that the action of the following verbs is more mental/emotional than physical.

Verbs in this category:

	present	**preterite**
conocer	to know (a person/place)	to meet *Conocí* a Juan hace dos años. *I met* John two years ago.
poder	to be able (to do something)	to manage (to do something) *Ella pudo* encontrarlo. *She managed* to find it.
no poder	not to be able (to do something)	to fail (to do something) *No pudimos* encontrarlo. *We couldn't/failed* to find it.
querer	to want	to try *Quise* salir. *I tried* to leave/*I wanted* to leave *very badly*.
no querer	not to want	to refuse *Él no quiso* comer. *He refused* to eat.
saber	to know (a fact/information)	to find out (learn) ¿Cuándo lo *supiste*? When *did you find* (it) *out*?
sentir	to feel	to regret, be sorry *Sentí* llamarla. *I regretted* calling/*I was sorry* I called her.
tener	to have	to have (at a certain time) *Ella tuvo* un bebé ayer. *She had* a baby yesterday.

Para ti, ¿cuál es verdadero o falso?

_____   1. No pude dormir anoche.

_____   2. Conocí a mi mejor amigo/a hace más de cinco años.

_____   3. Tuve un accidente de coche el año pasado.

_____   4. Pude pagar los impuestos el año pasado antes del quince de abril.

_____   5. Leí el periódico esta mañana y supe mucho de los dilemas políticos.

_____   6. En mi cumpleaños pasado no quise comer nada.

_____   7. Una amiga mía tuvo un bebé este año.

_____   8. Mis padres se conocieron en una cita a ciegas (*blind date*).

_____ 9. Muchos políticos no pudieron cumplir la palabra este año.

_____ 10. Mi mejor amigo/a tuvo una fiesta en su casa el sábado pasado.

ejercicio   II-1-12

1. I met Phillip a year and a half ago (*hace un año y medio*). _____

   _____

2. He failed to see my point of view. _____

3. They didn't find (it) out until yesterday. _____

4. My sister had a baby last May. _____

5. Why did you (*pl. fam.*) refuse to leave? _____

6. He regretted winning the money. _____

7. She tried to leave but couldn't (failed to) find her keys. _____

   _____

8. I managed to pay the bills on time this month. _____

9. We met each other on an elevator. _____

10. When I found out that Juana managed to forge (*falsificar*) my signature, I couldn't think. _____

    _____

The Imperfect Tense

We use the imperfect when referring to actions that took place in the past *either repeatedly* or *over an extended period of time.* Unlike the preterite, which is used to specify an action either at a particular point in time or number of times, the imperfect indicates that an action took place during a non-specified amount of time or was repeated an indefinite number of times.

The element of time, though certainly in the past, is necessarily *not* specific. It is impossible to determine when the action began or ended, or the exact time or number of times it occurred, for this specificity is irrelevant.

Consider the following sentences:

> I used to live in St. Louis.
>
> John always ate cereal for breakfast.
>
> Mary was a good conversationalist.

In the first sentence, the message clearly states that I lived in St. Louis in the past; however, *when* or *for how long* is not mentioned. While this action could be quantified (i.e., I lived in St. Louis *for four years*), in this sentence the speaker has chosen not to do so. Thus, in this case, the length of time is irrelevant.

In the second sentence, we know that in the past John ate cereal for breakfast. The addition of the word *always,* however, indicates (1) that he did so many, many times and (2) it would be virtually impossible to find out exactly how many times he did eat cereal for breakfast. In this case, the number of times cannot be determined.

The last sentence is a description of something that was ongoing. In fact, there is no real action involved other than being. The time involved most likely would be "most of Mary's life." As in the first sentence, the exact amount of time is irrelevant in this context, and as in the second example, it would be impossible to determine *exactly* how long she was able to keep up her end of a conversation.

The essence of the imperfect tense is that the specific elements of time are missing. Messages in the imperfect do not tell us *when specifically,* rather *when in general.*

Regular Verbs in the Imperfect

Nearly all verbs in the imperfect are regular. Only three verbs—*ser, ir,* and *ver*—are irregular. To form the imperfect, you will do the following:

-ar verbs: drop the **-ar** and add:

-aba	-ábamos
-abas	-abais
-aba	-aban

Consider the verbs **hablar** and **estudiar:**

(I used to speak, you used to speak, etc.)		*(I used to study, you used to study, etc.)*	
hablaba	hablábamos	estudiaba	estudiábamos
hablabas	hablabais	estudiabas	estudiabais
hablaba	hablaban	estudiaba	estudiaban

-er and **-ir** verbs: drop the **-er** or **-ir** and add:

-ía	-íamos
-ías	-íais
-ía	-ían

Consider the verbs **comer** and **vivir:**

(I used to eat, you used to eat, etc.)		*(I used to live, you used to live, etc.)*	
comía	comíamos	vivía	vivíamos
comías	comíais	vivías	vivíais
comía	comían	vivía	vivían

Irregular Verbs in the Imperfect

Only the following three verbs are formed irregularly in the imperfect:

ser		ir		ver	
(I used to be, etc.)		*(I used to go, etc.)*		*(I used to see, etc.)*	
era	éramos	iba	íbamos	veía	veíamos
eras	erais	ibas	ibais	veías	veíais
era	eran	iba	iban	veía	veían

Note that in *all* verbs—regular and irregular—the first and third person singular are identical.

When to Use the Imperfect

Habitual or continuous action in the past: In English we often use the phrase "used to," as in "I *used to* live in Texas" or "They *used to* eat in that restaurant." In these cases there is no indication of when or how many times this action occurred or for how long.

¿Cuál es verdadero o falso para ti?

_____ 1. Vivías en Nueva York.

_____ 2. Jugabas con muñecas.

_____ 3. De niño/a, tenías un perro.

_____ 4. Mirabas "Barrio Sésamo" ("Sesame Street").

_____ 5. Trabajabas en un restaurante.

_____ 6. Leías la revista "Highlights."

_____ 7. Masticabas chicle en la escuela.

_____ 8. Montabas en triciclo.

_____ 9. Almorzabas en una cafetería.

_____ 10. Ibas a la escuela en autobús.

_____ 11. Saltabas en la cama.

_____ 12. Tomabas muchas vitaminas.

ejercicio   II-2-1

1. I used to study with John. _____

2. He used to work in a bank. _____

3. We used to live in an apartment. _____

4. They used to write notes in class. _____

5. You used to read lots of magazines. _____

6. You (_pl. fam._) used to open the windows in January. _____

_____

7. I used to make my bed every morning. _____

8. Mickey Mantle played (used to play) baseball for the Yankees. _____

_____

9. They used to call us every night. _____

10. Where did you use to work? _____

11. Where did you (*pl. form.*) use to live? _____

12. He used to swim in our pool. _____

13. Mark used to be president of our club. _____

14. I used to go to Florida every winter. _____

15. We used to invite everybody to our parties. _____

Basic, simple description: Very often an important element in sentences in the imperfect is simply a description of how things were. Whereas the preterite often emphasizes physical action, the imperfect frequently focuses on background description. The reference is to what things were like, rather than what happened. Note that the verbs *ser,* which is used for description, origin, and time and *estar,* used to denote location, short-term conditions, and the result of an action, are used frequently in such situations. Consider the following sentences:

I *bought* a car. **preterite** (specific action)
Compré un coche.

The car *was* red. **imperfect** (description)
El coche era rojo.

Ana *got married.* **preterite** (specific action)
Ana se casó.

Ana *was married.* **imperfect** (description)
Ana estaba casada.

ejercicio	II-2-2

¿Qué era?
(What was each of the following people? Choose from the selections that follow.)

1. Jimmy Carter era _____.

2. Frank Lloyd Wright era _____.

3. Bozo era _____.

4. Margaret Mead era _____.

5. Andy Taylor y Barney Fife eran _____.

6. John Steinbeck era _____.

7. Liberace era _____.

8. Aristóteles era _____.

9. Pablo Picasso era _____.

10. Sigmund Freud era _____.

11. Fred Astaire y Ginger Rogers eran _____.

12. Cristóbal Colón era _____.

filósofo	payaso	antropóloga
psiquiatra	pianista	explorador
policía	bailarines	escritor
arquitecto	Presidente	pintor

ejercicio   11-2-3

1. My father was a farmer (*granjero*). _____

2. Mary had a little lamb (*corderito*). _____

3. We wore uniforms to school. _____

4. I was embarrassed (*avergonzado*). _____

5. The store didn't have the shirt that I wanted. _____

_____

6. The windows were open, but the door was closed. _____

_____

7. Susana was pregnant (*embarazada*). _____

8. You (*pl. fam.*) wore (were wearing) silly hats. _____

_____

9. George was tall and handsome. _____

10. The cat was in the attic (*el desván*). _____

11. My pen didn't work. _____

12. Where was the money? _____

13. I had lots of friends at camp (*el campamento*). _____

_____

14. The cat was black and white. _____

15. The monster had two heads. _____

"-ing" in the past: The addition of *-ing* to a verb in English indicates an action in progress, e.g., "I am working." References to such actions in the past ("I was working") generally omit mention of a specific length of time, and thus are in the imperfect. We often use this format to describe two actions going on at the same time, e.g., I *was playing* the guitar and John *was singing* (Yo **tocaba** la guitarra y Juan **cantaba**). See also the Progressive mood in the past (page 117).

---

ejercicio   **II-2-4**

1. I was washing the dishes. _____

2. Nobody was listening while the politician was speaking. _____
    _____

3. He was walking and I was running. _____

4. They were listening to the radio while they were studying. _____
    _____

5. We were trying to sleep, but the baby was crying (*llorar*). _____
    _____

6. Why were you watching television while I was studying? _____
    _____

7. The children were playing in the garden. _____

8. We were living in a glass house. _____

9. You (*pl. fam.*) were selling T-shirts (*camisetas*) on the corner (*la esquina*). _____
    _____

10. I was suffering from a cold (*el resfriado*). _____

11. The frogs were jumping (*saltar*) near the lake. _____

12. I was taking a shower while they were eating breakfast. _____
    _____

13. Carmen was preparing dinner. _____

14. We were thinking about you a lot. _____

15. While she was explaining the theory (*la teoría*), everybody was leaving. _____
    _____

Mental or emotional action or physical sensation: Feelings and mental actions usually are not bound by time or number of occurrences. These actions are not physical; rather, they describe a state of being, and thus are continuous. In fact, several of the verbs listed below change meaning significantly when used in the preterite (see preterite, page 99).

examples:

Yo **esperaba** el bus.
I waited/was waiting for the bus.

Estabas cansado.
You were tired.

Romeo **amaba** mucho a Julieta.
Romeo *loved* Juliet a lot.

Hacía buen tiempo.
It was nice out.

No creíamos el cuento.
We didn't believe the story.

Queríais ir al cine.
You wanted to go to the movies.

Ellos **tenían** veinte dólares esta mañana.
They *had* twenty dollars this morning.

Me dolían los oídos.
My ears hurt.

Some verbs often used in the imperfect:

amar	to love	**molestar**	to be bothersome to
conocer	to know a person	**odiar**	to hate
creer	to believe	**pensar (en)**	to think (about)
doler	to be painful to	**poder**	to be able to
esperar	to hope, wait (for)	**querer**	to want
estar	to be	**saber**	to know
gustar	to be pleasing to	**sentir** (*e → ie*)	to regret, feel sorry
llevarse bien con	to get along with	**sentirse** (*e → ie*)	to feel

¿Verdadero o falso?

(Note that some of the following sentences contain both an imperfect and a preterite clause.)

_____ 1. Esta mañana no comí nada porque no tenía hambre.

_____ 2. Dumbo podía volar porque tenía unas orejas enormes.

_____ 3. Fui al cine la semana pasada porque quería ver una película.

_____ 4. Elvis Presley era un cantante muy popular que también actuó en varias películas.

_____ 5. John Lennon tocaba la guitarra para los Beatles y también escribió muchas canciones.

_____ 6. De niño, yo tenía un televisor en mi dormitorio y lo miraba mucho.

ejercicio   II-2-5

1. I knew the answer. _____

2. Jane hated the color red. _____

3. Did you know him? _____

4. They didn't believe me. _____

5. My family loved me a lot. _____

6. We were very sad for a long time. _____

7. He hated his new boss. _____

8. I liked the photo of your family. _____

9. I liked the flowers in their garden. _____

10. Even though he bothered me, I loved him. _____

11. She worried about you a lot. _____

12. Were you thinking about me? _____

13. What were you thinking about? _____

14. How did you feel during the trial (*el juicio*)? _____

_____

15. He didn't get along with his mother-in-law (*la suegra*). _____

_____

"Would" and "could" in the past: The words "would" and "could" are unusual with regard to tenses because they are markers for both the imperfect and the conditional tenses in English, and thus often present problems when shifting to another language. Consider the following sentences:

I would go to the movies but I don't have time.

I would go to the movies every weekend as a child. (*I used to go to the movies. . . .*)

The first sentence is in the conditional, because it refers to an action that *would* take place if a certain condition were met, namely, my having more time. The second sentence is in the imperfect, as it refers to an action that took place many times in the past. In the imperfect, "would" is the equivalent of "used to."

The same holds true for "could." Consider the following sentences:

I'm so hungry, *I could eat three hamburgers.*

When I was younger, *I could eat three hamburgers* without gaining weight.

The first sentence is conditional because it refers to an uncompleted action. The second, however, refers to what the person *used to be able* to do. In the imperfect, "could" is equivalent to "was/were able to."

examples:

Cuando yo era joven, **jugaba** al béisbol cada fin de semana.
When I was young, *I would play* baseball every weekend.

Cuando yo vivía en Florida, **podía** nadar todo el año.
When I lived in Florida, I *could* swim all year long.

Juan **no estudiaba** porque no le gustaba la clase.
John *wouldn't study* because he didn't like the class.

ejercicio	II-2-6

1. As a child, John would watch TV every day after school. _____

   _____

2. When we lived in France, we would drink wine with every meal. _____

   _____

3. Last year they couldn't speak Spanish. _____

4. Why couldn't you go with me? _____

5. When I was young I would look under the bed every night before turning out (*apagar*) the light.

   _____

6. Lou Gehrig could play baseball better than Ty Cobb. _____

   _____

7. When Jane worked (used to work) at the bank, she would drink fifteen cups (*tazas*) of coffee every

   day. _____

8. When you (*sing. form.*) were younger, you could remember the capitals of every state. _____

   _____

9. When Robert worked for the CIA, he would never tell anybody his real name. _____

   _____

10. They couldn't vote because they didn't have identification. _____

    _____

11. You were never home. Where would you go those nights? _____

    _____

12. We couldn't call you because the telephone wouldn't work. _____

    _____

13. For every party that we had, Mary would bring French fries and I would bring ketchup. _____

_____

14. The bread was moldy *(mohoso)*. I couldn't eat it. _____

_____

15. As a girl, Vicky would have to make her bed every morning before leaving for school. _____

_____

Key words and phrases: Certain words or phrases, when used to describe frequency of a past action, imply repetitive, uncounted occurrences of that action. When one of these words or phrases appears in a sentence describing an ongoing past action, you will use the imperfect tense. Several of these words and phrases are listed below:

a menudo	often	**nunca**	never
a veces	at times; sometimes	**por un rato**	for a while
cada día (año, etc.)	every day (year, etc.)	**siempre**	always
con frecuencia	frequently; often	**tantas veces**	so many times
cuando	whenever	**toda la vida**	all one's life
de vez en cuando	from time to time	**toda el día**	all day long
frecuentemente	frequently	**todo el tiempo**	all the time
muchas veces	many times	**varias veces**	various/several times

ejercicio   II-2-7

1. I always studied before a test. _____

2. He frequently called me after 10:00 p.m. _____

3. All my life I wanted to have a piano. _____

4. They always cheated *(engañar)* us whenever we played cards. _____

_____

5. You ate there frequently. _____

6. You *(pl. fam.)* often wrote long letters. _____

7. From time to time we sent money to the organization. _____

_____

8. Sometimes he didn't earn as much money as his wife. _____

_____

9. All the time that I was there, you (*pl. fam.*) never said anything. _____

_____

10. He always sent a thank-you note after receiving a gift. _____

_____

11. She never bought anything without a coupon (*el cupón*). _____

_____

12. He frequently lied to us, but we never said anything to him. _____

_____

13. I always wondered (*preguntarse*) why she washed her hands so many times every day. _____

_____

14. She was never happy. She complained every day, all day long. _____

_____

15. At times we read, and at times we wrote. _____

ejercicio   II-2-8

Fill in the blanks with the appropriate *preterite* or *imperfect* form of the verb. Look for the "markers," i.e., *anoche* (last night) will set up the preterite, while *con frecuencia* (frequently) will set up the imperfect.

1. Yo (hablar) _____ con Jorge esta mañana.

2. De niño, Felipe (vivir) _____ en México.

3. Anoche, Marcos (comer) _____ tres tacos.

4. De niño, Marcos (comer) _____ tacos cada noche.

5. Ayer, nosotros (ir) _____ al cine.

6. Yo (comprar) _____ esta camisa en Macy's.

7. Nosotros (llegar) _____ aquí a las dos de la tarde.

8. Juanita (llegar) _____ a la una.

9. María siempre (estudiar) _____ en la cocina.

10. Ayer María (estudiar) _____ por una hora.

11. A veces los señores Molino (comer) _____ en el patio.

12. El jueves pasado, los Yankees (jugar) _____ al béisbol contra los Twins.

13. Mi tío siempre (ser) _____ más alto que yo.

14. Tú nunca (ser) _____ tan alto como yo.

15. Ellos (ir) _____ al cine tres veces el fin de semana pasado.

Clock time and age in the past: When referring to the time of day or one's age in the past, *always* use the imperfect. There are only two verbs involved here: *ser* (for clock time) and *tener* (for age). Note that references to time and age often are made with regard to other actions, and that these actions often (but not always) are in the preterite.

examples:

Era la una cuando **llegué.**   **Eran** las siete y media cuando **me desperté.**
It was one o'clock when I *arrived.*   It *was* seven-thirty when *I woke up.*
imperfect   **preterite**   **imperfect**   **preterite**

Yo **tenía** diez años cuando **conocí** a Juan.   **No conocía** a Juan cuando **tenía** ocho años.
I *was* ten years old when I *met* John.   I *didn't know* John when I *was* eight.
imperfect   **preterite**   **imperfect**   **imperfect**

ejercicio   II-2-9

1. It was two-thirty when you called me. _____

2. Mary was twenty-two when she bought her first car. _____

   _____

3. It was quarter after four when I found the money. _____

   _____

4. They were eighteen years old when they graduated from high school. _____

   _____

5. It was five to five when the tree fell down. _____

6. We worked hard when we were fifteen. _____

7. When I got up, it was six-fifteen. _____ _____

8. I learned how to ride a bike when I was six years old. _____

   _____

9. It was quarter to four when the telephone rang. _____

_____

10. She had a baby when she was forty. _____

11. We didn't know that it was twelve-thirty. _____

12. It was three o'clock in the morning when they left. _____

_____

13. Where did you live when you were fourteen years old? _____

_____

14. What time was it when you finished the book? _____

_____

15. How old was John when he got married (*casarse*)? _____

_____

¡Te toca a ti!

Responde a las siguientes preguntas con frases completas:

1. ¿Qué hora era cuando te acostaste anoche? _____

_____

2. ¿Qué hora era cuando te levantaste esta mañana? _____

_____

3. ¿Cuántos años tenías cuando comenzaste la escuela? _____

_____

4. ¿Cuántos años tenías cuando aprendiste a montar en bicicleta? _____

_____

5. ¿Qué hora era cuando saliste de tu casa esta mañana? _____

_____

6. ¿Qué hora era cuando volviste a tu casa anoche? _____

_____

7. ¿Cuántos años tenías cuando comenzaste a estudiar español? _____

_____

8. ¿Cuántos años tenías cuando aprendiste a nadar? _____

_____

Había—the past of *hay:* Just as *hay* in the present is both singular and plural (there *is*, there *are*), its imperfect form, *había* (from the verb *haber*), means both *there was* and *there were*. *Había* is used to express existence, *not* action.

examples:

Había leche en el refrigerador.
There was milk in the refrigerator.

No había dinero en el banco.
There wasn't any money in the bank.

Había tres hombres y un bebé en la película.
There were three men and a baby in the movie.

No había hojas en el árbol.
There weren't any leaves on the tree.

ejercicio   **II-2-10**

1. There was a spider under my bed this morning. _____

2. There were twenty people at the party. _____

3. There was a fly in my soup. _____

4. There were one hundred questions on the test. _____

5. There was a lot of noise during the storm. _____

6. There were five hundred pages in the book. _____

7. There wasn't any gasoline in the tank. (*Any* does not translate here.) _____

_____

8. There weren't any leaves on the tree. _____

9. There wasn't enough time for questions. _____

10. There were more women than men at the meeting. _____

_____

11. There was garbage (*la basura*) on the table. _____

12. There was so much fog (*la niebla*) that I couldn't drive. _____

_____

13. In January there wasn't anybody outside. _____

14. In the summer there were lots of people in the streets. _____

_____

15. There weren't any women in that restaurant. _____

traducción   **II-2-11**

When I was young, there was an exhibit of insects at the zoo every summer. My family and I always went. There was a building just for butterflies, and there were ten kinds of butterflies flying around. There was also a building that had dozens of insects. I never knew that there were so many insects. There was information everywhere. I read that for every pound of humans, there are twelve pounds of insects. I also learned that Little Miss Muffet really existed. Her father, Thomas Muffet, was an entomologist who gave his daughter mashed spiders when she was sick. This was a common remedy for colds 200 years ago!

vocabulario

building	**el edificio**	flying around	**volando de un lado a otro**
butterfly	**la mariposa**	human (being)	**el ser humano**
cold	**el resfriado**	just	**sólo**
dozen	**la docena**	mashed spiders	**puré de arañas**
entomologist	**el entomólogo**	pound	**la libra**
exhibit	**la exposición**	really	**verdaderamente**

_____

_____

_____

_____

_____

_____

_____

_____

_____

_____

"Going to" do something in the past: The expression of intent, **ir + a + infinitive,** e.g., *"Voy a comprar* un carro" (*I am going to buy* a car) is a mental expression: there is no physical action taking place. Such sentences in the past, therefore, will be in the imperfect.

Yo **iba a comprar** un carro.
I *was* going *to buy* a car.

Íbamos a comer.
We were going to eat.

¿Ibas a llamarme?
Were you going to call me?

Ibais a darme dinero.
You were going to give me money.

Él **iba a cantar.**
He *was going to sing.*

Ellos **iban a contar** las ovejas.
They *were going to count* the sheep.

ejercicio   II-2-12

1. I was going to eat. _____

2. Were you going to tell me something? _____

3. He was going to wear his white shirt but it was dirty. _____

    _____

4. We were going to shovel (*quitar*) the snow. _____

5. They were going to spend the day in the country but it was bad weather out. _____

    _____

6. When were you (*pl. form.*) going to sit down? _____

7. I was going to go to bed at ten-thirty but there was a good program on television. _____

    _____

8. How were you going to do this? _____

9. Why was she going to build a house in the woods? _____

    _____

10. Who was going to fix this faucet (*el grifo*)? _____

11. We were going to brush our teeth but there wasn't any toothpaste (*la pasta de dientes*). _____

    _____

12. I was going to give him money for his birthday. _____

13. Where were you (*pl. fam.*) going to send this package? _____

    _____

14. When were you going to bring us the flowers? _____

15. Why wasn't he going to fill the glasses with water? _____

Progressive mood in the past: There are two ways to show *-ing* in the past in Spanish (and you may use whichever you wish): one is simply to use the imperfect tense (see "ing" in the past on page 106), or you can use *estar* in the imperfect + present participle. The structure of the latter is identical to that covered in Unit 12 of the Present Tense, **The Present Progressive;** however, in the past *estar* will be in the imperfect.

examples:

Yo estaba hablando.
I was speaking.

Estábamos comiendo.
We were eating.

Estabas leyendo un libro.
You were reading a book.

Estabais arreglando (reparando) el coche.
You were fixing the car.

Él estaba cepillándose los dientes.
He was brushing his teeth.

Ellas estaban mirándose.
They were looking at each other.

¿Qué estabas haciendo anoche?

Escribe una X delante de las cosas que hiciste.

_____ 1. Yo estaba estudiando español.

_____ 2. Yo estaba jugando a los naipes.

_____ 3. Yo estaba duchándome.

_____ 4. Yo estaba escribiendo una carta.

_____ 5. Yo estaba pagando las cuentas.

_____ 6. Yo estaba limpiando la casa.

_____ 7. Yo estaba cocinando.

_____ 8. Yo estaba contando el dinero.

_____ 9. Yo estaba durmiendo.

_____ 10. Yo estaba pensando en mis amigos.

_____ 11. Yo estaba sirviendo una comida especial a mi familia.

_____ 12. Yo estaba escuchando la radio.

ejercicio   **II-2-13**

1. I was eating. _____

2. You were studying. _____

3. Dumbo was flying. _____

4. She was eating lunch. _____

5. We were drinking milk. _____

6. You (*pl. fam.*) were telling the truth. _____

7. They were going to bed. _____

8. You (*pl. form.*) were brushing your hair. _____

9. I was taking a bath. _____

10. John was shaving. _____

11. Mary was playing the piano. _____

12. Mary was playing tennis. _____

traducción   **II-2-14**

(Preterite and imperfect mix)

I watched "The People's Court" this afternoon while I was eating lunch. I love that show. There was a woman—who was not happy—who was suing the owners of a pet store because she bought a puppy, took it home, didn't train it, and after a few weeks the puppy began to chew and destroy the furniture. This woman wanted a reimbursement for the cost of the dog, its food, shots, even for its toys! The owners seemed normal. This woman seemed to be nuts. The judge was probably thinking the same thing because she lost the case. Afterwards, she told the announcer that she was going to put the dog to sleep. After some commercials, the announcer told his faithful viewers that he bought the dog and named it P.C. (for People's Court).

vocabulario

announcer	**el locutor**	(to be) nuts	**estar desquiciado/a**
(to) chew (bite)	**morder**	people's	**del pueblo**
court	**la corte**	pet	**el animal doméstico**
(to) destroy	**destruir**	reimbursement	**el reembolso**
faithful	**fiel**	(to) seem, appear	**parecer**
furniture	**los muebles**	(to) sue	**demandar**
(to) kill, put to sleep	**matar**	television viewer	**el telespectador**
(to) name	**llamar**	(to) train	**entrenar**

The Future Tense

We use the future tense to describe actions that *will* take place. In English, the word *will* (or *shall*) is the essence of the future tense, and simply placed before any given verb, this tense is formed: **I *will* go; You *will* eat; We *will* study,** and so on.

In Spanish, the future tense is a simple tense in that no auxiliary (helping) verb, such as "will," is brought in; expression of the future is shown in the main verb itself.

Most verbs in the future tense are regular. To form the future tense regularly, use the infinitive itself as the stem, and then add the appropriate future tense ending:

-é	-emos
-ás	-éis
-á	-án

These are the endings for **all** verbs, whether regular or irregular, in the future tense (irregular verbs make a change in the stem, not in the ending). Note that all the endings, except the first person plural (*nosotros*) take an accent.

Regular Verbs

hablar	
(I will speak, you will speak, etc.)	
hablaré	hablaremos
hablarás	hablaréis
hablará	hablarán

comer	
(I will eat, you will eat, etc.)	
comeré	comeremos
comerás	comeréis
comerá	comerán

vivir
(I will live, you will live, etc.)

viviré	**viviremos**
vivirás	**viviréis**
vivirá	**vivirán**

examples:

Iré al teatro con Marcos.
I will go to the theater with Marcos.

¿Dónde **estarás** mañana?
Where *will you be* tomorrow?

¿Quién **será** el próximo Presidente?
Who *will be* the next President?

Nos levantaremos a las cinco.
We will get up at five o'clock.

Enviaréis la carta esta noche.
You will send the letter tonight.

Aquellas mujeres nos **oirán**.
Those women *will hear* us.

Some common expressions of future time:

mañana	tomorrow	**esta tarde**	this afternoon
más tarde	later	**esta noche**	tonight
la semana que viene	next week	**mañana por la mañana**	tomorrow morning
el mes que viene	next month	**mañana por la tarde**	tomorrow afternoon
el año que viene	next year	**mañana por la noche**	tomorrow night

En tu opinión, ¿cuál es verdadero o falso?

_____ 1. Comeré una hamburguesa mañana.

_____ 2. Snoopy será el próximo Presidente de los Estados Unidos.

_____ 3. Mi mejor amigo/a me dará un regalo para mi cumpleaños.

_____ 4. Iré al cine este fin de semana.

_____ 5. Los Mets de Nueva York ganarán la próxima Serie Mundial.

_____ 6. Viajaré a México el año que viene.

_____ 7. Celebraremos la Navidad en noviembre.

_____ 8. Si una persona deja abierta la puerta en el verano, muchas moscas entrarán en la casa.

_____ 9. Todos los aviones en todos los aeropuertos llegarán y partirán a su hora esta semana.

_____ 10. En veinticuatro horas estaré en mi casa.

_____ 11. El vampiro beberá la sangre.

_____ 12. Nadie leerá el periódico mañana.

_____ 13. Esta noche lavaré los platos y después los secaré.

_____ 14. Mi carro no funcionará sin aceite.

_____ 15. Nadaré en el océano este verano.

ejercicio   II-3-1

Fill in the blanks with the appropriate future form of the verb.

1. Mañana yo (comprar) _____ comida para la cena.

2. Los dos gatos (correr) _____ alrededor de la casa.

3. Vosotros (abrir) _____ las ventanas.

4. Tú (ser) _____ famoso/a algún día.

5. Mi primo (estar) _____ enfermo si come diez tamales.

6. Nosotros (jugar) _____ a los naipes esta noche.

7. Ella (llevar) _____ una mini-falda al baile.

8. Yo no (ducharse) _____ porque no hay agua.

9. Ellos (llegar) _____ a las ocho.

10. El perro (vomitar) _____ si come esos huesos.

11. Nunca (nevar) _____ en Costa Rica.

12. Ellos (acostarse) _____ a las once y media.

ejercicio   II-3-2

1. I'll speak with you tomorrow. _____

2. She'll buy a new car next year. _____

3. He will sleep until tomorrow afternoon. _____

4. We will arrive at ten o'clock tomorrow night. _____

5. What time will you go to bed? _____

6. How much money will you (*pl. fam.*) need? _____

7. They will stay (*quedarse*) in a hotel next month. _____

8. It will never snow (*nevar*) in Panama. _____

9. Where will you be tonight at eleven-thirty? _____

10. What time will the program begin? _____

11. I don't want to give him the money because I know that he'll lose it. _____

_____

12. I won't take off (*quitarse*) this sweater until next summer. _____

_____

13. We will attend the university next fall. _____

14. I won't sign (*firmar*) this letter because it's not true. _____

_____

15. If I buy this suit (*el traje*) instead of that one, I'll save (*ahorrar*) fifty dollars. _____

_____

¡Te toca a ti!

Responde a estas preguntas con frases completas:

1. ¿Qué comerás esta noche? _____

2. ¿Quién será el próximo Presidente de los Estados Unidos? _____

_____

3. ¿Adónde irás el verano que viene? _____

4. ¿Hablarás español mañana? _____

5. ¿Dónde estarás en tres horas? _____

6. ¿A qué hora te acostarás esta noche? _____

7. ¿Qué llevarás mañana? _____

8. ¿Qué programa mirarás en la televisión esta semana? _____

_____

9. ¿Qué país ganará la Copa Mundial? _____

10. ¿Colgarás tu ropa antes de acostarte esta noche? _____

11. ¿A qué hora te levantarás mañana? _____

12. ¿Por cuánto tiempo estudiarás español mañana?_____

traducción   **II-3-3**

(Includes present, preterite, imperfect, future)

Tomorrow is the first of January, and therefore I will try to do all the things I wrote on my list of resolutions for next year. Last year I made ten resolutions, and for a while I kept them, but one by one I broke my promises to myself. This year, however, I will lose weight—last year I gained ten pounds. I will work harder—I wasted a lot of time last year. I will read more—I read only two books this past year. I will go to the gym more often—I belong to a club, but I never go. I will spend less money—I used to go shopping two or three times every week. I will walk or ride my bicycle instead of driving (yesterday I drove three blocks in order to buy a newspaper—how ridiculous!). I will complain less—I was not a little angel this year. Finally, I will study Spanish more. I will be perfect—just like last year.

vocabulario

(to) belong	**pertenecer**	(to) keep (one's resolution)	**cumplir**
(to) break one's promise	**faltar a su palabra**	(to) lose weight	**adelgazar**
city block	**la manzana (cuadra)**	(to) ride a bike	**montar en bicicleta**
(to) complain (about)	**quejarse (de)**	(to) spend (money)	**gastar**
(to) gain (weight)	**engordar**	(to) try to (do something)	**tratar de + inf.**
(to) go shopping	**ir de compras**	(to) waste time	**perder el tiempo**

_____

_____

_____

_____

_____

_____

_____

_____

Irregular Verbs

The future tense is one of the more regular of Spanish tenses. There are, however, twelve standard verbs that are irregular. The endings remain the same (**é; ás; á; emos; éis; án**); however, there are changes in the stem. These twelve verbs are listed below in three groups to make things a bit easier. Each is followed by the first person singular (*yo*) form of that verb in the future.

Group 1: Infinitive stem remains the same, but the final vowel of its ending is dropped.

caber	to fit, have enough room	*yo cabré*
haber	auxiliary verb meaning "to have"	*yo habré*
poder	to be able to	*yo podré*
querer	to want	*yo querré*
saber	to know a fact; to know how	*yo sabré*

Group 2: Infinitive stem remains the same, but the final vowel of its ending is dropped and replaced with the letter *d*.

poner	to put, place	*yo pondré*
salir	to leave	*yo saldré*
tener	to have, hold	*yo tendré*
valer	to be worth	*yo valdré*
venir	to come	*yo vendré*

Group 3: Entirely different stem is used.

decir	to say, tell	*yo diré*
hacer	to do, make, make out [a check]	*yo haré*

examples:

Podré hacerlo mañana.
I will be able to do it tomorrow.

Saldremos a las cuatro.
We will leave at four o'clock.

Tú me **dirás.**
You will tell me.

Vendréis a nuestra fiesta.
You will come to our party.

La mesa **no cabrá** en este cuarto.
The table *won't fit* in this room.

Estos anillos **valdrán** mucho.
These rings *will be worth* a lot.

***Hay* in the future:**   The third person singular of *haber* in the future, *habrá,* is the future form of *hay* (there is; there are). Alone (not as an auxiliary), *habrá* translates into "there will be," singular and plural.

examples:

Habrá una fiesta en tu honor.
There will be a party in your honor.

Habrá veinte personas en la fiesta.
There will be twenty people at the party.

¿Cuál es verdadero o falso para ti?

_____ 1. Tendré una fiesta el sábado que viene.

_____ 2. Saldré de mi casa en una hora y media.

_____ 3. Sabré más mañana que lo que sé hoy.

_____ 4. Todos mis amigos vendrán a mi casa esta noche.

_____ 5. En un año podré hablar español muy bien.

_____ 6. Habrá una gran rebaja en Bloomingdale's en enero.

_____ 7. Los Padres de San Diego querrán ganar la Serie Mundial este año.

_____ 8. No haré nada este fin de semana.

_____ 9. No diré nada a nadie esta noche.

_____ 10. Un anillo de oro valdrá más en veinte años que ahora.

_____ 11. Una mesa y ocho sillas no cabrán en mi cocina.

_____ 12. Mañana me pondré a dieta.

ejercicio   11-3-4

Fill in the blanks with the appropriate verb forms.

1. Nosotros (hacer) _____ las camas mañana.

2. Ellos (poner) _____ los tenedores en el cajón.

3. Ella (tener) _____ quince años en julio.

4. El sofá no (caber) _____ en la sala.

5. ¿Quién (saber) _____ la respuesta?

6. Nadie (querer) _____ vivir en esta casa.

7. Los elefantes no (poder) _____ levantar este coche.

8. Nosotros no (decir) _____ nada acerca de tus problemas.

9. Vosotros (venir) _____ en septiembre.

10. Ellos (salir) _____ a las dos de la tarde.

11. Este collar de perlas (valer) _____ cinco mil dólares en diez años.

12. (Haber) _____ cuatro almohadas en la cama.

ejercicio   II-3-5

1. I'll want to see your photos. _____

2. Where will you put the sofa? I'll put it in the living room. _____

_____

3. Mary will make the bride's dress. _____

4. What time will they come? _____

5. You (*pl. form.*) won't be able to see the boat from there. _____

_____

6. There will be three hundred stores in the new mall (*el centro comercial*). ____

_____

7. John will know the answer. _____

8. How much will the car be worth next year? _____

9. There will not be any noise during the program. (*Note:* any *in a negative sentence does not translate.*)

_____

10. Will there be time for asking questions (*hacer preguntas*)? _____

_____

11. Will you be able to call me later today? _____

12. These hammers (*el martillo*) will never fit into that box. _____

_____

13. This house will be worth more than two million dollars in five years. _____

_____

14. I will not tell your secret to anyone. _____

15. They'll make their check for five hundred dollars. _____

_____

Derivatives of Irregular Verbs

Several verbs have as their root verbs found in the previous section. When the root verb is irregular, e.g., *tener*, its derivatives will be irregular also, e.g., *obtener* (to obtain, get):

Yo tendré empleo.
I will have work.

Yo obtendré empleo.
I will get work.

Él hará la tarea.
He will do the assignment.

Él rehará la tarea.
He will redo the assignment.

One exception is *bendecir* (to bless), derived from *decir*. You will conjugate *bendecir* regularly in the future:

El sacerdote te **dirá**.
The priest *will tell* you.

El sacerdote te **bendecirá**.
The priest *will bless* you.

Otherwise, the verbs listed below (shown also in the future *yo* form) are conjugated irregularly, as are their roots.

abstenerse de + inf.	to abstain from	*me abstendré de + inf.*
atenerse a	to depend on, rely on	*me atendré a*
componer	to compose	*compondré*
contener	to contain, hold	*contendré*
convenir en + inf.	to agree to do something	*convendré en + inf.*
deshacer	to undo, untie (a knot)	*desharé*
detener	to detain, stop, arrest	*detendré*
mantener to	maintain	*mantendré*
obtener	to obtain, get	*obtendré*
oponerse	to oppose	*me opondré*
ponerse	to become, put on (clothing), set (sun)	*me pondré*
rehacer	to redo, remake	*reharé*
sostener	to sustain, support, uphold	*sostendré*
suponer	to suppose, assume	*supondré*

Para ti, ¿cuál es verdadero o falso?

_____ 1. Compondré una canción este año.

_____ 2. Se pondrá el sol mañana antes de las seis.

_____ 3. Me abstendré de comer chocolate este año.

_____ 4. Si nadie me llama por teléfono hoy, supondré que todo el mundo está enojado conmigo.

_____ 5. Un buen policía detendrá a muchos criminales durante su carrera.

_____ 6. Antes de nadar, una persona se pondrá el traje de baño.

_____ 7. Si cometo un error en este capítulo, reharé todos los ejercicios.

_____ 8. Si hace mucho frío el invierno que viene, me pondré guantes antes de salir de casa.

ejercicio   II-3-6

1. I will put on my hat. _____

2. He will untie this knot. _____

3. Will you oppose the President? _____

4. You (*pl. fam.*) will abstain from smoking for two weeks. _____

_____

5. Who will compose the music? _____

6. We'll depend on you. _____

7. Will this pail hold all the paint (*pintura*)? _____

8. He'll remake his bed later. _____

9. I will assume that you know the answer. _____

10. The police will detain you if you drive drunk (*borracho*). _____

_____

11. She will maintain good grades in college. _____

12. Where will you get enough money in order to buy the new furniture? _____

_____

13. Will you (*pl. form.*) agree to stay with me for a while? _____

_____

14. These beams (*las vigas*) will not support a house. _____

_____

15. Tomorrow I will abstain from eating. _____

traducción   II-3-7

In a couple of weeks I'll quit this job and begin a new life. I sold my house and bought a van. Last night I put food, clothing, my camera, and a pillow—everything that I'll need—into the van. I can't believe it! Soon that vehicle will be my home. During the past five years I saved enough money to live for another ten years. I won't be able to go to fancy restaurants or buy Armani suits, but I will be able to travel. I'll visit new places and I'll meet new people. I always dreamed of doing this. I won't be rich, but I'll be happy. For the first time in my life, my reality and my dreams will be the same.

vocabulario

(a) couple	**un par**	pillow	**la almohada**
dream	**el sueño**	place	**el lugar**
(to) dream of	**soñar con**	(to) quit (a job, etc.)	**renunciar a**
for the first time	**por primera vez**	(the) same (things)	**iguales**
home	**el hogar**	(to) travel	**viajar**
life	**la vida**	van	**la camioneta**
(to) meet	**conocer a**	vehicle	**el vehículo**

_____

_____

_____

_____

_____

_____

_____

_____

_____

_____

_____

ejercicio   II-3-8

(Includes regular and irregular verbs.)

1. John will arrive at ten o'clock. _____

2. Where will you put the lawnmower (*el cortacéspedes*)? _____

3. We will eat the raisins (*las pasas*) from the box. _____

4. When will you find out (*averiguar*) if you have the job? _____

_____

5. They will not go to bed until midnight. _____

6. I will never know how to play the violin. _____

7. From time to time I will visit you in prison. _____

8. How much will this ring be worth in twenty years? _____

_____

9. Will you obey the laws of this city? _____

10. It will never snow in Panama, and it will never rain in the desert. _____

_____

11. They will tell us lies, but we will not believe anything. _____

_____

12. Will you have to travel much? Will you be able to travel much? _____

_____

13. My car will not fit into the garage. I'll have to leave it on the street. _____

_____

14. I will bury the treasure (*el tesoro*) tonight; otherwise (*de lo contrario*), it won't be here tomorrow.

_____

15. The entire treasure will not fit in this trunk (*el baúl*); I will have to put the diamonds in my pocket.

_____

The Conditional Tense

The conditional tense expresses the feeling of future uncertainty, generally translated into the English "would + verb." It differs from the future tense, which expresses future certainty (He *will be* here), in that it suggests probability or possibility were some condition met: He *would* be here (but he's sick) or He *would be* here (if he weren't so busy).

The inherent feature of the conditional tense is that some condition is *not* being met, and that *if* it were met, a certain action *would* take place. Sometimes this condition is stated:

> He would play pro basketball *if* he were taller.
>
> Would you call me *if* I gave you my number?
>
> I would eat in that restaurant, *but* it's too expensive.
>
> I would call her, *but* she was rude at the party.

Note that when using the conditional tense, there will usually be a "but" or an "if," or some other reason given to explain why or why not the action would be completed. At times this reason is implied or simply understood, as in the following examples:

> I would go (if I were you).
>
> They wouldn't sing this song (because the lyrics are stupid).
>
> They would spend the money (but you hid it).

Sentences that employ the conditional tense followed by a hypothetical *if* clause (e.g., *if* I were; *if* you had, *if* we saw, etc.) require the use of the subjunctive following the *if* clause. As we have not yet covered the subjunctive, none of the examples or exercises in this unit will include sentences containing a hypothetical *if* clause.

Regular Verbs

Most verbs are regular in the conditional tense. In fact, the future and the conditional tenses share the same irregular verbs. To regularly form verbs in the conditional tense, the infinitive itself is the stem, and you then add the appropriate tense ending:

-ía	-íamos
-ías	-íais
-ía	-ían

hablar	comer	vivir
(I would speak, you would speak, etc.) **hablaría** **hablaríamos** **hablarías** **hablaríais** **hablaría** **hablarían**	*(I would eat, you would eat, etc.)* **comería** **comeríamos** **comerías** **comeríais** **comería** **comerían**	*(I would live, you would live, etc.)* **viviría** **viviríamos** **vivirías** **viviríais** **viviríais** **vivirían**

examples:

Yo compraría el vestido, pero no tengo suficiente dinero.   ¿Cuándo **iríamos?**
I would buy the dress, but I don't have enough money.   When *would we go?*

¿**Comerías** en ese restaurante?   **Estaríais** allí a las diez, pero tenéis que estudiar.
Would you eat in that restaurant?   *You would be there* at ten, but you have to study.

Nadie **dormiría** allí.   Ellos no **cantarían** esta canción.
No one *would sleep* there.   They *wouldn't sing* this song.

Place an X by all the things you would do if you won the lottery worth $25,000,000.

_____ 1. Renunciaría al trabajo.

_____ 2. Daría parte del dinero a los pobres.

_____ 3. Viajaría por el mundo.

_____ 4. Depositaría todo el dinero en el banco.

_____ 5. Me mudaría a una casa enorme y muy elegante.

_____ 6. Compraría regalos para mi familia y todos mis amigos.

_____ 7. Celebraría el premio con mis amigos en un buen restaurante y pagaría todo.

_____ 8. Compraría un coche nuevo.

_____ 9. Escribiría un libro sobre mi vida.

_____ 10. No cambiaría ningún aspecto de mi vida.

ejercicio   1-4-1

1. I would eat the cookies but I'm on a diet (*estar a dieta*). _____

_____

2. Would she marry (*casarse con*) John? _____

3. Where would you go? _____

4. They wouldn't live in that house because it's haunted (*embrujada*). _____

_____

5. Would you (*pl. form.*) deliver (*entregar*) the newspapers to our house? _____

_____

6. If I teach this class, you (*pl. fam.*) would be my students. _____

_____

7. I'm not going to give them the money because they would lose it. _____

_____

8. We would change the words of the song, but it would be too difficult. _____

_____

9. I'd get up but my leg is sore. _____

10. I know that they would give you the money that you need. _____

_____

11. Would you buy a used car from this man? _____

12. Who would think such a thing (*tal cosa*)? _____

13. Why wouldn't he shave (*afeitarse*) with that razor (*la navaja*)? _____

_____

14. Why would anybody read this? _____

15. I wouldn't play the piano in front of a crowd (*la multitud*). _____

_____

Irregular Verbs

The conditional and the future tenses share the same irregular verbs.* The conditional endings remain the same (*ía; ías; ía; íamos; íais; ían*); however, the infinitive is not retained entirely. Listed below are the twelve standard verbs that are irregular in both tenses. Each is followed by the first person, singular (**yo**) form of that verb in the conditional.

*Refer to the unit on the future tense for a more complete listing of irregular verbs (derivatives of the twelve standard verbs listed below).

Group 1: Infinitive stem remains the same, but the final vowel of its ending is dropped.

caber	to fit, have enough room	*yo cabría*
haber	auxiliary verb meaning "to have"	*yo habría*
poder	to be able to	*yo podría*
querer	to want	*yo querría*
saber	to know a fact; to know how	*yo sabría*

Group 2: Infinitive stem remains the same, but the final vowel of its ending is dropped and replaced with the letter *d*.

poner	to put, place	*yo pondría*
salir	to leave	*yo saldría*
tener	to have, hold	*yo tendría*
valer	to be worth	*yo valdría*
venir	to come	*yo vendría*

Group 3: Entirely different stem is used.

decir	to say, tell	*yo diría*
hacer	to do, make, make out (a check)	*yo haría*

examples:

Yo le **diría** a Juan cualquier cosa.
I *would tell* John anything.

¿Qué **haríamos?**
What *would we do?*

¿Cuándo **saldrías?**
When *would you leave?*

Sabríais sus nombres.
You would know their names.

Nuestro sofá **no cabría** en ese cuarto.
Our sofa *wouldn't fit* in that room.

Estos anillos **no valdrían** nada.
These rings *wouldn't be worth* anything.

***Hay* in the conditional:**   The third person singular of *haber* in the conditional, *habría*, is the conditional form of *hay* (there is; there are). Alone (not used as an auxiliary), *habría* translates into "there would be," singular and plural.

examples:

Habría más dinero aquí, pero tuvimos que comprar comida.
There would be more money here, but we had to buy food.

Juan perdió cinco libros; de otra manera, **habría** treinta en el estante.
John lost five books; otherwise, *there would be* thirty on the shelf.

ejercicio II-4-2

Fill in each blank with the appropriate conditional form of the verb.

1. Yo (poner) _____ estos libros en ese estante.

2. Tú (poder) _____ tocar el violín, pero nunca lo practicas.

3. Juan (tener) _____ una fiesta, pero no es su cumpleaños.

4. Esta pulsera (valer) _____ mucho, pero no es de oro.

5. ¿Qué (hacer) _____ Sherlock Holmes en esta situación?

6. Estas sillas (caber) _____ en la sala, pero no en el dormitorio.

7. Nosotros (venir) _____ a su fiesta, pero estamos enfermos.

8. (Haber) _____ mucha comida, pero Juan estaba aquí anoche y se comió todo.

9. ¿Qué (decir) _____ tú en esta situación?

10. Yo no (decir) _____ nada.

ejercicio   II-4-3

1. I would come to your party, but I'm sick. _____

2. Where would you put these chairs? _____

3. This bracelet would be worth more, but it's broken. _____

_____

4. What would you (*pl. fam.*) say to that man? _____

5. We would have the reception in our house, but there isn't enough room. _____

_____

6. Do you think that Robert would know the answer? _____

_____

7. Who would be able to do such a thing? _____

8. I would want the car, but it isn't my choice. _____

_____

9. There would be two dozen eggs in the refrigerator, but we ate four for breakfast. _____

_____

10. Would these plates fit into the cabinet? _____

11. What would you do during a hurricane? _____

12. I wouldn't tell him because he can't keep a secret (*guardar un secreto*). _____

_____

13. We would make out the check, but there isn't enough (*suficiente*) money in the bank. _____

14. I'm not going to give these shoes to Marcos because I know that he wouldn't be able to wear them.

15. I would put the flowers in front of the house, not in back. _____

traducción   II-4-4

When I was young, I loved to read fairy tales. One of my favorite characters was Aladdin because he was always granting people their fantasies in the form of three wishes. What would I do? First, I would ask him for a million wishes, but I know that he wouldn't do that. Therefore, these are my three wishes: 1. My cat would be able to speak, and she and I would have long conversations. 2. I would never have to worry about my weight. 3. And the most important wish is that no one in the world would suffer another minute: there would be no war; there would be no hunger; there would be no poverty; there would be no sadness.

vocabulario

(to) ask for, request	**pedir**	(to) suffer	**sufrir**
character	**el personaje**	therefore	**por eso**
fairy tale	**el cuento de hadas**	war	**la guerra**
(to) grant	**conceder**	weight	**el peso**
poverty	**la pobreza**	wish	**el deseo**
sadness	**la tristeza**	(to) worry about	**preocuparse por**

The Present Perfect Tense

The present perfect tense is a *compound tense,* which means that it requires an auxiliary, or *helping,* verb. This is true also in English, where the auxiliary is *have* or *has,* as in "I *have* spoken"; "She *has* studied." In Spanish, the auxiliary is formed from the auxiliary verb **haber** which means "to have." Do *not* confuse **haber** with **tener** (which means "to have; to possess").

We often use the present perfect tense when speaking about something that was true in the past and *is still true.* The sentence, "I have lived here for ten years," means that ten years ago I lived here, I still live here, and I have lived here all the time in between.

We also use this tense to indicate that an action was completed recently: I can't go out to dinner because *I have eaten.*

An important aspect of the present perfect tense is that there is a *scope* of time, either stated or implied, which includes the present, and that the action(s) referred to within this scope are not time specific (as they are in the preterite).

In the sentence, "I've gone to the club three times this year," the scope of time includes all of this year *until now;* we do not know *when* specifically (i.e., on which dates) the person visited the club. If you ask a person, "How have you been?" the implied scope is *lately.*

Formation of the Present Perfect Tense

Because the present perfect tense is a compound tense, you will be working with two verbs, not one. To form verbs in this tense you first conjugate **haber** in the present tense:

he	hemos
has	habéis
ha	han

The conjugated form of **haber** is then followed by the past participle of the desired verb. Most of the past participles in Spanish are regular, and we shall consider these first.

Regular Past Participles

The patterns for regularly formed past participles are below:

-ar verbs: drop the *-ar*, and replace it with **-ado**   hablar → **hablado**
-er verbs: drop the *-er*, and replace it with **-ido**   comer → **comido**
-ir verbs: drop the *-ir*, and replace it with **-ido**   vivir → **vivido**

hablar	comer	vivir
(I have spoken, etc.) **he hablado** **hemos hablado** **has hablado** **habéis hablado** **ha hablado** **han hablado**	*(I have eaten, etc.)* **he comido** **hemos comido** **has comido** **habéis comido** **ha comido** **han comido**	*(I have lived, etc.)* **he vivido** **hemos vivido** **has vivido** **habéis vivido** **ha vivido** **han vivido**

examples:

Yo **he hablado** con Roberto.
I *have spoken* with Robert.

Tú **has estado** aquí por diez minutos.
You have been here for ten minutes.

Tomás **ha sido** mi amigo por nueve años.
Tom *has been* my friend for nine years.

Nos hemos acostado.
We have gone to bed.

¿Habéis recibido los regalos?
Have you received the presents?

No lo **han visitado.**
They haven't visited him.

Note:

1. The conjugated verb *haber* and the past participle are not separated by any other words.

2. Object pronouns precede the conjugated verb *haber.*

Check the things that you have done today:

_____   1. He hablado por teléfono.

_____   2. He tomado café.

_____   3. He comido una ensalada.

_____   4. He comprado una camisa.

_____   5. He almorzado.

_____   6. Me he duchado.

_____   7. He contado mi dinero.

_____   8. He recibido un regalo.

_____   9. He cometido un error.

_____ 10. He escuchado la radio.

_____ 11. Me he lavado el pelo.

_____ 12. He lavado el coche.

| ejercicio | 11-5-1 |

1. I have worked. _____

2. You have listened. _____

3. She has drunk the milk. _____

4. We have understood. _____

5. They have received a present. _____

6. We have sold the house. _____

7. Have you watched television today? _____

8. Where have they lived? _____

9. I have showered. _____

10. He has been with me. _____

11. You (*sing. form.*) have learned a lot. _____

12. Have you brushed your teeth? _____

13. He has called me six times. _____

14. I've run three miles. _____

15. She hasn't washed her hair. _____

Irregular Past Participles

All conjugations in the present perfect begin with **haber** conjugated in the present tense, followed by a past participle. Most past participles are regular (see the previous section). Below is a list of verbs which have irregularly formed past participles. These verbs form two distinct groups.

1. Most *-er* and *-ir* verbs in which a vowel immediately precedes the infinitive ending are formed regularly, but take an accent over the *-i* in *-ido*. (This does *not* include verbs ending with *-uir*; such verbs are regular; for example, the past participle of *construir* is *construido*.)

atraer	to attract	**atraído**
caer	to fall	**caído**
creer	to believe	**creído**
leer	to read	**leído**
oír	to hear	**oído**

poseer	to possess	**poseído**
sonreír	to smile	**sonreído**
traer	to bring	**traído**

2. Other irregular past participles have no pattern and thus must be learned individually:

abrir	to open	**abierto**
cubrir	to cover	**cubierto**
decir	to say, tell	**dicho**
describir	to describe	**descrito**
descubrir	to discover	**descubierto**
devolver	to return (something)	**devuelto**
disolver	to dissolve	**disuelto**
envolver	to wrap, wrap up	**envuelto**
escribir	to write	**escrito**
freír	to fry	**frito**
hacer	to make, do	**hecho**
morir	to die	**muerto**
oponer	to oppose	**opuesto**
poner	to put, place	**puesto**
proveer	to provide, furnish	**provisto**
pudrir	to rot, languish	**podrido**
resolver	to resolve	**resuelto**
romper	to break, break through or up	**roto**
ver	to see	**visto**
volver	to return	**vuelto**

examples:

He abierto la puerta.
I have opened the door.

¿No has escrito la carta?
Haven't you written the letter?

Él me **ha dicho** una mentira.
He *has told* me a lie.

No hemos hecho nada.
We haven't done anything.

¿Habéis visto la película?
Have you seen the movie?

Los huevos **se han podrido.**
The eggs *have rotted.*

¿Qué has hecho esta semana?

Escribe una "X" delante de todo lo que has hecho.

_____ 1. He visto una película.

_____ 2. He escrito una carta.

_____ 3. He resuelto todos mis problemas.

_____ 4. He leído un libro.

_____ 5. He abierto las ventanas de mi casa.

_____ 6. He dicho una mentira.

_____ 7. He frito una hamburguesa.

_____ 8. He roto un plato.

_____ 9. He devuelto libros a la biblioteca.

_____ 10. He envuelto un regalo.

ejercicio   II-5-2

1. I have read twenty pages. _____

2. She has opened the book. _____

3. Where have you put the dishes? _____

4. The rabbit has died. _____

5. Have you told her the truth? _____

6. What have you seen? _____

7. The cook has fried all the eggs. _____

8. What have you done today? _____

9. The store has provided us with clothing. _____

10. She has broken another fingernail. _____

11. Has he resolved his problems? _____

12. We haven't said anything. _____

13. The politician has not told the truth. _____

14. Why haven't they returned? _____

15. What have you made for us? _____

ejercicio   II-5-3

Advanced exercises: regular and irregular past participles

1. I have had the money for more than twenty years. _____

_____

2. She has opened the window, and I have closed the door. _____

_____

3. My neighbor's dog has barked (*ladrar*) all night long, and I haven't been able to sleep. _____

_____

4. Where have you put your suitcase? _____

5. How many times have you brushed your teeth today? _____

_____

6. Why haven't you shaved today? _____

7. For how many years have you known Charles? _____

8. You've been (arrived) late every day this week. _____

9. Have you (*pl. form.*) seen her? _____

10. The thieves have robbed our jewels and have broken all my records. _____

_____

11. Have the newlyweds (*los recién casados*) returned from their honeymoon (*la luna de miel*)? _____

_____

12. Your manners (*los modales*) have attracted me. _____

13. They have demonstrated their love for Beethoven's music. _____

_____

14. If she is as rich as you say, then why has she robbed the bank? _____

_____

15. The telephone has rung twenty times. Why haven't you answered it? _____

_____

traducción   II-5-4

I want to go shopping because I haven't left this house in more than a week. I need to buy a pair of tennis shoes. I think I've lost my other pair. I've looked everywhere: under the bed, in the closet, in the basement, even in the trunk of my car, but I haven't been able to find them anywhere. My sister has borrowed them from time to time in the past, but she always returns things. Therefore, I've come to the conclusion that I've lost them forever and that if I want to play tennis again, I have to buy a new pair.

vocabulario

(to) borrow	**pedir prestado**
(to) come to the conclusion	**llegar a la conclusión**
even	**hasta**
everywhere	**en todas partes**
forever	**para siempre**
from time to time	**de vez en cuando**
(to) go shopping	**ir de compras**
nowhere; not anywhere	**en ninguna parte**
(to) return (a thing)	**devolver**
tennis shoes	**los zapatos tenis**
trunk	**el maletero (baúl)**

_____

_____

_____

_____

_____

_____

_____

_____

_____

The Past Perfect Tense

The past perfect tense is a compound tense, which means that it requires an auxiliary verb, followed by a past participle. We form the past perfect tense in the same manner in English, using for all persons the auxiliary "had," as in "You *had* written the letter"; "She *had* bought three suits."

We use the past perfect tense (sometimes called the pluperfect tense) when referring to an action which occurred prior to something else. When using this tense there is always a stated or implied cut-off point. Consider the following sentence:

I had taken three pictures before realizing that there wasn't any film in the camera.

The action, taking pictures, stopped at the cut-off point of discovering that there wasn't any film. The act of taking pictures, in a sense, is hidden behind the discovery. In this sense there is always something that stops the action referred to in the past perfect.

The past perfect differs from the present perfect in that sentences in the latter are still true: the cut-off point is *now*. In the past perfect, the cut-off point is some time in the past.

Formation of the Past Perfect Tense

Because the past perfect tense is a compound tense, you will be working with an auxiliary verb and a past participle. To form verbs in this tense you first conjugate **haber** in the imperfect tense:

había	habíamos
habías	habíais
había	habían

Note that the first and third person singular forms are identical.

The formation of the past perfect is identical to that of the present perfect, except that the conjugation of **haber,** the auxiliary verb, is in the imperfect. The conjugated form of **haber** is then followed by the past participle of the desired verb.

Regular Past Participles

The patterns for regularly formed past participles can be found in the preceding unit that deals with the present perfect.

examples:

Yo **había preparado** la cena.
I *had prepared* dinner.

No habíamos probado ese método.
We hadn't tried that method.

Habías estado aquí.
You had been here.

Habíais trabajado duro.
You had worked hard.

Él **no había visitado** a mi tío.
He *hadn't visited* my uncle.

¿Se habían acostado?
Had they gone to bed?

The following examples include the cut-off point. **Remember:** After a preposition the verb is not conjugated.

Yo había comido antes de llamarte.
I had eaten before calling you.

¿Te habías lavado las manos antes de comer?
Had you washed your hands before eating?

Él no había cerrado la puerta antes de salir.
He hadn't closed the door before leaving.

No habíamos escuchado los discos hasta el martes.
We hadn't listened to the records until Tuesday.

Habíais conocido a Jorge antes de la fiesta, ¿no?
You had met George before the party, right?

Ellos no habían manejado el coche antes de comprarlo.
They hadn't driven the car before buying it.

Para ti, ¿cuál es verdadero o falso?

_____   1. Antes de comenzar este ejercicio, yo había conseguido una pluma.

_____   2. Antes de ducharme esta mañana, me había cepillado los dientes.

_____   3. Antes de comprar este libro, yo nunca había estudiado español.

_____   4. Antes de acostarme anoche, había apagado todas las luces en la casa.

_____   5. Antes de graduarme de la escuela secundaria, había conseguido trabajo para el verano.

_____   6. Me había lavado las manos antes de almorzar ayer.

_____   7. Yo había aprendido a nadar antes de cumplir seis años.

_____   8. Antes de mi trabajo actual *(present)*, había trabajado en un banco.

_____   9. Antes de tener una bicicleta, yo había montado en triciclo.

_____   10. Yo había volado en un avión antes de cumplir tres años.

ejercicio   II-6-1

1. I had paid. _____

2. She had lived in Texas. _____

3. They had lost all the letters. _____

4. We hadn't received an invitation. _____

5. Had you worn those shoes before the wedding? _____

6. I had eaten all the candy before discovering the prize. _____

7. We had practiced for four hours before the concert. _____

8. How long had you smoked before quitting? _____

9. She had lived in St. Louis before moving to St. Paul. _____

10. We had dated (*salir*) for three years before getting married. _____

_____

11. The soldiers had suffered a lot before the end of the war. _____

_____

12. Before the party I had cleaned the house from top to bottom (*de cabo a rabo*). _____

_____

13. He hadn't washed his hair in three weeks. _____

14. I had never enjoyed (*disfrutar*) the theater as much as he. _____

_____

15. Before going to bed, had you (*pl. fam.*) turned off (*apagar*) the lights? _____

_____

Irregular Past Participles

Whether the participle is regular or irregular, using the past perfect tense requires first conjugating *haber* in the imperfect (*había; habías; había; habíamos; habíais; habían*).

Past participles never change. Thus, those past participles that were irregular in the present perfect will be irregular in the past perfect (and in *all* compound tenses).

Irregularly formed past participles can be found in the previous unit on the present perfect.

examples:

Yo había visto la película.
I had seen the movie.

Habías vuelto del mercado.
You had returned from the market.

La comida **se había podrido.**
The food *had rotted.*

Habíamos abierto todas las ventanas.
We had opened all the windows.

Habíais envuelto los regalos.
You had wrapped the gifts.

Los científicos **habían descubierto** otro elemento.
The scientists *had discovered* another element.

¿Cuál es verdadero o falso para ti?

_____ 1. Antes de leer *Huck Finn,* yo había leído *Tom Sawyer.*

_____ 2. Yo había visto "Batman" antes de ver "Jurassic Park".

_____ 3. Antes del año 1900, George Washington había muerto.

_____ 4. Agatha Christie había escrito muchas novelas de misterio antes de morir.

_____ 5. Pinocho había dicho muchas mentiras y por eso su nariz era muy larga.

_____ 6. Durante su vida, Martin Luther King, hijo, había hecho muchas cosas buenas para la gente.

_____ 7. Alguien había descubierto las Américas antes que Cristóbal Colón.

_____ 8. Para el año 1960, Sears había abierto muchas tiendas en los Estados Unidos.

_____ 9. Durante su vida, Gandhi había descrito su visión de la paz.

_____ 10. Al principio, Caperucita Roja había creído que el lobo era su abuela.

ejercicio   II-6-2

1. I hadn't opened the windows until May of that year. _____

_____

2. They hadn't done anything. _____

3. She hadn't seen the movie before Saturday. _____

4. All the trees had died. _____

5. We hadn't solved the problems before the meeting. _____

_____

6. The thieves had broken the chairs and the windows. _____

_____

7. Had you (*pl. form.*) covered the tables before the storm (*la tormenta*)? _____

_____

8. Where had you put the money? _____

9. I had written fifty letters before receiving an answer. _____

_____

10. Had they provided you with enough information? _____

_____

11. The food had rotted in the refrigerator. _____

12. We had fried enough potatoes for an army. _____

_____

13. What had you done in order to help them? _____

14. The dog hadn't discovered the bones (*los huesos*) under the bed. _____

_____

15. The books had fallen from the shelf (*el estante*). _____

_____

¡Te toca a ti!

¿Qué habías hecho hoy antes de abrir este libro? Responde con frases completas.

1. _____

2. _____

3. _____

4. _____

5. _____

traducción   **II-6-3**

We had never been to (*in*) Europe before. We'd traveled a lot in South America and, of course, the United States, but never anywhere in Europe. My husband had won the trip on a game show (he'd always liked "Your Place or Mine," but had never dreamed of being a contestant on it). Anyway, before winning two million dollars (he has won more money on TV than anyone else in the world), Fenton already had decided on Europe—all of it. Before leaving, we had bought new luggage, sunglasses and, of course, lots of film for the new camera. I still haven't gotten used to that camera. It must be defective. Now that we've been (gone) to Europe, we want to conquer the South Pole.

"all of it"	**nada menos**	game show	**el concurso**
anyway	**de cualquier forma**	(to) get used to	**acostumbrarse a**
(to) be pleasing to, like	**gustar algo a alguien**	luggage	**las maletas**
(to) conquer	**conquistar**	must	**debe de + inf.**
contestant	**el participante**	not anywhere	**por ninguna parte**
(to) decide on	**decidir**	of course	**por supuesto**
defective	**defectuoso**	sunglasses	**gafas de sol**
(to) dream of being	**soñar con ser**	(to) travel	**viajar**
film (camera)	**el rollo de película**	trip	**el viaje**

_____

_____

_____

_____

_____

_____

_____

_____

_____

_____

_____

_____

_____

PART III

The Imperative, Subjunctive, and Compound Tenses, and the Passive Voice

MOOD: Imperative

TIME: Refers to the present

KEY PHRASES: Any command

STRUCTURE: Simple: single verb with modified ending

The Imperative

The imperative deals with one aspect of the language, and that is giving commands. We call the imperative a mood because commands do not move among the various time frames as do the tenses. The only time frame involved in a command is now, as in "Clean your room, *now.*"

Statements in the imperative are direct. There are no qualifiers, such as "*I want you to* clean your room" or "*You should* clean your room." The message is straightforward, and often can contain as little as one word: *Go! Stop! Look! Wait! Listen!*

The understood recipient of any command is *you.* Even when admonishing yourself to do something, you are speaking to yourself as *you* (in Spanish, in the *tú* form). We can, however, give *we* commands, meaning "you *and* I," which in English usually begin with *Let's. Let's dance; Let's eat; Let's go.*

This unit will have five sections: one section for each of the four forms of *you* in Spanish (*tú, usted, vosotros,* and *ustedes*), and finally a section for *nosotros.* In some cases the affirmative command (*Go!*) differs from the negative command (*Don't go!*). These will be noted, as well as the use of object pronouns with commands in Spanish.

One final note: By learning to work with the imperative now, you will be laying a good deal of groundwork for working with the present subjunctive, which is introduced in the next unit.

Commands in the *tú* (singular, informal) form:

To form a **regular affirmative** command, simply drop the *s* from the conjugated verb form of the second person singular:

Hablas	You speak	becomes	*¡Habla!*	Speak!
Comes	You eat	becomes	*¡Come!*	Eat!
Vives	You live	becomes	*¡Vive!*	Live!

ejercicio   III-1-1

*Write the following affirmative commands in the **tú** form:*

1. Study! _____
2. Work! _____
3. Look! _____
4. Listen! _____
5. Read! _____
6. Run! _____
7. Walk! _____
8. Dance! _____
9. Write! _____
10. Decide! _____
11. Sell! _____
12. Pay! _____
13. Suffer! _____
14. Count! _____
15. Fly! _____
16. Begin! _____
17. Think! _____
18. Sleep! _____
19. Continue! _____
20. Confess! _____

For **regular** verbs, to form a **negative** command do the following:

1. Take the present tense *yo* form of the verb.

2. Remove the *o* (or the *oy* in the verb *estar*). This is called the "*yo* stem."

3. For *-ar* verbs, add *-es;* for *-er* and *-ir* verbs, add *-as.*

¡No hables!	Don't speak!	*¡No compres el pescado!*	Don't buy the fish!
¡No comas!	Don't eat!	*¡No vendas la casa!*	Don't sell the house!
¡No escribas!	Don't write!	*¡No abras la puerta!*	Don't open the door!

Standard orthographic (spelling) changes: When preceding an *e,* the following orthographic changes come into play (*c* → *qu, g* → *gu, z* → *c*):

No tocas el piano (You don't play the piano) becomes *¡No toques el piano!* (Don't play the piano!)

No juegas al béisbol (You don't play baseball) becomes *¡No juegues al béisbol!* (Don't play baseball!)

No comienzas (You don't begin) becomes *¡No comiences!* (Don't begin!)

ejercicio   III-1-2

*Write the following negative commands in the **tú** form:*

1. Don't look! _____
2. Don't sing! _____
3. Don't study! _____
4. Don't run! _____

5. Don't think! _____

6. Don't drink the water! _____

_____

7. Don't arrive late! _____

_____

8. Don't practice now! _____

_____

9. Don't pay the bill! _____

_____

10. Don't organize the papers! _____

_____

11. Don't read my diary! _____

_____

12. Don't dance on the table! _____

_____

13. Don't open the windows! _____

_____

14. Don't admit anything! _____

_____

15. Don't believe anything! _____

_____

There are very few **irregular verbs** in the *tú* form. Listed below are the most common of these in both their affirmative and negative forms:

infinitive	affirmative	negative
decir	**di**	**no digas**
hacer	**haz**	**no hagas**
ir	**ve**	**no vayas**
poner	**pon**	**no pongas**
salir	**sal**	**no salgas**
ser	**sé**	**no seas**
tener	**ten**	**no tengas**
venir	**ven**	**no vengas**

ejercicio   III-1-3

*Write the following irregular commands in the **tú** form:*

1. Put the book here! _____

2. Tell the truth! _____

3. Make the bed! _____

4. Leave the house! _____

5. Come to the kitchen! _____

6. Be kind! _____

7. Go to the living room! _____

8. Have the money by tomorrow! _____

9. Don't put the shoes on the table! _____

10. Don't say anything! _____

11. Don't make the beds! _____

12. Don't leave now! _____

13. Don't come tomorrow! _____

14. Don't be selfish! _____

15. Don't go shopping today! _____

16. Don't have animals in the house! _____

Affirmative commands with object pronouns: With an affirmative command, the object pronoun(s) will be attached directly to the end of the verb in its imperative form.

¡Estúdialo!	Study it!	*¡Hazme* **un favor!**	Do me a favor!
¡Tráemelo!	Bring it to me!	*¡Dinos* **el secreto!**	Tell us the secret!
¡Deme **el libro!**	Give me the book!	*¡Levántate!*	Stand up!
¡Déjame en paz!	Leave me alone!	*¡Tráigame* **el libro!**	Bring me the book!

Note that the original stress will be retained. In Spanish words that end with a vowel, an "n," or an "s," the natural stress will fall on the next-to-the-last syllable. When the addition of an object pronoun (or pronouns) affects the original stress, you will add an accent mark: **¡Cómelo! ¡Háblame! ¡Míralos!**

When two object pronouns are involved, remember the **RID** Rule: **R**eflexive; **I**ndirect; **D**irect. In other words, a reflexive pronoun will precede an indirect or direct pronoun, and an indirect pronoun will precede a direct pronoun. If both the indirect and direct pronouns begin with the letter "l," the indirect pronoun will change to *se* (see the last example below).

These same rules for object pronouns will apply in all imperative forms (*tú; usted; vosotros; ustedes; nosotros*).

¡Dímelo!	Tell it to me!	*¡Cómpratelo!*	Buy it for yourself!
¡Dámelas!	Give them (*f.*) to me!	*¡Dáselo!*	Give it to him!

ejercicio   III-1-4

*Write the following affirmative commands in the **tú** form:*

1. Buy it! (*m.*) _____

2. Sell it! (*f.*) _____

3. Sit down! _____

4. Go to bed! _____

5. Take a bath! _____

6. Tell me a story! _____

7. Put it (*m.*) here! _____

8. Go away! _____

9. Put them (*f.*) there! _____

10. Leave us alone! _____

11. Tell it (*m.*) to us! _____

12. Write it (*f.*) to me! _____

13. Sing it (*f.*) to her! _____

14. Buy it (*m.*) for me! _____

15. Do it (*m.*) for yourself! _____

Negative commands with object pronouns: With a negative command, the object pronoun(s) will precede the verb in its imperative form. The object pronoun will be independent of the verb. When there are two object pronouns, the **RID** rule will apply.

¡No me mires!	Don't look at me!	*¡No lo hagas!*	Don't do it!
¡No le des el dinero!	Don't give him the money!	*¡No se lo digas!*	Don't tell it to him!
¡No lo pongas allí!	Don't put it there!	*¡No los compres!*	Don't buy them!

ejercicio   III-1-5

*Write the following negative commands in the **tú** form:*

1. Don't read it! (*m.*) _____

2. Don't drink it! (*f.*) _____

3. Don't kiss it! (*m.*) _____

4. Don't tell me lies! _____

5. Don't lie to me! _____

6. Don't go away! _____

7. Don't stand up! _____

8. Don't take a shower! _____

9. Don't go to bed! _____

10. Don't hate me! _____

11. Don't give it (*f.*) to him! _____

12. Don't tell it (*m.*) to them! _____

13. Don't sell it (*m.*) to us! _____

14. Don't read it (*m.*) to me! _____

15. Don't sing it (*f.*) to her! _____

Commands in the *usted* (singular, formal) form:

For **regular** verbs, to form an **affirmative** or a **negative** command, do the following:

1. Take the present tense *yo* form of the verb.

2. Drop the *-o* ending (or *-oy* in the verb *estar*)—the "*yo* stem."

3. For *-ar* verbs, add an *e;* for *-er* and *-ir* verbs, add an *a* (don't forget the standard orthographic changes, as discussed previously).

¡Hable!	Speak!	*¡Ponga!*	Put!	*¡Esté!*	Be!
¡Coma!	Eat!	*¡Tenga!*	Have!	*¡Dé!*	Give!
¡Escriba!	Write!	*¡Traiga!*	Bring!	*¡Comience!*	Begin!

ejercicio   III-1-6

Write the following regular commands in the **usted** *form:*

1. Sing! _____
2. Sell! _____
3. Count! _____
4. Pay! _____
5. Run! _____
6. Do it! _____
7. Play the piano! _____
8. Read it! _____
9. Bring it here! _____
10. Stand up! _____

11. Give it to me! _____
12. Tell it to me! _____
13. Don't tell me a lie! _____
14. Don't wait for us! _____
15. Don't rob the bank! _____
16. Give me the money! _____
17. Sit down! _____
18. Put it there! _____
19. Don't do it! _____
20. Tell him a story! _____

Irregularly formed *usted* commands: In the *usted* form, only three verbs have irregularly formed commands. These are:

ir	*¡Vaya!*	Go!
saber	*¡Sepa!*	Know!
ser	*¡Sea!*	Be!

ejercicio   III-1-7

*Write the following irregular commands in the **usted** form:*

1. Go away! _____

2. Know it! *(m.)* _____

3. Be good! _____

4. Don't go away! _____

5. Don't be bad! *(f.)* _____

6. Don't go to the party! _____

7. Know everything for tomorrow! _____

8. Go to the front of the room! _____

Commands in the *ustedes* (plural, formal) form*:

Commands in the *ustedes* form are identical to those in the *usted* form, with the single exception that an *n* is added to the *usted* imperative. This is true for **all** verbs, regular and irregular.

¡Hablen!	Speak!	*¡Váyanse!*	Go away!
¡No coman!	Don't eat!	*¡Sépanlo!*	Know it!
¡Escriban!	Write!	*¡Sean amables!*	Be kind!

*The *ustedes* form is used in both formal and informal situations in Spanish America. The *vosotros* form is used in Spain.

ejercicio   III-1-8

*Write the following commands in the **ustedes** form:*

1. Work! _____

2. Think! _____

3. Don't do that! _____

4. Don't leave! _____

5. Sit down! _____

6. Put them here! *(m.)* _____

7. Don't tell me anything! _____

8. Play the piano! _____

9. Play baseball! _____

10. Bring me the food! _____

11. Tell him the secret! _____

12. Don't go away angry! *(f.)* _____

13. Go to bed! _____

14. Wash your hands! _____

15. Brush your teeth! _____

Commands in the *vosotros* (plural, familiar) form:

For **all** verbs (except reflexive verbs), to form a **regular, affirmative** command in the *vosotros* form, simply drop the *r* from the infinitive and add *d*.

¡Trabajad!	Work!	*¡Decídmelo!*	Tell it to me!
¡Bebed!	Drink!	*¡Traednos la foto!*	Bring us the photo!
¡Escribid!	Write!	*¡Sed simpáticos!*	Be kind!
¡Sabedlo!	Know it!	*¡Idos!*	Go away!

With reflexive verbs in the affirmative, *vosotros* form, this *d* is not added before the reflexive pronoun is attached directly to the stem.

¡Levantaos!	Stand up!	*¡Sentaos!*	Sit down!
¡Acostaos!	Go to bed!	*¡Callaos!*	Be quiet!

ejercicio   III-1-9

*Write the following affirmative commands in the **vosotros** form:*

1. Fly! _____

2. Return! _____

3. Come! _____

4. Stop! _____

5. Run! _____

6. Boil the water! _____

7. Sleep! _____

8. Read it! *(m.)* _____

9. Go to the store! _____

10. Put it *(f.)* in the house! _____

11. Do us a favor! _____

12. Arrive at ten o'clock! _____

To regularly form **negative** commands in the *vosotros* form, do the following:

add *-éis* to the "*yo* stem" of *-ar* verbs

add *-áis* to the "*yo* stem" of *-er* and *-ir* verbs

¡No trabajéis!	Don't work!	*¡No me lo digáis!*	Don't tell it to me!
¡No bebáis!	Don't drink!	*¡No nos traigáis nada!*	Don't bring us anything!
¡No escribáis!	Don't write!	*¡No se lo deis!*	Don't give it to him!

Note that the negative *vosotros* command of *ir, saber,* and *ser* mirrors that of the *usted* command for these verbs:

ir	*¡No vayáis conmigo!*	Don't go with me!
saber	*¡No sepáis todo!*	Don't know everything!
ser	*¡No seáis antipáticos!*	Don't be mean!

Finally, in the *vosotros* negative form, *-ir* stem-changing verbs undergo a little twist. These verbs change the *e* or *o* of the stem to *i* and *u* respectively:

pedir	*¡No pidáis!*	Don't request!	**dormir**	*¡No durmáis!*	Don't sleep!
servir	*¡No sirváis!*	Don't serve!	**morirse**	*¡No os muráis!*	Don't die!
seguir	*¡No sigáis!*	Don't follow!	**repetir**	*¡No repitáis!*	Don't repeat!

ejercicio   III-1-10

*Write the following negative commands in the **vosotros** form:*

1. Don't eat! _____

2. Don't speak! _____

3. Don't play here! _____

4. Don't sing! _____

5. Don't sleep in the park! _____

6. Don't boil the water! _____

7. Don't fall asleep! _____

8. Don't leave! _____

9. Don't take the money! _____

10. Don't follow me! _____

11. Don't go to bed! _____

12. Don't go away! _____

Commands in the *nosotros* form:

Commands in the *nosotros* (we) form generally translate to "Let's" statements in English: "Let's eat"; "Let's dance"; "Let's go." To form these commands in regular Spanish verbs, you will do the following:

Take the present tense *yo* form of the verb.

Remove the *o* or *oy*. You now have the "*yo* stem."

For *-ar* verbs, add *-emos;* for *-er* and *-ir* verbs, add *-amos*.

¡Hablemos!	Let's talk!
¡Comamos!	Let's eat!
¡Escribamos!	Let's write!

You have seen this same set of rules several times in this unit. Knowing this format will help you greatly when studying the present subjunctive.

Things to note:

1. Stem-changing verbs—except stem-changing *-ir* verbs—will *not* change (the stem change does not occur in the *nosotros* form).

¡Contemos el dinero!	Let's count the money!
¡Pensemos!	Let's think!
¡Movamos los muebles!	Let's move the furniture!
¡Volvamos!	Let's return!

2. Stem-changing *ir* verbs will make the following changes in *nosotros* commands:

    o → *ue* verbs: the *o* changes to *u*. dormir → *¡Durmamos!* Let's sleep!

    e → *ie* verbs: the *e* changes to *i*. mentir → *¡Mintamos!* Let's lie!

    e → *i* verbs: the *e* changes to *i*. pedir → *¡Pidamos!* Let's ask!

3. Verbs ending in *-car*, *-gar*, and *-zar* will make the necessary standard orthographic changes (*c* → *qu; g* → *gu, z* → *c*, respectively).

¡Toquemos el piano!	Let's play the piano!
¡Paguemos la cuenta!	Let's pay the bill!
¡Comencemos!	Let's begin!

4. With reflexive verbs, you will drop the *s* of the conjugated verb before adding *nos*. Otherwise, add all object pronouns directly.

Levantemos + nos = ¡Levantémonos!   Let's stand up!
Sentemos + nos = ¡Sentémonos!   Let's sit down!
Acostemos + nos = ¡Acostémonos!   Let's go to bed!

5. To make a negative command, just add **no** before the verb:

¡No trabajemos!   Let's not work!
¡No volemos!   Let's not fly!
¡No nos bañemos!   Let's not take a bath!

---

ejercicio   III-1-11

*Write the following regular commands in the **nosotros** form:*

1. Let's study! _____

2. Let's walk! _____

3. Let's not study! _____

4. Let's not eat! _____

5. Let's sell the car! _____

6. Let's do something! _____

7. Let's not do anything! _____

_____

8. Let's eat lunch! _____

9. Let's put the dog outside! _____

_____

10. Let's sing to them! _____

11. Let's not lie! _____

12. Let's not begin now! _____

_____

13. Let's tell the truth! _____

14. Let's not say anything! _____

15. Let's buy it (*m.*)! _____

As with several of the other command forms, there are only three irregularly formed verbs in the *nosotros* form (with *ir* having both reflexive and non-reflexive forms). Note that *ir* has different affirmative and negative forms:

ir	*¡Vamos!*	Let's go!	*¡No vayamos!*	Let's not go!
irse	*¡Vámonos!*	Let's go away!	*¡No nos vayamos!*	Let's not go away!
saber	*¡Sepamos!*	Let's know!	*¡No sepamos!*	Let's not know!
ser	*¡Seamos!*	Let's be!	*¡No seamos!*	Let's not be!

---

ejercicio   III-1-12

*Write the following irregular commands in the **nosotros** form:*

1. Let's know everything! _____

2. Let's be kind! _____

3. Let's not go to the party! _____

4. Let's go away tonight! _____

5. Let's not be cowards *(cobardes)*! _____

6. Let's go to the movies tomorrow! _____

7. Let's be honest people! _____

8. Let's not go away this afternoon! _____

The Present Subjunctive

The subjunctive mood (there are four subjunctive tenses) could be reduced to seven subheadings:

1. **desire**
2. **ignorance**
3. **impersonal opinion**
4. **uncompleted action**
5. **vague or indefinite antecedent**
6. **maybe/perhaps**
7. **"even if"**

At the root of every subjunctive sentence, there is always some aspect not known or not controllable.

Sentences that are not **subjunctive** are **indicative,** and do what the name implies: they indicate or report something. Consider the following sentences:

I know that you speak Spanish.

I hope that you speak Spanish.

The first sentence is in the indicative. The speaker is certain of something (that you speak Spanish) and is reporting that information.

The second clause of the second sentence is in the subjunctive. The speaker does not know that you speak Spanish, but has a *desire* that you do.

In sentences where there is a subjunctive clause, often there is also an indicative clause which reports desire, ignorance, or an impersonal opinion.

examples of desire sentences:

I hope *that you are happy.*

I suggest *that you buy the red car.*

We demand *that he pay in cash.*

He prays *that you get well.*

You insist *that we wash the dishes.*

examples of ignorance sentences:

I doubt *that he lives here.*

I don't think *that she knows my name.*

She doesn't believe *that you live here.*

examples of impersonal opinion sentences:

It's great *that you can dance so well.*

It's better *that we sit here.*

It's terrible *that we have to wait.*

It's advisable *that you sign your name in ink.*

examples of uncompleted action sentences:

We'll eat *after we wash our hands.*

I'll feel better *when I sit down.*

He won't work here *unless he gets a raise.*

I'll wear clean clothes *in case I have an accident.*

examples of vague or indefinite antecedent sentences:

I need an assistant *who is punctual.*

He wants a wife *who cooks as well as his mother.*

We want a car *that has a television.*

Isn't there anyone *who can read this?*

examples of maybe/perhaps sentences:

Maybe *he has the money.*

Perhaps *she'll call us tonight.*

examples of "even if" sentences:

Even if he knows, he won't tell us.

Even if she is Miss America, we won't hire her.

Formation of the Present Subjunctive:

Nearly all verbs in the present subjunctive are formed in the same way. There are three steps involved in this formation:

1. Take the *yo* form of the present indicative:

hablar	**hablo**
comer	**como**
vivir	**vivo**
conocer	**conozco**
tener	**tengo**
hacer	**hago**
querer	**quiero**
salir	**salgo**
ver	**veo**

2. Remove the *-o* ending:

hablar	**habl**
comer	**com**
vivir	**viv**
conocer	**conozc**
tener	**teng**
hacer	**hag**
querer	**quier**
salir	**salg**
ver	**ve**

3. Add the following endings:

    -ar verbs: **-e; -es; -e; -emos; -éis; -en**
    -er verbs: **-a; -as; -a; -amos; -áis; -an**
    -ir verbs: **-a; -as; -a; -amos; -áis; -an**

Thus:

hablar: hable; hables; hable; hablemos; habléis; hablen
comer: coma; comas; coma; comamos; comáis; coman
vivir: viva; vivas; viva; vivamos; viváis; vivan
conocer: conozca; conozcas; conozca; conozcamos; conozcáis; conozcan
tener: tenga; tengas; tenga; tengamos; tengáis; tengan
hacer: haga; hagas; haga; hagamos; hagáis; hagan
querer: quiera; quieras; quiera; queramos;* queráis;* quieran
salir: salga; salgas; salga; salgamos; salgáis; salgan
ver: vea; veas; vea; veamos; veáis; vean

*Note: There is no stem change in the *nosotros* or *vosotros* forms, except in *-ir* stem-changing verbs. With these verbs, the following changes will take place:

o → *ue* verbs: *o* changes to *u*. ***durmamos; durmáis***

e → *ie* verbs: *e* changes to *i*. ***mintamos; mintáis***

e → *i* verbs: *e* changes to *i*. ***pidamos; pidáis***

Irregularly formed verbs in the present subjunctive:

There are six verbs that do not follow the format described above. These, along with their present subjunctive conjugations, are:

> **dar:** dé; des; dé; demos; deis; den
> **estar:** esté; estés; esté; estemos; estéis; estén (**note:** accented vowels are retained)
> **haber:** haya; hayas; haya; hayamos; hayáis; hayan
> **ir:** vaya; vayas; vaya; vayamos; vayáis; vayan
> **saber:** sepa; sepas; sepa; sepamos; sepáis; sepan
> **ser:** sea; seas; sea; seamos; seáis; sean

Using the Present Subjunctive

You will use the subjunctive when there is a degree of desire, ignorance, or impersonal opinion on the part of the subject. There are two parts of the sentence containing a subjunctive clause: (1) the main clause and (2) the subordinate clause. These two clauses generally are separated by *que,* which translates into "that."

The *main clause* contains the statement of desire, ignorance, or opinion: this is in the indicative. The *subordinate* clause contains that which is being considered: this is in the subjunctive. Consider the following sentence:

> ***I doubt** that he works much.*

The main clause is "I doubt." The subordinate clause, "he works much," is in the subjunctive due to the uncertainty expressed in the main clause. This sentence would translate as:

> ***Yo dudo** que él trabaje mucho.*

1. Expressions of Desire: Verbs in the main clause which express a wish, a preference, a request, etc., will set up the need for the subjunctive in the subordinate clause. In these situations, the subject tells what he or she would like to happen: whether it will actually happen is not certain.

Listed below are some commonly used verbs of desire that require the use of the subjunctive:

esperar	to hope
exigir (*e → i*)	to demand
insistir en	to insist (on)
ojalá	God willing; I strongly hope
pedir (*e → i*)	to request
preferir (*e → ie*)	to prefer
querer (*e → ie*)	to want
rogar (*o → ue*)	to pray, beg
sugerir (*e → ie*)	to suggest

examples:

Él prefiere que **yo hable.**
He prefers that *I speak.*

Insistimos en que **tengas** el dinero.
We insist that *you have* the money.

Quiero que **Juan estudie.**
I want *John to study*—
literally: I want *that John study.*

Ellos esperan que **podamos** bailar.
They hope that *we can* dance.

Ella pide que **sirváis** el café.
She requests that *you serve* the coffee.

Espero que **ellos vivan** en esa casa.
I hope that *they live* in that house.

¿Cuál es verdadero o falso para ti?

_____ 1. Ojalá que no tenga un examen hoy.

_____ 2. Espero que haga buen tiempo mañana.

_____ 3. Espero que el próximo Presidente sea demócrata.

_____ 4. Quiero que mis amigos sean amables.

_____ 5. Prefiero que haya nieve en la Navidad.

_____ 6. Espero que llueva el fin de semana que viene.

_____ 7. Excepto en caso de emergencia, sugiero que nadie me llame después de las diez de la noche.

_____ 8. Cuando tengo una fiesta, quiero que los invitados lleguen a tiempo.

_____ 9. Pido que mis vecinos no tengan muchas fiestas ruidosas.

_____ 10. Espero que no haya cucarachas en mi cocina.

_____ 11. Cuando asisto a una reunión, prefiero que no sea larga (ni aburrida).

_____ 12. Insisto en que las personas me den el mismo respeto que yo les doy a ellos.

ejercicio   III-2-1

1. I hope that she speaks with me tomorrow. _____

2. I want you to eat the bread (I want that you eat the bread). _____

3. He wants me to write a letter. _____

4. We pray that you are well. _____

5. They want us to do it. _____

6. She hopes that you can come to the party. _____

7. They suggest that you do it. _____

8. I insist (on) that you (_pl. fam._) work. _____

9. He requests that we be here at nine o'clock. _____

10. Why do you request that I do it? _____

11. I prefer that we not leave the house until five o'clock. _____

12. She hopes that you know her. _____

13. We insist (on) that you eat with us. _____

14. Do you want me to count the money? _____

15. They suggest that we put the papers in the cabinet (*el gabinete*). _____

traducción   **III-2-2**

(Verbs in the present subjunctive are *in italics*.)

Tomorrow is the first day of my new job. I hope that everything *goes* well for me. My boss seems very friendly, but I prefer that she *be* more fair than friendly. I want her *to understand* that if I make a mistake (and I'm sure that I'll make many), I want her *to tell* me directly. Before the first week ends, I'm going to request that she *tell* me what she thinks of my performance. If she suggests that I *change* some aspect of my work, it will be easier to do so then than after working there for a few months.

vocabulario

boss	**el jefe/la jefa**	friendly	**amable**
(to) change	**cambiar**	(to) make a mistake	**cometer un error**
fair	**justo**	performance	**el desempeño**

_____

_____

_____

_____

_____

_____

_____

2. Ignorance: Verbs in the main clause that express ignorance or doubt will set up the need for the subjunctive in the subordinate clause. In these situations, the subject acknowledges uncertainty or ignorance of the outcome of the action described in the subordinate clause.

Some commonly used verbs of ignorance which require the use of the subjunctive:

dudar que	to doubt that
no creer que*	to not believe that
no estar convencido/a de que	to not be convinced that
no estar seguro/a que	to not be sure that
no imaginarse que	to not imagine that
no parecer que	to not seem that
no pensar que	to not think that
no suponer que	to not suppose that
temer que	to suspect, fear that

*Note: While the verbs listed in the negative will set up the use of the subjunctive, these same verbs in the affirmative (e.g., *creer, suponer,* etc.) will set up the indicative in the subordinate clause.

affirmative/indicative:	negative/subjunctive:
Yo *creo* que Juan *tiene* el dinero. I *think* that John *has* the money.	**Yo *no creo* que Juan *tenga* el dinero.** I *don't think* that John *has* the money.

ejercicio   III-2-3

1. I doubt that she eats in that restaurant. _____

2. I don't suppose that you'll tell me his name. _____

3. They don't believe that he plays the piano. _____

4. She isn't sure that the coffee is ready. _____

5. We don't think that the Vikings will win the game. _____

6. He is not convinced that I need so much money. _____

7. Why don't you believe that we know him? _____

8. We aren't convinced that the moon (*la luna*) is made (*ser*) of green cheese. _____

    _____

9. He doubts that they know the answer. _____

10. She isn't sure that we always tell the truth. _____

11. Why aren't you convinced that I am always right (*tener razón*)? _____

_____

12. It doesn't seem that he wants to be here. _____

13. I'm not sure that you can read this. _____

14. He doesn't believe that I'm his cousin. _____

15. I don't imagine that you believe my story (*la historia*). _____

traducción   **III-2-4**

(Verbs in *italics* are in the present subjunctive.)

I doubt that John *knows* that we're planning a party for him. It doesn't seem possible that he *is* the new president of this company, and I don't imagine that he *believes* it either. I doubt that he *likes* this new position. I'm not convinced that he *is ready* for so great a responsibility; on the other hand, I don't suppose that anyone *can* become a great leader overnight. I want everything *to go well* for him.

vocabulario

(to) be ready	**estar listo**	not either	**tampoco**
(to) become	**hacerse**	on the other hand	**en cambio**
company	**la compañía**	overnight	**de la noche a la mañana**
(to) go well	**salir bien**	(to) plan	**planear**
leader	**el líder**	so; such	**tan**

_____

_____

_____

_____

_____

_____

3. Impersonal Opinion: An impersonal expression in the main clause which expresses emotion, uncertainty, unreality, or an indirect or implied command will set up the need for the subjunctive in the subordinate clause.

Some commonly used impersonal expressions are listed below. Each is followed by *que,* then the subordinate clause which contains a verb in the subjunctive.

conviene que	it is advisable that
es fantástico que	it is fantastic that
es importante que	it is important that
es imposible que	it is impossible that
es improbable que	it is unlikely that
es increíble que	it is incredible that
es (una) lástima que	it is a pity that; it is a shame that
es mejor que	it is better that
es necesario que	it is necessary that
es posible que	it is possible that
es probable que	it is probable that
es preferible que	it is preferable that
es ridículo que	it is ridiculous that
es terrible que	it is terrible that
más vale que	it is better that
ojalá (que)	I hope (that); if only he (it, they, etc.) would, could, might; God willing (that)
puede ser que	it may be that

examples:

Es una lástima que **yo esté** enfermo.
It's a pity that *I'm* sick.

Es necesario que **te vayas** ahora.
It is necessary that *you go* now.

Ojalá que **no llueva** mañana.
I hope *it doesn't rain* tomorrow.

Es mejor que **comamos** el apio.
It's better that *we eat* the celery.

Es importante que **miréis** este programa.
It's important that *you watch* this program.

Conviene que **ellos sepan** su dirección.
It's advisable that *they know* their address.

ejercicio   III-2-5

1. It's better that we eat in the kitchen. _____

2. It's necessary that you call them tomorrow. _____

3. It's preferable that you buy the eggs by the dozen (*por docenas*). _____

_____

4. It's unlikely that they'll be ready by five o'clock. _____

5. It's advisable that you (*sing., form.*) have an attorney (*abogado*) with you. _____

_____

6. It's important that no one know that secret. _____

7. It may be that Alice doesn't work here anymore (not anymore = *ya no* + conjugated verb). _____

_____

8. It's ridiculous that so many politicians (*políticos*) don't tell the truth. _____

_____

9. It's impossible that I be in two places at the same time (*al mismo tiempo*). _____

_____

10. It's incredible that he speaks twelve languages (*idiomas*). _____

_____

11. It's a shame that ice cream has so many calories (*calorías*). _____

_____

12. If only Jane wouldn't sing at (*en*) the wedding (*la boda*). _____

13. It's fantastic that we don't have to sit next to (*al lado de*) them. _____

_____

14. It may be that Steven isn't what (*lo que*) he says he is. _____

_____

15. It's impossible that I remain (*quedarse*) in this room one more minute. _____

_____

traducción   **III-2-6**

(Verbs in *italics* are in the present subjunctive.)

Last night I read for the first time the rules and regulations of the company where I have worked for six years. It is possible that I *am* the only person who has read this pamphlet. There are so many absurd rules. For example, it's ridiculous that we *should* keep our desks neat at all times. It's better that a person *have* the freedom to be a slob if that is what he/she needs in order to work well. Also, it's incredible that we *have to* attend all meetings, including the ones that have nothing to do with our own work (nobody ever goes to these meetings). It's better that we *work* at a messy desk than attend a meeting in a neat boardroom and twiddle our thumbs. If only no one would *enforce* these rules!

---

vocabulario

boardroom	**la sala de juntas**	neat	**ordenado**
(to) enforce	**imponer**	pamphlet	**el folleto**
(to) have nothing	**no tener nada**	regulation	**el reglamento**
to do with	**que ver con**	rule	**la regla**
meeting	**la reunión**	slob	**el cochino**
messy	**desordenado**	(to) twiddle one's thumbs	**voltear los pulgares**

---

4. Uncompleted Action: When the action of the subordinate clause is pending or indefinite, as in "I'll speak with John *when he arrives,*" that verb will be in the subjunctive. Spanish is very precise: You may be absolutely certain that John will arrive (absence of ignorance), but you cannot know **exactly when** until you see the whites of his eyes!

Some common connecting phrases which frequently set up the subjunctive:

a menos que	unless
antes (de) que*	before
con tal (de) que	provided that
cuando	when
después (de) que*	after
en caso de que	in case
hasta que	until
mientras que	while
para que	so that; in order that
sin que	without
tan pronto como	as soon as

*The *de* is optional.

examples:

Ella te llamará **tan pronto como yo llegue.**
She'll call you *as soon as I arrive.*

Él no irá **a menos que tú vayas.**
He will not go *unless you go.*

Estudiaré **en caso de que haya** un examen.
I will study *in case there is* a test.

Cocinaré **para que podamos** comer.
I'll cook *so that we can* eat.

Tocaré el piano **con tal de que cantéis.**
I'll play the piano *provided that you sing.*

Trabajaremos **hasta que cierren** la oficina.
We will work *until they close* the office.

ejercicio   III-2-7

(Note that in most cases the main clause will be in the future tense.)

1. I won't eat until I'm hungry. _____

2. I'll write you a note so that you remember to buy milk. _____

_____

3. You'll feel (*sentirse*) better after you take this medicine. _____

_____

4. He won't marry (*casarse con*) a woman unless she's rich. _____

_____

5. You (*pl. fam.*) can't hunt (*cazar*) unless you have a license (*la licencia*). _____

_____

6. I'll wipe (dry) the dishes while you wash them. _____

7. The priest can't baptize (*bautizar*) the baby before the godparents (*los padrinos*) arrive. _____

_____

8. The game's not over (*acabarse*) till it's over. _____

9. I'll believe it when I see it. _____

10. He's going to read this book another time in case we have a quiz (*la prueba*). _____

_____

11. He won't eat anything unless he has a napkin (*la servilleta*) in his lap (*el regazo*). _____

_____

12. Every week I save (*ahorrar*) twenty-five dollars so that I have enough money for my vacation.

_____

13. She'll never be happy until she knows how to conjugate (*conjugar*) verbs. _____

_____

14. You should brush your teeth before we leave for the dentist's office (*la consulta del dentista*).

_____

15. I can't wear these pants until I lose (*perder*) ten pounds. _____

_____

traducción   III-2-8

(Italicized verbs are in the present subjunctive.)

"I'll write you as soon as I *get* (arrive) there." These were Marco's famous last words. What he should have said (*debería haber dicho*) was, "I'll write you unless I'm *having* a good time," or "I'll send you a letter when *there is* nothing else to do," or, more simply, "I'll tell you about my trip after I *get* (arrive) home." The day that I *get* (receive) a letter from Marco will be the day that miracles happen everywhere. Unless someone *puts* a gun to his head, Marco will never write anyone a letter.

vocabulario

gun	**la pistola**	(to) send	**mandar**
(to) happen	**ocurrir**	(to) tell	**contar**
(to) have a good time	**divertirse** (*e → ie*)	trip	**el viaje**
miracle	**el milagro**	word	**la palabra**

_____

_____

_____

_____

_____

_____

_____

_____

_____

_____

5. Vague or Indefinite Antecedent: When the object or person being referred to in the main clause is not known to actually exist, you will need to use the subjunctive in the subordinate clause. This difference can be seen in the following sentences:

> _I have a secretary_ who is efficient. (**definite antecedent**)

> _I want a secretary_ who is efficient. (**indefinite antecedent**)

examples:

Él quiere* una esposa que **gane** mucho dinero.   No conozco a nadie que **sepa zapatear.**
He wants a wife who _earns_ a lot of money.   I don't know anyone who _knows how to tap-dance._

*The personal _a_ is not required with verbs of desire for a person who does not necessarily exist.

ejercicio   III-2-9

1. We're looking for a house that has three bedrooms. _____

2. She wants a dog that doesn't bark (_ladrar_). _____

3. Is there anyone here who can play the guitar? _____

4. I need a maid (_la criada_) who washes (_limpiar_) windows. _____

5. Is there anybody in the world who knows how to express (_expresarse_) himself clearly? _____

_____

6. I'm looking for a cat that doesn't scratch (_arañar_) the furniture (_los muebles_). _____

_____

7. Where can I buy a shirt that isn't polyester (_de poliéster_)? _____

8. There isn't anyone here who can help you. _____

9. For his birthday this year he wants a parrot (_el loro_) that speaks three languages. _____

_____

10. I want to live in a city where there isn't any crime (_crimen_). _____

_____

traducción   III-2-10

(Verbs in *italics* are in the present subjunctive.)

I went shopping with Giralda this morning. I will never, ever, put myself through that torture again. Giralda is impossible! First, she wants a parking space that *is* no more than ten feet from the front door of the mall. This took half an hour. Next, she wants a dress that *has* detachable sleeves so that she *can* wear it all year. She also wants a necklace that *looks like* something a queen would wear, but she also wants this necklace *to cost* less than ten dollars. She wants shoes that *have* jewels on the heels and she wants gloves that *have* little pearls at the wrists. In each store she told the clerk exactly what she wanted, and each clerk told Giralda that there is no store in that mall, or in any mall on this planet, that *sells* such items. Giralda was furious and said that there is no one in this world who *understands* her fabulous taste.

vocabulario

clerk	**la dependienta**	never, ever	**nunca jamás**
detachable	**de quita y pon**	parking space	**el aparcamiento**
front door	**la puerta principal**	planet	**el planeta**
(to) go shopping	**ir de compras**	(to) put oneself through	**meterse en**
glove	**el guante**	queen	**la reina**
heel	**el tacón**	shopping mall	**el centro comercial**
item	**el artículo**	sleeve	**la manga**
jewel	**la joya**	store	**la tienda**
little pearl	**la perlita**	(to) take time	**tardar (en)**
(to) look like	**parecer**	taste	**el gusto**
necklace	**el collar**	wrist	**la muñeca**

6. "Perhaps"; "Maybe":   Phrases that are set up by the words "perhaps" or "maybe" are usually cloaked in uncertainty, and therefore require the use of the subjunctive. The words **acaso, quizá,*** and **tal vez** all mean "perhaps" and "maybe," and for the most part are used interchangeably.

Acaso, however, is generally reserved for writing, while **quizá(s)** and **tal vez** are used more in daily conversation.

*Some people use **quizás** instead of **quizá.** There is no difference, though **quizá** is more commonly used. The important thing for each person is to choose one form and use that consistently.

examples:

Quizá **él no te conteste.**
Perhaps/Maybe *he won't answer you.*

Tal vez **ella esté enferma.**
Maybe/Perhaps *she's sick.*

Acaso **ellos no vayan de compras.**
Maybe/Perhaps *they won't go shopping.*

Quizá **no la conozcamos.**
Perhaps/Maybe *we don't know her.*

ejercicio	III-2-11

1. Maybe he has the money. _____

2. Perhaps we can go. _____

3. Maybe they live here. _____

4. Perhaps you know him. _____

5. Maybe they'll buy the house today. _____

6. Perhaps we are lost (*perdidos*). _____

7. Maybe he isn't the smartest person in the world. _____

8. Perhaps you (*pl. fam.*) shouldn't drink this milk. _____

9. Maybe the politician isn't telling the truth. _____

10. Perhaps the cat has only eight lives. _____

traducción	III-2-12

(Each "maybe" appears as *tal vez* in the answers.)

Let's see. I don't have to work today. What should I do? Maybe I'll read a book. Maybe I'll buy a book. Maybe I'll go to the movies. Maybe I'll study Spanish. Maybe I'll fly a kite. Maybe I'll mow the lawn. Maybe I'll eat an egg. Maybe I'll go for a walk. Maybe I'll take out the garbage. Maybe I'll do nothing. That's it! I'll do nothing!

<table>
<tr><td>**vocabulario**</td></tr>
</table>

egg	**el huevo**	Let's see	**A ver**
(to) fly a kite	**remontar una cometa**	(to) mow	**cortar**
garbage	**la basura**	(to) take out	**sacar**
(to) go to the movies	**ir al cine**	(to) take a walk	**dar un paseo**
lawn	**el césped**	That's it!	**¡Ajá!**

_____

_____

_____

_____

_____

7. *Aunque,* **Meaning "Even if":**   *Aunque* is the Spanish word for "even if," "although," and "even though." When the action **has not yet occurred or is not known to be occurring,** *aunque* sets up the subjunctive, as in, "We will go *even if it rains*" (Iremos *aunque llueva*). When the action already has occurred or is occurring, you will use the indicative, as in, "We will go *even though it is raining*" (Iremos *aunque llueve*).

examples:

Aunque él no hable español, lo contrataré.   **Aunque no ganemos,** estaremos felices.
Even if he doesn't speak Spanish, I'll hire him.   *Although we may not win,* we'll be happy.

ejercicio   **III-2-13**

1. Even if Jane cooks, I won't stay (*quedarse*). _____

2. Although they may want to watch television, we won't let (*dejar*) them. _____

_____

3. Even if you yell (*gritar*) at me, I won't change my mind (*cambiar mi idea*). _____

_____

4. Although he may think he's a genius (*el genio*), everyone knows that he isn't. _____

_____

5. Even if you offer the policeman a thousand dollars, he'll still (*todavía*) give you a ticket (*la multa*).

_____

6. Although we may be ignorant (*ignorar*) of the candidates, we still have the right (*el derecho*) to vote.

_____

7. Even if you put the cat in the basement, Barbara will still sneeze (*estornudar*). _____

_____

8. Although you (*pl. fam.*) may feel sick, you still have to take the test. _____

_____

9. Even if you wind your watch (*dar cuerda al reloj*) fifty times, it will never work. _____

_____

10. Although he may smile (*sonreír*) all the time, inside (*en su interior*) he is evil (*malo*). _____

_____

11. Even if I know the answer, I won't tell you. _____

12. Although you (*pl. form.*) may think I'm crazy, I know that I'm right. _____

_____

traducción   III-2-14

Oh no! Someone is at the door. I'm looking through the window. It doesn't look like anyone that I know. It's possible that it's a politician, but it's more likely that it's a salesperson. Or maybe it's UPS. No—they always carry packages. Maybe it's the florist with a bouquet of flowers for me. No—they always have flowers. I don't know who this person can be. Maybe it's Publishers' Clearing House because I've won ten million dollars. No—they always have that giant check. I'm not going to open the door. I hope that the intruder will go away.

vocabulario

bouquet	**el ramo**	(to) look like	**parecerse a**
florist	**el florista**	(to) look through the window	**mirar por la ventana**
giant	**gigante**	salesperson	**el vendedor**
intruder	**el intruso**	someone	**alguien**

_____

_____

_____

_____

_____

_____

traducción	**III-2-15**

(Includes subjunctive themes from all seven categories.)

There isn't anyone who can cook as well as my friend Catarina. It's great that she's having a party this weekend because I haven't eaten a good meal in a long time (that is to say, since the last time I ate at her house). I hope that she makes her famous apple tart again, but I doubt that she will make it this weekend, because she served it less than a year ago and she rarely repeats herself. Even if she prepares this treat, it won't be the same because she always changes (improves) every recipe a little each time she uses it. I fear that I will never taste that same tart again. Maybe I'll beg her, so that she will prepare the tart for me for my birthday. I know that when I taste that tart again I will either be in heaven or in Catarina's dining room.

vocabulario

apple	**la manzana**	rarely	**rara vez**
(to) change	**cambiar**	recipe	**la receta**
either . . . or	**o . . . o . . . .**	(to) repeat oneself	**repetirse**
heaven	**el cielo**	tart	**la tarta**
(to) improve	**mejorar**	treat	**la delicia**

_____

_____

_____

_____

_____

The Imperfect Subjunctive

MOOD: Imperfect Subjunctive

TIME: Refers to the past

KEY PHRASE: Hypothetical "if"; "as if"

STRUCTURE: Simple tense: verb root + ending

We use the imperfect subjunctive in the same situations that we use the present subjunctive: in times of uncertainty and after certain words and expressions. However, the time is in the past.

When studying the indicative tenses, we do a great deal of work to distinguish between the preterite and the imperfect. This is not an issue in the subjunctive mood, where the imperfect subjunctive refers to actions simply in the past.

Consider the following two sentences:

> Espero que Ricardo **tenga** el libro.
> I hope that Richard *has* the book.

> Esperaba que Ricardo **tuviera** el libro.
> I hoped that Richard *had* the book.

The first sentence is in the present, as indicated by the main clause *Espero* (I hope), and is followed by the present subjunctive in the subordinate clause.

In the second sentence, the main clause *Esperaba* (I hoped) is in the past (imperfect indicative) and thus sets the stage for the imperfect subjunctive.

First we are going to look at the formation of the imperfect subjunctive tense, and then at the situations in which it is used.

Formation of the Imperfect Subjunctive

For *all* verbs you will drop the *-ron* ending of the third person plural of the preterite. This gives you the base for *all* forms of the imperfect subjunctive.

Third Person Preterite	Imperfect Subjunctive Base
hablaron (they spoke)	**habla**
comieron (they ate)	**comie**
abrieron (they opened)	**abrie**
tuvieron (they had)	**tuvie**
dijeron (they said)	**dije**
fueron (they were/went)	**fue**
estuvieron (they were)	**estuvie**
hicieron (they made/did)	**hicie**
pusieron (they put)	**pusie**

To this base, you add the following endings:

-ra	**-´ramos***		**-se**	**-´semos***
-ras	**-rais**	OR	**-ses**	**-seis**
-ra	**-ran**		**-se**	**-sen**

Of these two endings, which may be used interchangeably, the first (**-ra; -ras; -ra . . .**) form is more commonly used. This is the one we will use in this book.

*Note that an accent falls on the vowel which precedes the first person plural (*nosotros*) ending (e.g., *habláramos; dijéramos; tuviéramos; fuéramos*, etc.).

When to Use the Imperfect Subjunctive

1. Main Clause in the Past: When the main clause is in the past *and* calls for the subjunctive, you will use the imperfect subjunctive in the subordinate clause.

examples:

Ella quería que **yo hablara** en español.
She wanted *me to speak* in Spanish.

Fue terrible que **estuviéramos enfermos.**
It was terrible that *we were sick.*

Querían que **supieras** la respuesta.
They wanted *you to know* the answer.

Él dudaba que **pudierais** bailar.
He doubted that *you (pl. fam.) could* dance.

Yo esperaba que **no hubiera** un accidente.
I hoped that *there wasn't* an accident.

Comimos antes de que **ellos llegaran.**
We ate before *they arrived.*

ejercicio	III-3-1

1. I wanted John to buy the towels (*las toallas*). _____

2. It was a pity that you had to work last Sunday. _____

3. There wasn't anyone in the class who spoke French. _____

_____

4. We doubted that Humpty Dumpty fell from the wall (*el muro*). _____

_____

5. No one believed that Mary had a little lamb (*el corderito*). _____

_____

6. Mr. Clean requested that we take off our shoes before entering his palace (*el palacio*). _____

_____

7. Was it necessary that you (*pl. fam.*) call me in the middle (*en medio*) of the night? _____

_____

8. They weren't sure that I could take care of myself (*cuidarse*). _____

_____

9. She prepared dinner so that we wouldn't die (*morirse*) of hunger. _____

_____

10. We cleaned the house before they arrived. _____

11. She studied in case there was a test the next day. _____

12. He begged me not to order the lobster (*la langosta*). _____

_____

13. We didn't think that anyone heard us. _____

14. Was anybody there who knew all the state capitals? _____

_____

15. We asked that they continue without us. _____

2. Main Clause in the Present; Subordinate in the Past: When the main clause is in the present and is one which calls for the subjunctive, but refers to an action in the past, the subordinate clause will be in the imperfect subjunctive.

examples:

Ella espera que yo no **gastara** todo el dinero.
She hopes that *I didn't spend* all the money.

Estoy contento/a de que él **estudiara.**
I'm happy that he *studied.*

Siento que **no conociéramos** a Felipe.
I'm sorry that *we didn't meet* Philip.

Es absurdo que **tuvieran** que pagar.
It's absurd that *they had* to pay.

ejercicio   **III-3-2**

1. They don't believe that I made these cookies (*la galleta*). _____

_____

2. It's unlikely that Francis Bacon wrote these plays (*el drama*). _____

_____

3. We're not convinced that Little Miss Muffet was afraid of the spider (*la araña*). _____

_____

4. I'm sorry that you were sick and couldn't come to our party. _____

_____

5. I don't suppose that you knew that she was the thief (*la ladrona*). _____

_____

6. It doesn't seem that the maid cleaned the house this morning. _____

_____

7. God willing you paid the bills (*la cuenta*) on time this month. _____

_____

8. It may be that no one heard your speech (*el discurso*). _____

_____

9. He behaves (*portarse*) as if he were three years old. _____

_____

10. I don't think that he studied last night. _____

11. He hopes that you washed your hands before eating. _____

_____

12. It may be that she didn't want to take (*sacar*) our picture. _____

_____

13. It's a miracle that the airline (*la aerolínea*) didn't lose your luggage (*el equipaje*). _____

_____

14. Is it possible that you left (*dejar*) your keys in the car? _____

_____

15. It's incredible that you were born (*nacer*) the same day as I. _____

_____

3. Hypothetical "if" Clauses in the Past: Most "if" clauses in the past fall under the heading "hypothetical," and are therefore at best presumptive, leading us straight into the clutches of the subjunctive. Consider the sentence, "*If I were taller,* I would play basketball." My being taller is clearly hypothetical, and therefore the verb, **were,** is in the subjunctive. A few important things to know regarding this type of sentence:

- An "if" (or hypothetical) subordinate clause in the past is very often linked with a main clause in the conditional indicative: **If I *were* taller** ("if" clause in the past), **I *would play* basketball** (conditional indicative).

- Only hypothetical "if" clauses in the past are in the subjunctive. If they are not hypothetical, and their intent is to elicit true information, the clause remains in the indicative: **Pregunté a Juan si él sabía la respuesta** (I asked John if he knew the answer). Two things tip you off that the form of **saber** remains in the indicative:

    1. The information is clearly verifiable (all you have to do is ask John).

    2. Note that the main clause (**Pregunté a Juan**) is in the preterite, and not in the conditional.

- "If" clauses in the present do *not* take the subjunctive: *Si Juan tiene* el dinero, te pagará (*If John has* the money, he will pay you).

examples:

Si yo fuera más alto, jugaría al baloncesto.	Recibirías buenas notas **si estudiaras.**
If I were taller, I would play basketball.	You would get good grades *if you studied.*
Yo no iría **si fuera** tú.	¿Te quedarías **si hubiera** un incendio?
I wouldn't go *if I were* you.	Would you stay *if there were* a fire?

ejercicio   III-3-3

1. If I had a hammer (*el martillo*), I'd hammer (*martillar*) in the morning. _____

_____

2. She wouldn't marry him if he were the last man on earth (*la Tierra*). _____

_____

3. What would you do if I sang out of tune (*desafinadamente*)? _____

_____

4. If you knew the answer, would you tell us? _____

5. If giraffes (*la jirafa*) didn't have long necks (*el cuello*), they couldn't eat leaves (*la hoja*). _____

_____

6. If it weren't for gravity (*la gravedad*), we would float (*flotar*) like bubbles (*la burbuja*). _____

_____

7. The bears wouldn't eat your food if you hung (*colgar*) it from a tree. _____

_____

8. If Pinocchio didn't lie so much, people would believe him once in a while (*de vez en cuando*). _____

_____

9. If there were no cars, there wouldn't be so much pollution (*la contaminación*). _____

_____

10. If he weren't so lazy (*perezoso*), I'd hire (*contratar*) him. _____

_____

11. If it weren't raining, we could take a walk in the park. _____

_____

12. If it weren't so cold, I would ride my bicycle (*ir en bicicleta*) to work. _____

_____

13. This ring (*el anillo*) would be worth (*valer*) a lot more money if the diamond were genuine. _____

_____

14. If my car started (*arrancar*) in this weather, it would be a miracle (*el milagro*). _____

_____

15. If pigs could fly, where would they go? _____

4. "As if" and "as though" Clauses: The verb in a subordinate clause which begins with "as if" or "as though" (*como si*) will be in the imperfect subjunctive. The main clause can be either in the present, the past, or the conditional:

Te ves como si **fueras** culpable.   Actuábamos como si **estuviéramos** enfermos.
You look as if *you were* guilty.   We acted (were acting) as if *we were* sick.

Él se puso el sombrero como si **fuera** el Rey.   Hablaban como si **supieran** todo.
He put on his hat as though *he were* the King.   They were talking as if *they knew* everything.

ejercicio   III-3-4

1. He speaks as if he were Daniel Webster himself (*el mismo Daniel Webster*). _____

   _____

2. In your situation, I would act (*actuar*) as if I didn't know anything. _____

   _____

3. She talks as if she were the owner (*la dueña*) of this company. _____

   _____

4. We danced as if we were Fred Astaire and Ginger Rogers. _____

   _____

5. He spends (*gastar*) money as though (as if) there were no tomorrow. _____

   _____

6. You look (*verse*) as if you saw a ghost (*el fantasma*). _____

   _____

7. He looks as if he lost his best friend. _____

8. The critic (*el crítico*) looks as though he liked the play. _____

   _____

9. You sing as though you swallowed (*tragar*) a bird. _____

10. It was as if I couldn't remember anything. _____

11. He felt as if he already knew her. _____

12. She lived each day as though it were the last. _____

13. He spoke to me as though I didn't have (a) brain (*el cerebro*). _____

    _____

14. She looked as though she lost (*perder*) a lot of weight. _____

    _____

15. You used to smoke as if you were a chimney (*la chimenea*). _____

    _____

5. *Querer* and *Poder:* The verbs *querer* and *poder* operate in a unique manner within the framework of the imperfect subjunctive. Each verb takes on a special meaning when used in the main clause in a sentence. Consider the following two sentences, each spoken in a restaurant:

> I want a cup of coffee.
> I would like a cup of coffee.

The first is direct and brusque and, if spoken with great emphasis, could come out sounding rude. The second sentence, merely by changing "want" to "would like" softens the effect and makes the speaker appear more civil.

At first glance, the second sentence appears to be in the conditional. However, remember that the conditional tense is used to tell what *would* happen *if a certain condition were met,* i.e., "I would like a cup of coffee *if I hadn't already drunk ten cups this morning.*" But that is not the speaker's intent. He clearly wants a cup of coffee *and* he also wants to appear reasonably courteous, so he changes "want" to "would like" and probably gets better service as a result! To achieve this same sort of gallantry in Spanish, you need only to use *querer* in the imperfect subjunctive:

> **Yo quisiera** una taza de café.   **¿Quisieras leer** mi diario?
> *I would like* a cup of coffee.   *Would you like to read* my diary?

A similar situation occurs with the verb *poder.* Consider the following inquiries:

> Can you wash the windows?
> Will you wash the windows?
> Could you wash the windows? *or* Would you wash the windows?

The first inquiry is in the present tense and implies that the speaker wants to know if the addressee has the talent required to wash windows.

The second inquiry in the future tense is a request, is quite direct and, spoken with enough emphasis, could be considered pushy.

As with our discussion of *querer,* the third inquiry, also a request, appears to be in the conditional. And it would be were the question actually, "Could you wash the windows *if your hands weren't broken?*" But this speaker isn't seeking information, rather someone to perform an odious task for her.

In English she would use either "could" or "would" with a slightly ingratiating tone and probably add "please." In Spanish, the speaker begins with *Si* (If), followed by the imperfect subjunctive form of *poder,* then the conditional form of the verb which refers to whatever the speaker wants done:

> **¿Si pudieras,** limpiarías las ventanas?   **¿Si pudieras,** te sentarías, por favor?
> *Could you* wash the windows?   *Would you* sit down, please?
> *If you could,* would you wash the windows?   *If you could,* would you sit down, please?

---

ejercicio   III-3-5

1. I would like a cold lemonade, please. _____

2. What would you like to do tonight? _____

3. Could you mail (*echar al correo*) these letters for me? _____

4. Would you (could you) do a favor for me? _____

5. We would like a room (*la habitación*) with a view of the river. _____

   _____

6. Could you move (*moverse*) a little to the right (*a la derecha*)? _____

   _____

7. Where would you like to go for your honeymoon (*la luna de miel*)? _____

   _____

8. Where would you (*pl. fam.*) like to eat tomorrow night (*mañana por la noche*)? _____

   _____

9. The Queen (*La Reina*) would like to speak. _____

10. Could you be quiet (*callarse*), please? _____

11. What would you (*pl. form.*) like to do this afternoon? _____

   _____

12. We would like to roller skate (*patinar sobre ruedas*) in the shopping mall (*el centro comercial*).

   _____

13. Could you (*s. form.*) make me a cup of coffee? _____

14. Could you (*s. form.*) take me to your leader? _____

15. Would you like to eat these houseflies (*la mosca*) covered (*cubierto*) with chocolate? _____

   _____

6. Querer as "To wish":   The other specialized use of **querer** (to want) in the imperfect subjunctive is the context in which it means "to wish." To form wish-filled sentences, you will use **querer** in the imperfect subjunctive in the main clause and when there is no change of subject (*I wish that I had a million dollars*), follow the conjugated **querer** with an infinitive:

Yo quisiera tener un millón de dólares.	*Quisiéramos conocer* a más personas.
I wish that *I had* a million dollars.	*We wish* that *we knew* more people.

If there is a change of subject (*I wish that you were here*), the imperfect subjunctive form of **querer** is followed by *que* and then the imperfect subjunctive form of that second verb:

Yo quisiera que **estuvieras** aquí.	**Quisiéramos** que él nos **llamara.**
I wish that *you were* here.	*We wish* that *he would call* us.
Quisieras que **no lloviera.**	**Quisierais** que Juan **estuviera** aquí.
You wish that *it wouldn't rain.*	*All of you wish* that *John were* here.
Ella quisiera que **hubiera** comida en la casa.	**Quisieran** que **yo tuviera** un coche.
She wishes that *there were* food in the house.	*They wish* that *I had* a car.

¿Estás de acuerdo? ¿Sí o no?

_____ 1. (Yo) quisiera ser más alto/a.

_____ 2. (Yo) quisiera que el dinero creciera en los árboles.

_____ 3. (Yo) quisiera que los políticos siempre nos dijeran la verdad.

_____ 4. (Yo) quisiera tener más tiempo.

_____ 5. (Yo) quisiera que la gente leyera más y mirara la televisión menos.

_____ 6. (Yo) quisiera que los aviones salieran y llegaran a su hora.

_____ 7. (Yo) quisiera que más personas montaran en bicicleta en vez de conducir todo el tiempo.

_____ 8. (Yo) quisiera que no hubiera guerras.

_____ 9. (Yo) quisiera que no tuviéramos que pagar tanto por la comida en el cine.

_____ 10. (Yo) quisiera que la gente hiciera más ejercicio y comiera menos.

_____ 11. (Yo) quisiera que el Presidente me conociera personalmente.

_____ 12. (Yo) quisiera vivir en Madrid.

_____ 13. (Yo) quisiera que estuviéramos de vacaciones ahora.

_____ 14. (Yo) quisiera correr en un maratón.

ejercicio   III-3-6

1. I wish that you weren't so nervous. _____

2. We wish that you were here. _____

3. I wish that there were a machine (*la máquina*) that could wash and dry clothes at the same time.

_____

4. I wish that you didn't have to hear this. _____

5. Jane wishes that her husband didn't watch so much television. _____

_____

6. Children always wish that they were older and adults, younger. _____

_____

7. I wish that I spoke Spanish fluently (*con soltura*). _____

8. He wishes that he could (were able to) drive. _____

9. He wishes that he could see through (*a través de*) walls (*la pared*). _____

_____

10. I wish that we weren't behind (*detrás de*) the horses in the parade (*el desfile*). _____

_____

11. I wish that I made (*ganar*) more money. _____

12. I wish that it would snow. _____

13. We wish that they would go (*irse*) home. _____

14. I wish that there weren't any calories in ice cream. _____

_____

15. Luisa wishes that she didn't have to pay taxes (*los impuestos*). _____

_____

traducción   **III-3-7**

In "The Wizard of Oz," everybody wishes that his or her life were different. The Scarecrow wishes that he had a brain. The Tinman wishes that he had a heart. The Lion wishes that he were brave. Toto wishes that the flying monkeys would disappear. The tree wishes that people wouldn't eat his apples. The wizard wishes that he were a wizard, and the witch wishes two things: that she had Dorothy's shoes and that she could tolerate water better. Most of all, Dorothy wishes that she were in Kansas.

vocabulario

brain	**el cerebro**	monkey	**el mono**
brave	**valiente**	scarecrow	**el espantapájaros**
(to) disappear	**desaparecer**	tin	**el estaño**
everybody	**todo el mundo**	(to) tolerate	**tolerar**
flying	**volante**	tree	**el árbol**
heart	**el corazón**	witch	**la bruja**
lion	**el león**	wizard	**el mago**

_____

_____

_____

_____

_____

_____

_____

_____

_____

_____

_____

_____

_____

_____

_____

_____

The Future Perfect

The future perfect tense refers to an action that *will have* taken place in the future at or by a specified time, e.g., "I *will have* finished this book by Friday" (or "*I'll have* this book *finished* by Friday").

The future perfect tense also can be used to express probability or conjecture, as in: "He has *probably* already left."

Formation of the Future Perfect

The future perfect is a compound tense, which means that an auxiliary verb is required before the main verb. The auxiliary verb **haber** is conjugated in the future tense and followed by the past participle of the main verb:

habré + past participle	habremos + past participle
habrás + past participle	habréis + past participle
habrá + past participle	habrán + past participle

Uses of the Future Perfect

1. Expresses what will have happened: The future perfect expresses an action that *will have* taken place by a specified time in the future. In English one can say, "I *will*

195

have written this letter by three o'clock," or, more commonly, "I *will have* this letter *written* by three o'clock." Both versions will translate into:

$$\textbf{\textit{Habré escrito}} \textbf{ esta carta para las tres.}$$

examples:

Habré pintado la casa para el sábado.
I will have the house *painted* by Saturday.

Habremos leído el libro para el jueves.
We will have read the book by Thursday.

¿Cuándo **habrás hecho** esto?
When *will you have* this *done?*

Habréis comido para las siete.
You will have eaten by seven o'clock.

Él no lo **habrá visto** para entonces.
He won't have seen it by then.

Habrán vendido su coche para mañana.
They will have sold their car by tomorrow.

---

ejercicio   III-4-1

1. In two weeks, I will have lived here for four years. _____

_____

2. By next year McDonald's will have sold another billion (*billón*) hamburgers. _____

_____

3. She won't have prepared dinner by five-thirty. _____

4. When will they have the work finished (*terminar*)? _____

_____

5. We will have known each other for twelve years this August. _____

_____

6. Will you (*pl. fam.*) have your dresses ironed (*planchar*) by this afternoon? _____

_____

7. Will you have all this clothing washed by tonight? _____

_____

8. He won't have the pharmacy (*la farmacia*) opened by then. _____

_____

9. We have to go now; if we go later, they'll have left already. _____

_____

10. If you give all the food to the dog, he'll have all of it eaten by tomorrow. _____

_____

11. You needn't worry: I'm sure they'll have told her everything by now (*para este momento*). _____

_____

12. I suppose that everyone will have gone to bed by midnight (*la medianoche*). _____

_____

13. At this rate (*A este paso*), you'll have fried more potatoes than McDonald's by the end of the week.

_____

14. If you lose this election, you will have lost more elections than anybody (*nadie*). _____

_____

15. If you win this election, you will have proven that it is possible to fool (*engañar*) all the people all

the time. _____

_____

2. Expresses probability: You also can use the future perfect to express probability or conjecture with regard to something that took place in the *recent past*.

It is in the conjecture that the future perfect differs from the present perfect tense. Note this difference in the following two sentences:

present perfect	future perfect
Él lo **ha hecho.** He *has done* it.	Él lo **habrá hecho.** He *must have done* it; he's *probably done* it.

The first sentence is simply reporting an action; there is no uncertainty on the speaker's part.

In the second sentence, though the speaker appears reasonably certain, there is still a little room left for doubt. It is this slight uncertainty which is expressed in this use of the future perfect.

examples:

Lo siento. **Me habré dormido.**
I'm sorry. *I must have fallen asleep.*

Nos habremos perdido.
We must have gotten lost.

Habrás estado aquí.
You must have been here.

Habréis leído el libro.
You must have read the book.

¿Quién **habrá escrito** tal cosa?
Who *could have written* such a thing?

¿Adónde **habrán ido?**
Where *could they have gone?*

ejercicio   III-4-2

1. Fernando must have sent these flowers to me. _____

2. He must have paid our bill. How nice! _____

3. Fido must have stolen these slippers (*las zapatillas*). _____

   _____

4. Where has my little dog gone (can my little dog have gone)? _____

   _____

5. Abdul looks (*verse*) pretty (*bien*) mad; Farrah must have told him everything. _____

   _____

6. The kitchen stinks (*oler mal*)! Dorothy must have made (prepared) dinner again. _____

   _____

7. That is a lie! You must have heard it from Roger. _____

8. How does he know these things? He must have read my diary (*el diario*). _____

   _____

9. When could this have happened? _____

10. Arthur must have known that Mary burned (*quemar*) all his love letters (*cartas de amor*). _____

    _____

11. You must have known that he was married. _____

12. I must have been crazy (in order) to buy vitamins (*la vitamina*) over the telephone (*por teléfono*).

    _____

13. Bears must have eaten our food. _____

14. It must have been terrible to discover that cockroaches were the real owners of your house.

    _____

15. She must have given you a fake (*falso*) telephone number. _____

    _____

traducción   III-4-3

I can't believe it! By the end of this month (*Para finales de mes*) I will have paid for this house completely. I never thought that this would happen. I thought that either I would move or die before making out that last miserable check. When I make out that last check, taking into account all the interest I've paid, I will have bought this house almost three times. A year from now, I suppose that I'll have forgotten that the bank owned (had) more of this house than I did for many years, and the bank will have forgotten that I ever (*una vez*) existed. I must have been crazy to think that a forty-year mortgage would make me feel as if I were a mature adult. It only made me feel poor. In two years, I'll have saved thousands of dollars and taken at least two long vacations. I wish I were in Tahiti right now.

vocabulario

ever	**una vez**	mortgage	**la hipoteca**
(to) forget	**olvidar**	(to) move	**mudarse**
interest	**el interés**	poor	**pobre**
last	**último**	(to) save (money)	**ahorrar**
(to) make out a check	**hacer un cheque**	(to) take into account	**tomar en consideración**

The Conditional Perfect

TENSE: Conditional
Perfect

TIME: Refers to an
uncompleted action

KEY PHRASE: "Would
have"

STRUCTURE: Com-
pound tense: "haber"
in the conditional +
past participle

Of all the tenses, the conditional perfect holds the dubious honor of being the only one to express no action. It is the favorite tense of excuse makers. The conditional perfect is used to refer to an action that *would have* taken place, but did not because something got in the way or some specified condition was not met.

In any sentence containing the conditional perfect, there will always be an "if" or a "but" lurking about, either stated or implied. People whose verbiage contains a good deal of conditional perfect sentences most likely are those who don't get a lot done and have loads of excuses for all that they don't do, for example:

I *would have paid* you, but I couldn't find my checkbook.

If it weren't so difficult, I *would have baked* you a pie.

The conditional perfect also can express probability or conjecture with regard to an action in the remote past (Where do you *suppose they had been?*) or time (*It must have been three o'clock* when he arrived).

Formation of the Conditional Perfect

The conditional perfect is a compound tense, which means that an auxiliary verb is required before the main verb. The auxiliary verb **haber** is conjugated in the conditional tense and followed by the past participle of the main verb:

habría + past participle	habríamos + past participle
habrías + past participle	habríais + past participle
habría + past participle	habrían + past participle

Uses of the Conditional Perfect

1. Expresses what *would have* happened: The conditional perfect expresses an action that *would have* taken place, but did not. In such sentences it is important to note that when the dependent clause is introduced with "but," the verb in that clause will be in the indicative:

Él habría trabajado, **pero estaba cansado.**   Yo habría comido, **pero no tenía hambre.**
He would have worked, *but he was tired.*   I would have eaten, *but I wasn't hungry.*

When the dependent clause is introduced with "if," the verb in that clause will be in the imperfect subjunctive:

Él habría trabajado **si no estuviera cansado.**   Yo habría comido **si tuviera hambre.**
He would have worked *if he weren't tired.*   I would have eaten *if I were hungry.*

ejercicio   III-5-1

1. I would have called you, but my telephone doesn't work (*funcionar*). _____

_____

2. He would have gone to the movies with us, but he had a headache. _____

_____

3. Would you have told me the answer if you knew it? _____

4. We would have given you a bigger piece (*el pedazo*) of cake if you weren't on a diet (*estar a dieta*).

_____

5. Sherlock Holmes is the only person who would have known who stole (*robar*) the diamonds.

_____

6. He would have hired (*contratar*) me if I spoke Spanish. _____

_____

7. Would you (*pl. fam.*) have gone to the beach if it weren't raining? _____

_____

8. We would have invited the Joneses, but the last time they were here they got sick (*enfermarse*).

_____

9. What would you have done if you didn't have your credit card (*la tarjeta de crédito*)? _____

_____

10. I would have bought the dress if it were one size (*la talla*) smaller. _____

_____

11. If she weren't so selfish (*egoísta*), she would have helped you. _____

_____

12. I would have gone on a diet (*ponerse a dieta*), but I don't have any willpower (*la voluntad*). _____

_____

13. I would have made dinner, but I was in a bad mood (*estar de mal humor*). _____

_____

14. He would have changed the lightbulb, but there was no one to turn (*girar*) the ladder (*la escalera*).

_____

15. He would have turned in (*entregar*) his assignment (*la tarea*), but the dog ate it. _____

_____

2. Expresses conjecture: The conditional perfect also expresses probability or conjecture with regard to:

   1. An action in the (relatively) remote past, e.g.:

¿Adónde **habrían ido?**	Él lo **habría visto.**
Where do you think *they had gone?*	I suppose he *had seen* it.

   In a question, the "do you think?" aspect is understood, as is the speaker's "I suppose" in a statement.

   2. The (clock) time or reference to a date of a specific action, e.g.:

Habría sido la una cuando él llegó.	**Habrían sido** las dos cuando me dormí.
It must have been one o'clock when he arrived.	*It must have been* two when I fell asleep.
Habría sido febrero cuando nació Fido.	**Habría sido** el domingo pasado cuando se cayó.
It must have been February when Fido was born.	*It must have been* last Sunday when he fell.

ejercicio   III-5-2

1. I suppose I had worn the ring only two or three times before the robbery (*el robo*). _____

_____

2. Where do you suppose she had hidden (*esconder*) the money? _____

_____

3. It must have been one o'clock in the morning when the telephone rang (*sonar*). _____

_____

4. It must have been July or August when I met you because it was very hot. _____

_____

5. I suppose they'd never met anyone like you. _____

6. It must have been November when I bought this because I remember that there were turkeys (*el pavo*) everywhere (*en todas partes*). _____

_____

7. Do you suppose they had lied to us? _____

8. It must have been a Tuesday when we met because that day everybody was voting. _____

_____

9. It must have been February when I received this letter because there was a valentine in the envelope.

_____

_____

10. I don't suppose they had studied very much. _____

11. It must have been four in the morning when Barbie returned from her date (*la cita*) with Ken.

_____

12. It must have been the Fourth of July because I had on (*tener puesto*) a red, white, and blue T-shirt (*la camiseta*). _____

_____

13. It must have been a holiday (*el día de fiesta*) because the post office (*la oficina de correos*) was closed.

_____

14. Who do you suppose had left (*dejar*) those shoes on the highway (*la carretera*)? _____

_____

15. Why do you suppose Peter had put his wife inside a pumpkin (*la calabaza*)? _____

_____

traducción   **III-5-3**

Yesterday, while I was walking through the park, I found a box filled with money. At first I was happy because, well, who wouldn't be happy in this situation? But after a while I began to worry, and I decided to take it to the police station. Last night I asked some of my friends what they would have done. John said that he would have bought a new car—there were at least ten thousand dollars. Ana told me that she would have donated the money to charity. Roberto said he would have left the box alone and (would have) left (from) the park immediately. What would you have done?

vocabulario

at first	**al principio**	(to) leave from	**salir de**
box	**la caja**	police station	**la estación de policía**
charity	**la caridad**	situation	**la situación**
(to) donate	**donar**	thousand	**mil**
immediately	**inmediatamente**	well	**pues**
(to) leave alone	**dejar solo**	(a)while	**un rato**

_____

_____

_____

_____

_____

_____

_____

_____

_____

_____

_____

The Present Perfect Subjunctive

As its name implies, the present perfect subjunctive mood is in the time of the present perfect (John *has eaten*), but also is in a sentence which requires the use of the subjunctive (*I hope* that John *has eaten*). Keeping in mind the general time of the present perfect, i.e., completed action, often in the recent past, as well as the situations in which one uses the subjunctive, you will know when to use the present perfect subjunctive.

> **Yo sé** que Juan **ha comido.**
> *I know* that John *has eaten.* (present perfect indicative)

> **Yo dudo** que Juan **haya comido.**
> *I doubt* that John *has eaten.* (present perfect subjunctive)

Formation of the Present Perfect Subjunctive

The present perfect subjunctive is a compound tense, which means that an auxiliary verb is required before the main verb. The auxiliary verb **haber** is conjugated in the present subjunctive and followed by the past participle of the main verb:

haya + past participle	hayamos + past participle
hayas + past participle	hayáis + past participle
haya + past participle	hayan + past participle

Use of the Present Perfect Subjunctive

Main clause in present; subordinate in present perfect subjunctive: When the main clause in the present (or present perfect) requires the use of the subjunctive and refers to an action that *may have taken place,* that subordinate clause will be in the present perfect subjunctive.

examples:

Es posible que **yo lo haya leído.**
It's possible that *I've read it.*

Es improbable que **nos hayamos conocido** antes.
It's unlikely that *we've met* before.

Espero que **hayas comido.**
I hope that *you have eaten.*

Espero que **hayáis comido.**
I hope that *you have eaten.*

Dudamos que **él haya estado** aquí.
We doubt that *he has been* here.

Podemos comenzar después que **hayan llegado.**
We can begin after *they have arrived.*

ejercicio   III-6-1

1. I hope that the cat hasn't eaten my goldfish (*la carpa dorada*). _____

_____

2. It's unlikely that anyone here has driven a Rolls Royce. _____

_____

3. I don't believe that those people in Michigan have seen Elvis. _____

_____

4. You haven't lived until you've seen the Grand Canyon (*el Gran Cañón*). _____

_____

5. Do you know anyone who has read all of Shakespeare's plays? _____

_____

6. The jury (*el jurado*) doubts that the defendant (*el acusado*) has told the truth. _____

_____

7. It's incredible that no one has found the money we buried (*enterrar*) in the back yard (*jardín de*

casa). _____

8. You (*pl. fam.*) can dance after the band (*la banda*) has begun to play. _____

_____

9. It's a miracle that the bank has loaned (*prestar*) him money. _____

_____

10. It may be that they have never learned to read. _____

11. It's ridiculous that I've had to wait in this line (*la cola*) for over (more than) an hour. _____

_____

12. We can't go until after everyone has voted. _____

13. We hope that you (*sing. form.*) have enjoyed (*gozar de*) your stay (*la estancia*) here. _____

_____

14. Is there anyone in the world who hasn't read *The Cat in the Hat?* _____

_____

15. I'm looking for a student who has never failed (*suspender*) a test. _____

_____

2. Main clause in the future; subordinate in the present perfect subjunctive: When the main clause in the future refers to an action in the subordinate clause that *may have* or *will have* taken place (uncompleted action), that subordinate clause will be in the present perfect subjunctive.

examples:

¿Te quedarás después que **me haya ido?**
Will you stay after *I've gone?*

Será estupendo que **hayamos leído** tanto.
It will be great that *we've read* so much.

¿Qué harás cuando **hayas terminado** esto?
What will you do when *you've finished* this?

Volveremos después que **os hayáis ido.**
We'll return after *you have left.*

Hablaremos cuando Juan **haya terminado.**
We will talk when John *has finished.*

Jugarán después que **hayan trabajado.**
They will play after *they've worked.*

ejercicio	III-6-2

1. I will not hire anyone who has gotten his or her diploma from the back (*el fondo*) of a tabloid (*el*

tabloide). _____

2. What will you do after you have conquered (*vencer*) all your fears (*el temor*)? _____

_____

3. After we've counted our money, we'll deposit it in the bank. _____

_____

4. The program will begin when they have arrived. _____

_____

5. He will not tell you anything until you have paid him. _____

_____

6. As soon as you have set the table, we will eat dinner. _____

_____

7. I will bring a salad to the party in case the host (*el anfitrión*) hasn't prepared enough food. _____

_____

8. He will not go to bed until he's brushed his teeth. _____

_____

9. You will never know true happiness until you have appeared on the *Oprah Winfrey Show.* _____

_____

10. He will never be able to run a mile (*la milla*) in four minutes until he has quit (*dejar de*) smoking.

_____

11. What will we do after we've spent all our money? _____

_____

12. I will not drink milk that has sat (been) on the counter (*el mostrador*) all day long. _____

_____

13. We will not make (*tomar*) any financial (*financiero*) decisions until we've paid this year's taxes.

_____

14. Captain Kirk will go where no man has gone before. _____

_____

15. As soon as he has taken this medicine, he will feel better. _____

_____

traducción   **III-6-3**

"It's great that you've saved so much money with all these seeds, but what will you do next year when nothing has grown?" This is what I would like to say to my neighbor who frequently "steps over a dollar to pick up a dime." Last year he invested three thousand dollars in an absurd little company that makes air-conditioners for dog houses. I can hear him now: "In two years, when this country has finally realized that dogs also get hot in the summer, I will have earned many thousands of dollars with this investment." That was the last I heard of that venture. I continue praying that he has learned his lesson, but I fear that he will always be this way.

vocabulario

air-conditioner	**el acondicionador**	(to) pray	**rezar**
(to) grow	**crecer**	(to) save (money)	**ahorrar**
(to) invest	**invertir**	seed	**la semilla**
(to) learn one's lesson	**escarmentar**	(to) step over	**pasar sobre**
neighbor	**el vecino**	this way	**así**
(to) pick up	**recoger**	venture	**la empresa**

The Pluperfect Subjunctive

The time of the pluperfect subjunctive (also referred to as the "past perfect subjunctive") is the same time as the pluperfect (also referred to as the "past perfect"), but is used in situations which require the use of the subjunctive: I hoped *that Mary had spoken.* The action in the pluperfect refers to something which happened before another action occurred: I hoped that Mary had spoken (*before she left*).

> **Yo sabía** que María **había hablado.** *I knew* that Mary *had spoken.* (pluperfect indicative)
>
> **Yo esperaba** que María **hubiera hablado.** *I hoped* that Mary *had spoken.* (pluperfect subjunctive)

Formation of the Pluperfect Subjunctive

The pluperfect subjunctive is a compound tense, which means that an auxiliary is required before the main verb. The auxiliary verb **haber** is conjugated in the imperfect subjunctive and followed by the past participle of the main verb.

hubiera + past participle	hubiéramos + past participle
hubieras + past participle	hubierais + past participle
hubiera + past participle	hubieran + past participle

Use of the Pluperfect Subjunctive

1. Main clause in past; subordinate in pluperfect subjunctive: When the main clause in the past (preterite or imperfect) requires the use of the subjunctive, and refers to an action which *possibly had taken place,* that subordinate clause will be in the pluperfect subjunctive.

examples:

¿Fue posible que **yo hubiera hecho** tal cosa?
Was it possible that *I had done* such a thing?

Él actuaba como si **nos hubiéramos conocido** antes.
He acted as if *we had met* before.

Yo esperaba que **hubieras comido.**
I hoped that *you had eaten.*

Ella dudaba que **hubierais leído** la tarea.
She doubted that *you had read* the assignment.

No había nadie que **hubiera escuchado.**
There wasn't anybody who *had listened.*

Fue terrible que **no hubieran pagado** la cuenta.
It was terrible that *they hadn't paid* the bill.

ejercicio   III-7-1

1. I wasn't sure that they had heard me. _____

2. John hoped that the students had studied the lesson. _____

_____

3. It was a pity that the plumber (*el fontanero*) hadn't fixed the drain (*el desagüe*). _____

_____

4. We wrote them a letter in case they hadn't understood us. _____

_____

5. Was it possible that they had never heard of Leo Tolstoy? _____

_____

6. They were acting as if they had never met (*conocerse*) before. _____

_____

7. He didn't believe that I had said such a thing. _____

8. It was unlikely that she had paid for the car in cash (*al contado*). _____

_____

9. There wasn't anyone at the party who had traveled around the world. _____

_____

10. I never believed that she had been Miss America. _____

11. He refused (*negarse a*) to speak until we had locked (*cerrar*) the doors. _____

_____

12. I sent him a telegram (*el telegrama*) in case he hadn't yet heard the good news (*las buenas noticias*).

_____

13. It was tragic that the gardener (*el jardinero*)—not the butler (*el criado*)—had done it. _____

_____

14. She always doubted that he had been honest (*honrado*) with her. _____

_____

15. There wasn't anyone in the house who had gotten up before ten-thirty. _____

_____

2. Hypothetical "if" clause followed by pluperfect subjunctive: When the hypothetical "if" is followed by reference to an action that *possibly had taken place,* that clause will be in the pluperfect subjunctive. These "if" clauses often are balanced by a main clause in the conditional perfect.

examples:

(Yo) no te habría preguntado **si hubiera sabido** la respuesta.
I wouldn't have asked you *if I had known* the answer.

Si no me hubieras mentido, no me habría enojado contigo.
If you hadn't lied to me, I wouldn't have gotten mad at you.

Si hubiera habido más tiempo, yo habría aprobado el examen.
If there had been more time, I would have passed the test.

¿Qué habrías hecho **si ellos no te hubieran encontrado?**
What would you have done *if they hadn't found you?*

ejercicio   III-7-2

1. If I had read this book earlier (*antes*), I wouldn't have made so many mistakes in my life. _____

_____

2. If Barbara had known the truth about Ken, would she have married him? _____

_____

3. If you had warned (*advertir*) us of the earthquakes (*el terremoto*), we wouldn't have built our house

in this area (*el área*). _____

_____

4. It would have been nice (*bueno*) if you had included a photo (*la foto*) with this article (*este artículo*).

_____

5. If you had called me ten minutes earlier, I wouldn't have been home. _____

_____

6. I don't know where I'd be if I hadn't met you. _____

_____

7. If there had been one ounce (*la onza*) of truth in your speech (*el discurso*), somebody would have

believed you. _____

_____

8. If you had been born two days earlier, we would have had the same birthday. _____

_____

9. If there hadn't been a snowstorm (*la nevada*) yesterday, there would have been one today.

_____

10. If we had known that you were in trouble (*tener dificultades*), we would have offered you help.

_____

11. If you hadn't given me these mittens (*la manopla*), I think that I would have frozen to death (*morirse

de frío*). _____

_____

12. If you hadn't put another stamp (*el sello*) on that letter, the post office wouldn't have accepted it.

_____

13. If anyone had told me that, I wouldn't have believed it. _____

_____

14. If you hadn't given your goldfish so much food, it wouldn't have died. _____

_____

15. How would they have felt if you hadn't received an invitation? _____

_____

3. *Querer* ("to wish") in main clause; pluperfect subjunctive in subordinate: In the unit on the imperfect subjunctive, we discussed the use of *querer*, meaning "to wish." This special use of *querer* balances nicely with the pluperfect subjunctive.

examples:

(Yo) quisiera **que nunca lo hubiera conocido.**
I wish *that I'd never met him.*

Él quisiera **que lo hubiéramos escuchado.**
He wishes *that we had listened to him.*

(Yo) quisiera **que hubieras tenido más tiempo.**
I wish *that you had had more time.*

(Yo) quisiera **que hubierais estado** allí.
I wish *that you had been* there.

Quisiéramos **que hubiera hecho más calor.**
We wish *that it had been warmer.*

¿Quisieras **que no lo hubieran visto?**
Do you wish *that they hadn't seen it?*

Para ti, ¿cuál es verdadero o falso?

_____   1. (Yo) quisiera que hubiera nevado más el invierno pasado.

_____   2. (Yo) quisiera que yo hubiera nacido en otro siglo.

_____   3. (Yo) quisiera que yo hubiera comido menos ayer.

_____   4. (Yo) quisiera que yo hubiera estudiado más cuando era menor.

_____   5. (Yo) quisiera que yo hubiera aprendido a bailar como un/una profesional.

_____   6. (Yo) quisiera que yo hubiera tomado lecciones de cocinar.

_____   7. (Yo) quisiera que yo hubiera visto el cometa Halley.

_____   8. (Yo) quisiera que yo hubiera gastado menos dinero el año pasado.

_____   9. (Yo) quisiera que yo hubiera leído más este año.

_____ 10. (Yo) quisiera que yo hubiera hecho más ejercicio el año pasado.

_____ 11. (Yo) quisiera que yo no hubiera comprado tanto el diciembre pasado.

_____ 12. (Yo) quisiera que yo hubiera recibido un caballo para mi último cumpleaños.

ejercicio   III-7-3

1. I wish that he had studied more in high school. _____

_____

2. Do you wish that he had kept his word (*cumplir su palabra*)? _____

_____

3. He wishes that he hadn't eaten so much. _____

4. We wish that you had told us that this would be a formal party. _____

_____

5. I wish that we hadn't eaten lunch (*almorzar*) here. _____

_____

6. He wishes that he had saved (*ahorrar*) more money. _____

_____

7. I wish that I'd tried on (*probarse*) these pants before buying them. _____

_____

8. I wish that you hadn't fried these sausages (*la salchicha*) in lard (*la manteca*). _____

_____

9. Do you (*pl. fam.*) wish that there had been more variety (*la variedad*) in the program? _____

_____

10. I wish that it hadn't rained on my parade (*el desfile*). _____

_____

11. Do you sometimes wish that you'd been born (*nacer*) in another century (*el siglo*)? _____

_____

12. I wish that I had turned off (*apagar*) the lights three hours ago. _____

_____

13. I wish that it hadn't been so cold. _____

14. We wish that they had told us about the cockroaches in this hotel. _____

_____

15. I wish that you hadn't put so much cinnamon (*la canela*) in this tea. _____

_____

traducción   III-7-4

If I had been more careful, I wouldn't be here in this office fighting this parking ticket. I thought it was strange that there was a parking space open right in front of the theater five minutes before the play began, but who am I to question such good luck? In fact, there was a sign that said "No Parking" two feet from my car, but a very tall man was standing in front of it, blocking the view. No, nobody would believe that. There was a woman selling balloons and I couldn't see the sign through the balloons, so if anybody is going to pay this ticket, she should pay it—nobody will believe that, either. The truth is that I realize that if I had told anyone these absurd stories I would have to pay more money than I probably owe now. Where is the cashier's office?

vocabulario

balloon	**el globo**	(to) park	**aparcar**
(to) be careful	**tener cuidado**	parking space	**el aparcamiento**
(to) block	**bloquear**	parking ticket	**la multa de aparcamiento**
cashier	**el cajero**	(to) question	**cuestionar**
(to) fight (a ticket)	**disputar**	(to) realize	**darse cuenta de que**
luck	**la suerte**	sign	**el letrero**
no parking	**prohibido estacionar**	view	**la vista**

_____

_____

_____

_____

_____

_____

_____

_____

_____

_____

The Passive Voice

There are two kinds of passive voice: incomplete and complete. Each will be discussed in this unit; however, greater attention is paid to the incomplete passive voice due to its far greater use in everyday conversation.

The Incomplete Passive Voice

A sentence in the incomplete passive voice indicates that an action is performed, but there is no *named* actor, or *agent*. In the sentence, "Mary sells clothing at Bloomingdale's," *Mary* is the agent; thus the sentence is *not* in the passive voice. However, in the sentence, "Clothing is sold at Bloomingdale's," there is no named agent (we do not know *who* precisely is selling the clothing). Thus, the sentence is in the incomplete passive voice.

We often use the incomplete passive voice in English without even being aware of it. The ubiquitous "they," as in "they say . . . ," is the incomplete passive voice speaking: "They say that cats make nice pets." Who says so? *They* do. Who are *they*? Nobody knows.

When giving directions, the "you" is usually passive: "In order to get to the bank, *you* need to turn right at the corner." Who needs to turn right? You do, and so does anyone else wanting to get to the bank from here. In this case, the word *you* does not refer to *you* specifically, but rather to the collective *you*.

They say that you shouldn't swim after eating.

They don't accept applications after 4:00.

One should never make a telephone call after 9:00 p.m.

You should look both ways before crossing the street.

Spanish is spoken here.

This house was built in 1956.

In all the example sentences, while there are specific actions, there are no specific agents. This is the essence of the incomplete passive voice.

Formation of the Incomplete Passive Voice

There are only two possible verb conjugations in a sentence which employs the incomplete passive voice: third person singular and third person plural. Each conjugated verb, whether singular or plural, is preceded by **se.**

The noun that follows the conjugated verb determines if that verb will be conjugated in the singular or plural form: a singular noun is preceded by a verb in its singular form (third person); a plural noun is preceded by a verb in its plural form (third person):

Se construye la casa	**Se construyen las casas.**
The house is built.	The houses are built.

Note that in Spanish and English the word order of the noun and verb is reversed.

Se habla español aquí.	**Se hablan español y francés aquí.**
Spanish is spoken here.	Spanish and French are spoken here.

examples:

Se dice que la educación es la clave del éxito.	**Se necesitan huevos** para cocer una torta.
They say that education is the key to success.	*You need eggs* in order to bake a cake.
No se debe nadar después de una comida grande.	**Se apagan las luces** a las diez de la noche.
You shouldn't swim after a big meal.	*The lights are turned off* at ten p.m.
Se dobla a la izquierda en la calle Elm.	**Se pagan las cuentas** cada viernes.
You turn left on Elm Street.	*The bills are paid* every Friday.

¿Verdadero o falso?

_____   1. Se habla portugués en Brasil.

_____   2. Se venden libros en la biblioteca.

_____   3. Se dice que no se debe llevar zapatos blancos después de la primera semana de septiembre.

_____   4. En los Estados Unidos, no se puede fumar en los aviones.

_____   5. Para conseguir un doctorado, se necesita estudiar mucho.

_____   6. Para hablar en un teléfono público, se necesita introducir una moneda.

_____   7. En un hotel, normalmente se paga con tarjeta de crédito.

_____   8. Tradicionalmente, se sirven champaña y torta después de la boda.

_____   9. Se fabrican muchos televisores y cámaras en Japón.

_____ 10. Se cultivan naranjas en Alaska.

ejercicio   III-8-1

Fill in the blanks with the appropriate form of the verb:

1. Se (vender) _____ pan en la panadería.

2. Se (vender) _____ zapatos en la zapatería.

3. Se (jugar) _____ al béisbol en este estadio.

4. Se (jugar) _____ los partidos de béisbol en este estadio.

5. Se (mirar) _____ la televisión demasiado estos días.

6. Se (cultivar) _____ trigo (*wheat*) en este campo (*field*).

7. Se (cultivar) _____ manzanas en esta huerta (*orchard*).

8. Se (construir) _____ caminos (*paths*) para bicicletas en muchas ciudades.

9. No se (deber) _____ comer antes de operarse.

10. No se (poder) _____ nadar afuera cuando hace mucho frío.

.

ejercicio   III-8-2

¿Qué se habla en . . . ? Responde con una frase completa. ¡No te olvides de que en Suiza y en Canadá, hay más de un idioma oficial!

alemán	inglés	japonés	ruso
francés	italiano	portugués	suizo

1. ¿Qué se habla en Francia? _____

2. ¿Qué se habla en Japón? _____

3. ¿Qué se habla en Alemania? _____

4. ¿Qué se habla en Portugal? _____

5. ¿Qué se habla en Suiza? _____

6. ¿Qué se habla en Rusia? _____

7. ¿Qué se habla en Canadá? _____

8. ¿Qué se habla en Inglaterra? _____

ejercicio   III-8-3

1. You can't buy a good cigar (*el puro*) these days (*hoy en día*) for less than two dollars. _____

   _____

2. White wine is drunk with chicken and fish. _____

3. They say that Colombian coffee is the best. _____

4. One needs to be careful (*tener cuidado*) when driving in a snowstorm (*la tormenta de nieve*). _____

   _____

5. How do you say "dog" in French? _____

6. They speak Portuguese in Brazil. _____

7. Where is it written that the President has to be a man? _____

   _____

8. If you drive like a madman (*el loco*), you'll get a ticket (*la multa*). _____

   _____

9. It is said that a pig is smarter than a horse. _____

10. They always waste (*perder mucho tiempo*) a lot of time in these meetings. _____

    _____

11. If it is maintained (*mantener*) properly, a car will last (*durar*) for twenty years. _____

    _____

12. One never wears white shoes after the first of September. _____

    _____

13. If you exercise more (*hacer más ejercicio*) and eat less, you'll lose weight (*adelgazar*). _____

    _____

14. Where do you go in this town for a good hamburger? _____

    _____

15. If they can put a man on the moon, why can't they make (*fabricar*) a car that lasts more than five

    years? _____

The Incomplete Passive Voice in Other Tenses

When using the incomplete passive voice in other tenses, you will begin with **se** and then conjugate the desired verb (using the third person singular or plural form of that verb). The formation remains the same as discussed above:

Preterite:	**Se construyó** esta casa en 1956. This house *was built* in 1956.
Imperfect:	Cuando yo era joven, **no se podía comer** carne los viernes. When I was young, *you couldn't eat* meat on Fridays.
Future:	**Se terminará** esta casa el año que viene. This house *will be finished* next year.
Conditional:	**Se moriría** en Plutón. *A person would die* on Pluto.
Present Perfect:	**Se ha escrito** este libro para los enamorados de los gatos. *They've written* this book for cat lovers.
Past Perfect:	**No se había pintado** la casa hasta 1945. The house *hadn't been painted* until 1945.
Future Perfect:	**Se habrá terminado** el puente hace un año en abril. The bridge *will have been finished* one year in April.
Conditional Perfect:	**Se habría repintado** la casa, pero decidimos no venderla. The house *would have been repainted*, but we decided not to sell it.
Present Subjunctive:	Espero que **no se sirvan** perritos calientes en la recepción. I hope that *they don't serve* hot dogs at the reception.
Imperfect Subjunctive:	Fue ridículo que **se tuviera que pagar** tanto por televisión cable. It was ridiculous that *you had to pay* so much for cable TV.
Present Perfect Subjunctive:	Ella espera que **no se haya vendido** el vestido que quiere. She hopes that *they haven't sold* the dress she wants.
Pluperfect Subjunctive:	Ella esperaba que **no se hubiera vendido** el vestido que quería. She hoped that *they hadn't sold* the dress she wanted.

¿Qué piensas tú? ¿Verdadero o falso?

_____ 1. Un día se podrá vivir hasta los 150 años.

_____ 2. Hace cien años se viajaba con frecuencia a caballo.

_____ 3. Si se estudiara muchísimo, uno podría graduarse de la universidad en menos de tres años.

_____ 4. Espero que no se aumenten los impuestos este año.

_____ 5. Se añade el fluoruro al agua en muchas ciudades para prevenir caries.

_____ 6. En el futuro, se comprará todo con tarjeta de crédito.

_____ 7. Es trágico que se malgaste tanta comida cuando millones de personas tienen hambre.

_____ 8. Yo creía que se podía vivir bien con una dieta de sólo chocolate y Coca-Cola.

_____ 9. Se hizo mi coche en Japón.

_____ 10. Se mejorarían las escuelas si hubiera más maestros y menos administradores.

_____ 11. Se debe hacer ejercicios por lo menos tres o cuatro veces por semana.

_____ 12. Se tenía que leer en la noche con velas y lámparas de queroseno.

ejercicio   III-8-4

(These sentences use mixed tenses.)

1. When were these pictures taken? _____

2. Where was your sofa made? _____

3. They used to sell bread for five cents a loaf (*la barra*). _____

_____

4. The house was painted (*pintar*) last year. _____

5. There was so much noise (*el ruido*) in the restaurant that you couldn't think. _____

_____

6. I wanted the flowers delivered (*entregar*) by four-thirty. _____

_____

7. You couldn't hear anything; everybody was talking at the same time (*al mismo tiempo*). _____

_____

8. The party was a disaster (*el desastre*). The living room hadn't *even* been cleaned. (*Even* does not

translate here.) _____

9. You used to be able to smoke anywhere; now you can only smoke outside the building. _____

_____

10. The book will be published (*publicar*) next year. _____

_____

11. The element was discovered by accident (*por casualidad*). _____

_____

12. The house hadn't been painted in (*durante*) fifty years. _____

_____

13. They'll close the doors at eleven-thirty. _____

14. If you've seen one castle (*el castillo*), you've seen them all. _____

_____

15. You haven't lived until you've heard Van Morrison sing "Gloria." _____

_____

The Complete Passive Voice

At times, even when the agent is known and/or stated, we use the passive voice to lend special emphasis to the action. This is called the complete passive voice. The unstated message is that while we know who the agent is, our greater concern is with the action. When this is the case, we use the following format:

noun + *ser* **+ adjectival form of the past participle (+** *por* **+ agent)**

Though the mention of the agent with this format is not mandatory, it is common. When you mention the agent, you will precede his/her action with the preposition *por* (by). Since you are using the adjectival form of the past participle, don't forget that it must agree in gender and number with the noun!

Note the various tenses in play in the following:

El retrato **es visto** por todos.　　　　La pintura **fue vista** por todos.
The portrait *is seen* by everyone.　　　The painting *was seen* by everyone.

Los retratos **serán vistos** por todos.　Las pinturas **eran vistas** por todos.
The portraits *will be seen* by everyone.　The paintings *used to be seen* by everyone.

¿Verdadero o falso?

_____ 1. La Mona Lisa fue pintada por Leonardo da Vinci.

_____ 2. *Tom Sawyer* y *Huck Finn* fueron escritos por William Shakespeare.

_____ 3. Durante el siglo diecinueve, Abraham Lincoln fue elegido Presidente de los Estados Unidos.

_____ 4. En la Biblia, Goliath es matado por David.

_____ 5. La electricidad fue descubierta por Galileo.

_____ 6. El teléfono fue inventado por Alexander Graham Bell.

_____ 7. Mis zapatos fueron diseñados por Manolo Blahnik.

_____ 8. Hace muchos años, el español fue declarado el idioma oficial de España.

_____ 9. La novela *Guerra y Paz* fue escrita por Leo Tolstoi.

_____ 10. Mi coche fue hecho en Alemania.

_____ 11. Todos mis problemas serán resueltos durante el año que viene.

_____ 12. Cuando yo era joven, las camas en mi casa siempre eran hechas por los sirvientes.

ejercicio   III-8-5

1. The play (*el drama*) *Romeo and Juliet* was written by William Shakespeare. _____

_____

2. Many new houses were constructed after World War II (*la Segunda Guerra Mundial*). _____

_____

3. The leaflets (*el folleto*) will be distributed (*repartir*) by volunteers tomorrow. _____

_____

4. These cookies were made by elves (*el duende*). _____

_____

5. The spoiled child (*el niño consentido*) was given too many toys by his parents. _____

_____

6. The tires (*el neumático*) were slashed (*acuchillar*) by vandals. _____

_____

7. The television will be turned on (*poner*) when John enters this house. _____

_____

8. This quilt (*la colcha*) was sewn (*coser*) completely by hand (*a mano*). _____

_____

9. The doors will be opened and closed by armed guards. _____

_____

10. The grass was planted (*sembrar*) by Martin. _____

_____

11. These bills would have been paid by John, but he lost the checkbook (*el talonario de cheques*). _____

_____

_____

12. When I was young, my classes were always taught by excellent teachers. _____

_____

13. I hope that my house is bought by a nice person. _____

_____

14. I hope that this mess (*el lío*) wasn't made by mice. _____

_____

15. The national anthem (*el himno nacional*) was sung by my neighbor before the game. _____

_____

traducción   III-8-6

After the Super Bowl the winning quarterback was asked by a reporter how he felt. This is what he said: "Well, you work hard all year and you train every day. Of course you hope for something like this, but you know that it's just a dream, and then you win lots of games, but only because you have great teammates, and you're really happy. But you aren't prepared for a day like this. You wake up and you know that this is the most important day in your life and you think that you have a chance to win, but you can't be too sure, so you pray. And you play your best and hope that you win. And when you win, it's the most wonderful thing you've ever felt in your life, and when you're asked point-blank how you feel, you completely whitewash the whole thing and speak in the passive voice."

vocabulario

(to) ask, interview	**entrevistar**	reporter	**el reportero**
chance	**la oportunidad**	sure	**seguro**
dream	**el sueño**	teammate	**el compañero**
great	**estupendo**	(to) train	**entrenar**
point-blank	**categóricamente**	(to) wake up	**despertarse**
(to) pray	**rezar**	(to) whitewash	**encubrir**
quarterback	**el lanzador**	(the) whole thing	**toda la situación**

PART IV

Appendices

Preterite Conjugations

I. Regular Verbs

hablar	hablé	hablaste	habló	hablamos	hablasteis	hablaron
comer	comí	comiste	comió	comimos	comisteis	comieron
abrir	abrí	abriste	abrió	abrimos	abristeis	abrieron

Verbs with Standard Orthographic Changes (first person, singular only)

llegar	**llegué**	llegaste	llegó	llegamos	llegasteis	llegaron
comenzar	**comencé**	comenzaste	comenzó	comenzamos	comenzasteis	comenzaron
practicar	**practiqué**	practicaste	practicó	practicamos	practicasteis	practicaron

II. Irregular Verbs

andar	anduve	anduviste	anduvo	anduvimos	anduvisteis	anduvieron
caber	cupe	cupiste	cupo	cupimos	cupisteis	cupieron
dar	di	diste	dio	dimos	disteis	dieron
decir	dije	dijiste	dijo	dijimos	dijisteis	dijeron
estar	estuve	estuviste	estuvo	estuvimos	estuvisteis	estuvieron
haber	hube	hubiste	hubo	hubimos	hubisteis	hubieron
hacer	hice	hiciste	hizo	hicimos	hicisteis	hicieron
ir	fui	fuiste	fue	fuimos	fuisteis	fueron
poder	pude	pudiste	pudo	pudimos	pudisteis	pudieron
poner	puse	pusiste	puso	pusimos	pusisteis	pusieron
producir	produje	produjiste	produjo	produjimos	produjisteis	produjeron
querer	quise	quisiste	quiso	quisimos	quisisteis	quisieron
saber	supe	supiste	supo	supimos	supisteis	supieron
ser	fui	fuiste	fue	fuimos	fuisteis	fueron
tener	tuve	tuviste	tuvo	tuvimos	tuvisteis	tuvieron
traer	traje	trajiste	trajo	trajimos	trajisteis	trajeron
venir	vine	viniste	vino	vinimos	vinisteis	vinieron
ver	vi	viste	vio	vimos	visteis	vieron

Verbs with Stem Change in the Third Person

dormir	dormí	dormiste	**durmió**	dormimos	dormisteis	**durmieron**
mentir	mentí	mentiste	**mintió**	mentimos	mentisteis	**mintieron**
pedir	pedí	pediste	**pidió**	pedimos	pedisteis	**pidieron**
creer	creí	creíste	**creyó**	creímos	creísteis	**creyeron**
destruir	destruí	destruiste	**destruyó**	destruimos	destruisteis	**destruyeron**

Imperfect Conjugations

| I. | Regular Verbs |

hablar	hablaba	hablabas	hablaba	hablábamos	hablabais	hablaban
comer	comía	comías	comía	comíamos	comíais	comían
vivir	vivía	vivías	vivía	vivíamos	vivíais	vivían

| II. | Irregular Verbs |

ir	iba	ibas	iba	íbamos	ibais	iban
ser	era	eras	era	éramos	erais	eran
ver	veía	veías	veía	veíamos	veíais	veían

Future Conjugations

| I. | Regular Verbs |

hablar	hablaré	hablarás	hablará	hablaremos	hablaréis	hablarán
comer	comeré	comerás	comerá	comeremos	comeréis	comerán
vivir	viviré	vivirás	vivirá	viviremos	viviréis	vivirán

| II. | Irregular Verbs |

caber	cabré	cabrás	cabrá	cabremos	cabréis	cabrán
decir	diré	dirás	dirá	diremos	diréis	dirán
haber	habré	habrás	habrá	habremos	habréis	habrán
hacer	haré	harás	hará	haremos	haréis	harán
poder	podré	podrás	podrá	podremos	podréis	podrán
poner	pondré	pondrás	pondrá	pondremos	pondréis	pondrán
querer	querré	querrás	querrá	querremos	querréis	querrán
saber	sabré	sabrás	sabrá	sabremos	sabréis	sabrán
salir	saldré	saldrás	saldrá	saldremos	saldréis	saldrán
tener	tendré	tendrás	tendrá	tendremos	tendréis	tendrán
valer	valdré	valdrás	valdrá	valdremos	valdréis	valdrán
venir	vendré	vendrás	vendrá	vendremos	vendréis	vendrán

Conditional Conjugations

| I. | Regular Verbs |

hablar	hablaría	hablarías	hablaría	hablaríamos	hablaríais	hablarían
comer	comería	comerías	comería	comeríamos	comeríais	comerían
vivir	viviría	vivirías	viviría	viviríamos	viviríais	vivirían

| II. | Irregular Verbs |

caber	cabría	cabrías	cabría	cabríamos	cabríais	cabrían
decir	diría	dirías	diría	diríamos	diríais	dirían
haber	habría	habrías	habría	habríamos	habríais	habrían
hacer	haría	harías	haría	haríamos	haríais	harían
poder	podría	podrías	podría	podríamos	podríais	podrían
poner	pondría	pondrías	pondría	pondríamos	pondríais	pondrían
querer	querría	querrías	querría	querríamos	querríais	querrían
saber	sabría	sabrías	sabría	sabríamos	sabríais	sabrían
salir	saldría	saldrías	saldría	saldríamos	saldríais	saldrían
tener	tendría	tendrías	tendría	tendríamos	tendríais	tendrían
valer	valdría	valdrías	valdría	valdríamos	valdríais	valdrían
venir	vendría	vendrías	vendría	vendríamos	vendríais	vendrían

Present Subjunctive Conjugations

| I. | Regular Verbs |

hablar	hable	hables	hable	hablemos	habléis	hablen
comer	coma	comas	coma	comamos	comáis	coman
vivir	viva	vivas	viva	vivamos	viváis	vivan

| II. | Verbs with Standard Orthographic Changes |

llegar	llegue	llegues	llegue	lleguemos	lleguéis	lleguen
comenzar	comience	comiences	comience	comencemos	comencéis	comiencen
practicar	practique	practiques	practique	practiquemos	practiquéis	practiquen

III.   Irregular Verbs

dar	dé	des	dé	demos	deis	den
estar	esté	estés	esté	estemos	estéis	estén
haber	haya	hayas	haya	hayamos	hayáis	hayan
ir	vaya	vayas	vaya	vayamos	vayáis	vayan
saber	sepa	sepas	sepa	sepamos	sepáis	sepan
ser	sea	seas	sea	seamos	seáis	sean

Imperfect Subjunctive Conjugations

I.   Regular Verbs

hablar	hablara	hablaras	hablara	habláramos	hablarais	hablaran
comer	comiera	comieras	comiera	comiéramos	comierais	comieran
vivir	viviera	vivieras	viviera	viviéramos	vivierais	vivieran

II.   Irregular Verbs (verbs, and verb types, which are irregular, third person, preterite)

andar	anduviera	anduvieras	anduviera	anduviéramos	anduvierais	anduvieran
caber	cupiera	cupieras	cupiera	cupiéramos	cupierais	cupieran
creer	creyera	creyeras	creyera	creyéramos	creyerais	creyeran
dar	diera	dieras	diera	diéramos	dierais	dieran
decir	dijera	dijeras	dijera	dijéramos	dijerais	dijeran
destruir	destruyera	destruyeras	destruyera	destruyéramos	destruyerais	destruyeran
dormir	durmiera	durmieras	durmiera	durmiéramos	durmierais	durmieran
estar	estuviera	estuvieras	estuviera	estuviéramos	estuvierais	estuvieran
haber	hubiera	hubieras	hubiera	hubiéramos	hubierais	hubieran
hacer	hiciera	hicieras	hiciera	hiciéramos	hicierais	hicieran
ir	fuera	fueras	fuera	fuéramos	fuerais	fueran
mentir	mintiera	mintieras	mintiera	mintiéramos	mintierais	mintieran
pedir	pidiera	pidieras	pidiera	pidiéramos	pidierais	pidieran
poder	pudiera	pudieras	pudiera	pudiéramos	pudierais	pudieran
poner	pusiera	pusieras	pusiera	pusiéramos	pusierais	pusieran
producir	produjera	produjeras	produjera	produjéramos	produjerais	produjeran
querer	quisiera	quisieras	quisiera	quisiéramos	quisierais	quisieran
saber	supiera	supieras	supiera	supiéramos	supierais	supieran
ser	fuera	fueras	fuera	fuéramos	fuerais	fueran
tener	tuviera	tuvieras	tuviera	tuviéramos	tuvierais	tuvieran
traer	trajera	trajeras	trajera	trajéramos	trajerais	trajeran
venir	viniera	vinieras	viniera	viniéramos	vinierais	vinieran
ver	viera	vieras	viera	viéramos	vierais	vieran

Conjugations of Auxiliary *Haber*

present perfect:	he	has	ha	hemos	habéis	han
past perfect:	había	habías	había	habíamos	habíais	habían
future perfect:	habré	habrás	habrá	habremos	habréis	habrán
conditional perfect:	habría	habrías	habría	habríamos	habríais	habrían
present perfect subjunctive:	haya	hayas	haya	hayamos	hayáis	hayan
past perfect subjunctive:	hubiera	hubieras	hubiera	hubiéramos	hubierais	hubieran
or	hubiese	hubieses	hubiese	hubiésemos	hubieseis	hubiesen

Verbs That Take a Preposition

Listed below are several verbs that require prepositions when preceding another word. These verbs are arranged alphabetically, and are grouped according to the preposition each verb takes. Following each verb is the most common part of speech (or parts of speech) the verb will precede, then its English equivalent, and finally the result of the clause created, e.g.: **cuidar a (n.),** *to take care of (someone)*. This will result in: **Yo cuido a Juan** (*I take care of John*). Or, **acabar de (v.),** *to have just (done something)*. This gives us: **María acaba de escribir una carta** (*Mary has just written a letter*).

Important: In the entries below, when a verb takes **a,** note that this **a** is a preposition. Be careful not to confuse the preposition **a** with the personal **a** (as discussed on pages 33–34). The personal **a** is placed after *all* verbs when the stated direct object is a person.

Abbreviations below include: **(v.)** for *verb* and **(n.)** for *noun*.

a

acertar a *(v.)*   to manage to, succeed in *(doing something)*

acostumbrarse a *(n.)*   to become used to *(someone/something)*

adaptarse a *(n.)*   to adapt oneself to *(something—a situation)*

adelantarse a *(n.)*   to step forward to *(someone/something)*

animar a *(v.)*   to encourage to *(do something)*

animarse a *(v.)*   to make up one's mind to *(do something)*

aprender a *(v.)*   to learn to *(do something)*

apresurarse a *(n./v.)*   to hasten to, hurry to *(somewhere/do something)*

arriesgarse a *(v.)*   to risk *(doing something)*

asistir a *(n.)*   to attend *(something—a function)*

asomarse a *(n.)*   to appear at, look out from *(something)*

aspirar a *(v.)*   to aspire to *(do/be something/someone)*

atreverse a *(v.)*   to dare to *(do something)*

aventurarse a *(v.)*   to venture to *(do something)*

ayudar a alguien a *(v.)*   to help someone to *(do something)*

burlar a *(n.)*   to make fun of *(someone)*

comenzar a *(v.)*   to begin to *(do something)*

comprometerse a *(v.)*   to obligate oneself to *(do something)*

condenar a alguien a *(v.)*   to condemn someone to *(do something)*

consagrarse a *(n.)*   to devote oneself to *(someone/something)*

contribuir a *(n.)*   to contribute to *(something)*

convidar a *(n./v.)*   to invite to *(a function/do something)*

correr a *(n./v.)*   to run to *(somewhere/do something)*

cuidar a *(n.)*   to care for, take care of *(a person, pet)*

dar a *(n.)*   to face *(something)*

dar cuerda a *(n.)*   to wind *(a watch)*

decidirse a *(v.)*   to decide to *(do something)*

dirigirse a *(n.)*   to go to *(a place)*, address *(someone)*

disponerse a *(v.)*   to prepare to, be disposed to *(do something)*

empezar a *(v.)*   to begin to *(do something)*

enseñar a *(v.)*   to teach to *(do something)*

forzar a *(v.)*   to force to *(do something)*

impulsar a *(v.)*   to impel to *(do something)*

incitar a *(v.)*   to incite to *(do something)*

inducir a *(v.)*   to induce to *(do something)*

inspirar a *(v.)*   to inspire to *(do something)*

instar a *(v.)*   to urge to *(do something)*

invitar a *(v.)*   to invite to *(do something)*

ir a *(n./v.)*   to go to *(a place)*; to be going to *(do something)*

limitarse a *(v.)*   to limit oneself to *(do something)*

llegar a *(n./v.)*   to arrive at *(a place)*; to manage to *(do something)*

meterse a *(v.)*   to take up *(doing something)*

negarse a *(v.)*   to refuse to *(do something)*

obligar a *(v.)*   to oblige to *(do something)*

ofrecerse a *(v.)*   to offer to, promise to, volunteer to *(do something)*

oponerse a *(n./v.)*   to be opposite to *(something)*, oppose *(doing something)*

pararse a *(v.)* to stop *(doing something)*

parecerse a *(n.)* to resemble *(someone)* physically

pasar a *(n./v.)* to pass to, proceed to *(something/doing something)*

persuadir a *(v.)* to persuade to *(do something)*

ponerse a *(v.)* to begin to, set about to *(do something)*

prestarse a *(v.)* to lend oneself to *(doing something)*

probar a *(v.)* to try to *(do something)*

quedarse a *(v.)* to stay somewhere to *(do something)*

rebajarse a *(n./v.)* to stoop to *(a situation/doing something)*

reducirse a *(n./v.)* to reduce a situation or oneself to *(something/do something)*

rehusar a *(v.)* to refuse to *(do something)*

renunciar a *(n.)* to renounce, give up, quit *(something—a job)*

resignarse a *(n./v.)* to resign oneself to *(something/doing something)*

resistirse a *(n./v.)* to resist *(something/doing something)*

resolverse a *(n.)* to "come down to" *(something)*

retirarse a *(n./v.)* to retire to *(something/do something)*

romper a *(v.)* to begin *(to do something)* suddenly

saber a *(n.)* to taste like/of *(something)*

sentarse a *(n./v.)* to sit down to *(something/doing something)*

someterse a *(n./v.)* to submit oneself to *(something/doing something)*

sonar a *(n.)* to sound like *(something)*

subir a *(n.)* to go up to, climb, get on *(something)*

venir a *(n./v.)* to come to *(a place/doing something)*

volver a *(n./v.)* to return to *(a place/doing something)* again

con

aburrirse con *(n.)* to be or get bored *(with someone or something)*

acabar con *(n.)* to finish, exhaust *(something)*

amenazar con *(n./v.)* to threaten with *(something/doing something)*

asociarse con *(n.)* to associate, team up with *(someone)*

asustarse con *(n.)* to be afraid of *(someone/something)*

bastarle a alguien con *(n.)* to have enough of *(something)*

casarse con *(n.)* to marry *(someone)*

comerciar con *(n.)* to trade in or with *(a person/business)*

conformarse con *(n./v.)* to conform to *(something/doing something)*

contar con *(n.)* to count on *(someone/something)*

contentarse con *(n.)* to content oneself with *(something)*

dar con *(n.)* to come upon *(someone/something)*

disfrutar con *(n.)* to enjoy *(someone/something)*

divertirse con *(n.)* to enjoy, have fun or a good time with *(someone/something)*

enfadarse con *(n.)* to get mad/angry at *(someone/something)*

enojarse con *(n.)* to get mad/angry at *(someone/something)*

equivocarse con *(n.)* to make a mistake about *(someone)*

espantarse con *(n.)* to become afraid of *(someone/something)*

juntarse con *(n.)* to associate with *(someone)*

limpiar con *(n.)* to clean something with *(something)*

meterse con *(n.)* to provoke *(someone/something)*

preocuparse con *(n.)* to worry about *(someone/something)*

romper con *(n.)* to break up with, break off relations with *(someone)*

salir con *(n.)* to go out with, date *(someone)*

soñar con *(n.)* to dream of *or* about *(someone/something)*

tener sabor a *(n.)* to taste like *(something)*

tratarse con *(n.)* to be on good terms with *(someone)*, deal with *(something)*

tropezar con *(n.)* to come upon *(someone/something)*

tropezarse con *(n.)* to bump into *(something)* *[the reflexive use is more emphatic]*

de

abusar de *(n.)* to take advantage of *(someone/something)*

acabar de *(v.)* to have just *(done something)*

acordarse de *(n./v.)* to remember *(someone/something/to do something)*

alegrarse de *(n./v.)* to be glad *(of something/to do something)*

alejarse de *(n.)*　to go away from *(someone/something/somewhere)*

aprovecharse de *(n./v.)*　to take advantage of *(someone/something/doing something)*

arrepentirse de *(n./v.)*　to repent, be sorry for *(something/doing something)*

asombrarse de *(n.)*　to be astonished at *(something)*

avergonzarse de *(n.)*　to be ashamed of *(someone/something)*

brindar a la salud de *(n.)*　to toast *(someone)*

burlarse de *(n.)*　to make fun of *(someone/something)*

cansarse de *(n./v.)*　to get tired of *(someone/something/doing something)*

carecer de *(n.)*　to lack *(something)*

cesar de *(v.)*　to cease *(doing something)*

conseguir algo de *(n.)*　to obtain, get hold of something from *(someone/something)*

cuidar de *(n.)*　to care for, take care of *(something)*

deber de *(v.)*　to suppose *[conjecture]*, "must be" *(someone/something)*

dejar de *(v.)*　to stop *(doing something)*

depender de *(n./v.)*　to depend on *(someone/something/doing something)*

encargarse de *(n./v)*　to take charge of *(someone/something/doing something)*

estar encargado de *(n./v.)*　to be in charge of *(someone/something/doing something)*

gozar de *(n.)*　to enjoy, take pleasure in *(something)*

haber de *(v.)*　to suppose *[conjecture]* *(to be* or *do something)*

hablar de *(n./v.)*　to talk about *(someone/something/doing something)*

jactarse de *(n./v.)*　to brag about, boast of *(something/doing something)*

lastimarse de *(n.)*　to feel sorry for, complain about *(something)*

librarse de *(n.)*　to get rid of *(someone/something)*

maldecir de *(n.)*　to speak ill of *(someone/something)*

maravillarse de *(n.)*　to marvel at *(someone/something)*

marcharse de *(n.)*　to leave from, walk away from *(a place)*

morir de *(n.)*　to die *[literally (and from accidental or deliberate death)]* of/from *(an illness/a situation)*

morirse de *(n.)*　to be dying *[figuratively (and a gradual death)]* for *(something)*

ocuparse de *(n.)*　to pay attention to, mind *(someone/something)*

olvidarse de *(n./v.)*　to forget *(someone/something/to do something)*

parar de *(v.)*　to cease, stop *(doing something)*

pensar de *(n.)*　to think of, have an opinion about *(someone/something)*

preciarse de *(n.)*　to brag about, boast of *(something)*

prescindir de *(n./v.)*　to do without, neglect *(someone/something/doing something)*

probar de *(n.)*　to sample, take a taste of *(something)*

quejarse de *(n./v.)*　to complain of/about *(someone/something/doing something)*

salir de *(n.)*　to leave from *(a place)*

separarse de *(n.)*　to leave from *(someone/something/a place)*

servir de *(n.)*　to act as *(someone/something)*

sorprenderse de *(n.)*　to be surprised at, by *(someone/something)*

terminar de *(v.)*　to finish *(doing something)*

tratar de *(v.)*　to try to *(do something)*

tratarse de *(n./v.)*　to be a question of *(something/doing something)*

en

abdicar en *(n.)*　to abdicate to *(someone)*

complacerse en *(n./v.)*　to take pleasure in *(something/doing something)*

confiar en *(n./v.)*　to trust, confide in *(someone/a situation/doing something)*

consentir en *(v.)*　to consent to *(do something)*

consistir en *(n./v.)*　to consist of *(something/doing something)*

convenir en *(n./v.)*　to agree to *(something/do something)*

convertirse en *(n.)*　to become, change into *(someone/something)*

empeñarse en *(n./v.)*　to insist on *(something/doing something)*

equivocarse en *(n.)*　to make a mistake in *(something)*

esforzarse en *(n./v.)*　to try hard in *(something)*; to endeavor to *(do something)*

influir en *(n.)*　to influence *(someone/something)*

insistir en *(n./v.)*　to insist on *(something/doing something)*

interesarse en *(n.)*　to be interested in *(someone/something)*

meterse en *(n.)*　to become involved in *(something)*

mojarse en *(n.)*　to get mixed up in *(something)*

molestarse en *(v.)*   to take the trouble to *(do something)*

montar en *(n.)*   to ride *(something)*

obstinarse en *(n./v.)*   to persist in *(something/doing something)*

ocuparse en *(n./v.)*   to be busy with *(something/doing something)*

pararse en *(v.)*   to bother to *(do something)*

pensar en *(n./v.)*   to think about *(someone/something/doing something)*

persistir en *(n./v.)*   to persist in *(something/doing something)*

quedar en *(n./v.)*   to agree to *(something/do something)*

recrearse en *(n.)*   to amuse oneself with *(something)*

reflexionar en *(n.)*   to reflect on, think about *(something)*

tardar en *(n./v.)*   to delay in *(something)*, to take long to *(do something)*

trabajar en *(n.)*   to work at *(something)*

vacilar en *(v.)*   to hesitate to *(do something)*

para

bastarse para *(v.)*   to be sufficient in *(doing something)*

estar listo para *(v.)*   to be ready to *(do something)*

estar para *(v.)*   to be about to *(do something)*

quedarse para *(v.)*   to stay to *(do something)*

prepararse para *(n./v.)*   to prepare oneself *(for something, to do something)*

sentarse para *(v.)*   to sit down to *(do something)*

servir para *(n./v.)*   to be of use for *(something/doing something)*

trabajar para *(n./v.)*   to work for *(someone)*; strive to *(do something)*

por

abogar por *(n.)*   to plead on behalf of *(someone/something)*

acabar por *(v.)*   to end by, wind up *(doing something)*

apurarse por *(n.)*   to get worried by *(someone/something)*

clasificar por *(n.)*   to classify in *or* by *(something)*

esforzarse por *(n./v.)*   to strive for *(someone/something/doing something)*

estar por *(v.)*   to be inclined to *(do something)*

hacer por *(v.)*   to try to *(do something)*

impacientarse por *(n./v.)*   to grow impatient for *(someone/something/doing something)*

llorar por *(n./v.)*   to cry for, about *(someone/something/doing something)*

luchar por *(n./v.)*   to struggle for *(someone/something/doing something)*

mandar por *(n.)*   to send via *(something—mail)*

mirar por (n.)   to look after, tend to *(something)*

morirse por *(n./v.)*   to be dying for *(something/doing something)*

ofenderse por *(n.)*   to be offended by *(something)*

optar por *(n./v.)*   to choose, opt for *(something/doing something)*

preocuparse por *(n./v.)*   to worry about *(someone/something/doing something)*

rabiar por *(n./v.)*   to be crazy about *(someone/something/doing something)*

terminar por *(v.)*   to end by *(doing something)*

trabajar por *(n.)*   to work for *(someone—as a substitute)*

votar por *(n.)*   to vote for *(someone/something)*

PART V

Glossaries

Glossary: Spanish-English

a

a este paso at this rate
a menos que unless
a menudo often
a su hora on time
a tiempo on time
a veces at times; sometimes
A ver . . . Let's see . . .
abastecedor (*m.*) caterer
abogado (*m.*) lawyer
abrir to open
abstenerse de + inf. to abstain from doing something
abuelo (*m.*) grandfather
aburrido bored; boring
accidente (*m.*) accident
aceite (*m.*) oil
aceptar to accept
acerca de about
acostarse (o → ue) to go to bed
acostumbrarse (a) to get used (to)
actitud (*f.*) attitude
actuar to act
acusado (*m.*) defendant; accused
adelgazar to lose weight
adentro inside
admitir to admit
adolescente (*m./f.*) teenager; adolescent
¿adónde? (to) where?
adquirir (e → ie) to acquire, get
adulto (*m.*) adult
advertir (e → ie) to advise, warn
aerolínea (*f.*) airline
aeropuerto (*m.*) airport
afeitar(se) to shave (oneself)
afuera outside
afueras (*f.*) suburbs
agente de viajes (*m./f.*) travel agent
agradecer to be thankful

ahora now
ahorrar to save (money)
¡Ajá! Aha!; That's it!
ajedrez (*m.*) chess
al cine to the movies
al contado in cash
al lado de next to; next door to
al principio at first; in the beginning
alacena (*f.*) cabinet
alcanzar to reach (a goal)
alejarse to walk away
algo something; anything
alguien someone; somebody; anybody
allí there
almohada (*f.*) pillow
almorzar (o → ue) to eat lunch
almuerzo (*m.*) lunch
alrededor (de) around
amable nice; kind
amar to love
amarillo yellow
amistoso friendly
amor (*m.*) love
andar to walk
anfitrión (*m.*) host
anillo (*m.*) ring
animal doméstico (*m.*) pet
anoche last night
antes (de) before; beforehand
año (*m.*) year
apagar to turn off, switch off
aparcamiento (*m.*) parking space; parking lot
aparcar to park
aparecer to appear
apartamento (*m.*) apartment
aprender to learn
aprobar (o → ue) to approve
aquí here
araña (*f.*) spider
arañar to scratch
árbol (*m.*) tree
área (*f.*) area
arena (*f.*) sand

arete (*m.*) earring
armario (*m.*) closet; cabinet
arquitecto (*m.*) architect
arrancar to start (a car)
arreglar to fix, arrange
arroz (*m.*) rice
artículo (*m.*) item; article
ascensor (*m.*) elevator
asistir + a to attend a function
astronauta (*m./f.*) astronaut
atenerse (a) to depend (on), rely (on)
atleta (*m./f.*) athlete
atraer to attract
atrás (de) behind; in back (of)
aumento (*m.*) raise; increase
autobús (*m.*) bus
autorizar to authorize
ave (*f.*) bird
avergonzado embarrassed
averiguar to find out
avión (*m.*) airplane
¡ay! alas!
ayer yesterday
ayuda (*f.*) help
ayudar to help
azúcar (*m.*) sugar

b

bailar to dance
baile (*m.*) dance
balde (*m.*) pail
baloncesto (*m.*) basketball
banco (*m.*) bank
banda (*f.*) band
bandera (*f.*) flag
bañar(se) to bathe (oneself)
baño (*m.*) bathroom
baraja (*f.*) deck of cards
barco (*m.*) boat
barra (de pan) (*f.*) loaf (of bread)
barrer to sweep
bastante enough
bastar to be sufficient to, suffice

basura *(f.)*   garbage; trash

baúl *(m.)*   trunk

bautizar   baptize

bebé *(m./f.)*   baby

beber   to drink

béisbol *(m.)*   baseball

Bella Durmiente *(f.)*   Sleeping Beauty

biblioteca *(f.)*   library

bicicleta *(f.)*   bicycle

bien   well

bilingüe   bilingual

billar *(m.)*   billiards; pool

billón *(m.)*   billion

bendecir (e → i)   to bless

boca *(f.)*   mouth

boda *(f.)*   wedding

boleto *(m.)*   ticket

bolígrafo *(m.)*   pen

bolsa *(f.)*   purse; pocketbook; bag

bolsillo *(m.)*   pocket

bomba *(f.)*   bomb; pump

bombero *(m.)*   firefighter

bombilla *(f.)*   lightbulb

borracho   drunk

bosque *(m.)*   woods; forest

botón *(m.)*   button

bravo   brave

broma *(f.)*   joke

bruja *(f.)*   witch

bueno   good

burbuja *(f.)*   bubble

buscar   to look for, search for

(

caballo *(m.)*   horse

caber   to fit

cabeza *(f.)*   head

cada   every; each

caer(se)   to fall (down)

café *(m.)*   coffee; brown

cafeína *(f.)*   caffeine

cafetería *(f.)*   cafeteria; coffee shop

caja *(f.)*   box

calabaza *(f.)*   pumpkin

calcetines *(m.)*   socks

callarse   to be quiet, "shut up"

calle *(f.)*   street

calor *(m.)*   heat; warmth

caloría *(f.)*   calorie

cama *(f.)*   bed

cámara *(f.)*   camera

cambiar   to change

(en) cambio   on the other hand

camino *(m.)*   road

camioneta *(f.)*   van; small truck

camisa *(f.)*   shirt

camiseta *(f.)*   T-shirt

campamento *(m.)*   camp

canción *(f.)*   song

candidato *(m.)*   candidate

cansado   tired

cantar   to sing

Caperucita Roja *(f.)*   Little Red Riding Hood

capital *(f.)*   capital (city)

capital *(m.)*   capital (wealth)

capítulo *(m.)*   chapter

carácter *(m.)*   character

cárcel *(f.)*   jail; prison

carne *(f.)*   meat

carpa dorada *(f.)*   goldfish

carrera *(f.)*   career

carretera *(f.)*   highway

carta *(f.)*   letter; card

casado   married

casarse con (alguien)   to marry (someone)

caso *(m.)*   case

castillo *(m.)*   castle

categóricamente   point-blank

catálogo *(m.)*   catalogue

cazar   to hunt

celebrar   to celebrate

cena *(f.)*   dinner

cenar   to dine, eat dinner

Cenicienta *(f.)*   Cinderella

centro *(m.)*   center; downtown

centro comercial *(m.)*   shopping mall

centro de mesa *(m.)*   centerpiece

cepillar(se)   to brush (oneself)

cerdo *(m.)*   pig

cerveza *(f.)*   beer

cerebro *(m.)*   brain

ceremonia *(f.)*   ceremony

cerrado   closed

cerrar (e → ie)   to close, shut

césped *(m.)*   lawn

cheque *(m.)*   check

chimenea *(f.)*   chimney; fireplace

cierto   certain; true

cigarro *(m.)*   cigar

cine; [al _____] *(m.)*   movie theater; [to the movies]

cinta *(f.)*   ribbon; tape

cita *(f.)*   date; appointment

clarificar   to clarify

clase *(f.)*   class

clasificar   to classify

cliente *(m./f.)*   client; customer

club *(m.)*   club

cochino *(m.)*   slob

cocinar   to cook

cocinero *(m.)*   cook; chef

coger   to catch, seize, grab

cola *(f.)*   line; tail

colegir (e → i)   to deduce

colgar (o → ue)   to hang (up)

collar *(m.)*   necklace

comedor *(m.)*   dining room

comenzar (e → ie)   to begin, commence

comer   to eat

cometa *(f.)*   kite

cometer (un error)   to make (a mistake)

cómico   funny; comical

comida *(f.)*   food; meal

comisión *(f.)*   commission

¿Cómo?   How?

compañero *(m.)*   companion; colleague; roommate

compañía *(f.)*   company

competir (e → i)   to compete

componer   to compose

comportarse   to act, behave

compra *(f.)*   purchase

comprar   to buy, purchase

comprender   to understand, comprehend

con   with

con frecuencia   frequently; often

con tal que   provided that

conceder   to grant
concierto *(m.)*   concert
concluir   to conclude
concurso *(m.)*   contest; game show
conducir   to drive, conduct, lead
conejo *(m.)*   rabbit
confesar (e → ie)   to confess
conjugar   to conjugate
conmigo   with me
conocer   to know (a person), be familiar with
conquistar   to conquer
conseguir (e → i)   to obtain, get
consentir (e → ie)   to consent
constituir   to constitute
contribuir   to contribute
construir   to construct, build
contaminación *(f.)*   contamination; pollution
contar (o → ue)   to count
contener   to contain, hold
contestar   to answer
contra   against
contraer   to contract
contratar   to hire, contract
contribuir   to contribute
convencer   to convince, persuade
convenir en + inf.   to agree to do something
convertir (en) (e → ie)   to convert (into)
corazón *(m.)*   heart
corbata *(f.)*   necktie
cordero *(m.)*   lamb
correo *(m.)*   mail
corregir (e → i)   to correct
correr   to run
cortacéspedes *(m.)*   lawnmower
cortar [el césped]   to cut, mow [the lawn]
cortés   polite; courteous
cortina *(f.)*   curtain
cosa *(f.)*   thing
costar (o → ue)   to cost
credo *(m.)*   ethic; creed
crecer   to grow
creer   to believe

criada *(f.)*   maid; servant
criar   to raise (children, animals, etc.)
crimen *(m.)*   crime
cristal *(m.)*   glass; crystal
cuadra *(f.)*   (city) block
cuadro *(m.)*   square
¿Cuál(es)?   Which?
cualquier cosa   anything
cualquiera   any; anything
cuando; ¿Cuándo?   when; When?
¿Cuánto/a?   How much?
¿Cuántos/as?   How many?
cuarto *(m.)*   room
cubrir   to cover
cucaracha *(f.)*   cockroach
cuchara *(f.)*   spoon
cuchillo *(m.)*   knife
cuenta *(f.)*   bill
cuento *(m.)* **(de hadas)**   story; (fairy) tale
cuestión *(f.)*   issue; question
cuidado *(m.)*   care
cuidar a   to care for (a person)
cuidar de   to care for (an animal or thing)
cuidarse   to care for oneself
culebra *(f.)*   snake
cultivar   to grow (plants)
cumpleaños *(m.)*   birthday
cumplido *(m.)*   compliment
cumplir (la palabra)   to complete, keep (one's word, promise, resolution)
cupón *(m.)*   coupon

d

damas *(f.)*   checkers
dañado   broken; damaged
dar   to give
dar cuerda a (un reloj)   to wind (a watch)
dar un paseo   to take a walk
de cabo a rabo   from top to bottom
de cualquier forma   anyway
de lo contrario   otherwise
de niño/a   as a child

de pie   standing
de vez en cuando   from time to time; once in a while
debajo (de)   underneath; under
deber   to owe, ought, "should"
deber de + inf.   to "must" (conjecture)
decidir   to decide
decir (e → i)   to say, tell
deducir   to deduce, infer
defectuoso   defective
defender (e → ie)   to defend
dejar   to leave (behind); allow
dejar de + inf.   to stop doing something
delgado   thin; slim
demostrar (o → ue)   to demonstrate
dentro (de)   inside
dependiente *(m.)*   clerk
depositar   to deposit, put (money in the bank)
deprimido   depressed
(a la) derecha   (to the) right
derecho *(m.)*   right
desafinadamente   out of tune
desagüe *(m.)*   drain
desaparecer   to disappear
desastre *(m.)*   disaster
desayuno *(m.)*   breakfast
descansar   to rest
describir   to describe
descubrir   to discover
desempeño *(m.)*   performance (on the job)
deseo *(m.)*   wish; desire
desfile *(m.)*   parade
deshacer   to undo, untie (a knot)
desierto *(m.)*   desert
deslucir   to tarnish, spoil
desordenado   messy
despedir (e → i)   to fire
despedirse (e → i) (de alguien)   to say goodbye (to someone)
despertarse (e → ie)   to wake up
después (de)   after; afterwards; later

destacar   to stand out
destruir   to destroy
desván (*m.*)   attic
desvestir(se) (e → i)   to undress (oneself)
detener   to detain, stop; arrest
devolver (o → ue)   to return (an object)
día (*m.*)   day
diamante (*m.*)   diamond
diario (*m.*)   diary
diente (*m.*)   tooth
dieta (*f.*)   diet
difícil   difficult; hard
dificultad (*f.*)   difficulty
dinero (*m.*)   money
diploma (*m.*)   diploma
dirección (*f.*)   address
dirigir   to direct
disco (*m.*)   record
disculparse   to apologize, pardon oneself
discurso (*m.*)   speech
discutir   to discuss
disgustar   to be repugnant to
disolver (o → ue)   to dissolve
distancia (*f.*)   distance
distinguir   to distinguish
distinto   distinct; different
diversión (*f.*)   fun
docena (*f.*)   dozen
documento (*m.*)   document
dólar (*m.*)   dollar
doler (o → ue)   to be painful to
donde; ¿Dónde?   where; Where?
dormir (o → ue)   to sleep
dormirse (o → ue)   to fall asleep
drama (*m.*)   play; drama
ducha (*f.*)   shower
ducharse   to take a shower
dudar   to doubt
dueño (*m.*)   owner
dulce   sweet
dulces (*m.*)   candy
durante   during
durar   to last, take time
duro   hard

e

e   and (preceding a word beginning with *i* or *hi*)
echar   to pour
echar al correo   to mail
echar una siesta   to take a nap
edificio (*m.*)   building
educación (*f.*)   education
egoísta   selfish; egotistic
ejercer   to exert, exercise
ejército (*m.*)   army
elección (*f.*)   choice; election
elegir (e → i)   to elect
elemento (*m.*)   element
embarazada   pregnant
empacar   to pack
embrujado   haunted
empezar (e → ie)   to begin
empleado (*m.*)   employee
empleo (*m.*)   work
en caso (de que)   in case (of/that)
en ninguna parte   nowhere; not anywhere
en todas partes   everywhere
en vez de   instead of
encantar   to be enchanting to
encender (e → ie)   to light, kindle
encontrarse (con) (o → ue)   to meet (with)
encubrir   to whitewash, cover up
enemigo (*m.*)   enemy
energía (*f.*)   energy
enero   January
enfermarse   to get sick
enfermo   sick
enfrente (de)   in front (of)
engañar   to fool, trick, deceive, cheat
engordar   to gain weight
enigma (*m.*)   puzzle; enigma
enojado   angry; mad
enojarse   to get angry, mad
ensalada (*f.*)   salad
ensayo (*m.*)   essay
enseñar   to teach
entender (e → ie)   to understand

entero   entire
enterrar (e → ie)   to bury
entomólogo (*m.*)   entomologist
entonces   then
entrar (en)   to enter (into)
entre   between; among
entregar   to deliver
entrenar   to train
envolver (o → ue)   to wrap (up)
equipaje (*m.*)   equipment; luggage
erguir   to erect, lift up
error (*m.*)   error; mistake
escalera (*f.*)   stairway; staircase; ladder
escena (*f.*)   scene
escoger   to select
esconder   to hide
escribir   to write
escritorio (*m.*)   desk
escuchar   to listen (to)
escuela (secundaria) (*f.*)   (high) school
espacio (*m.*)   space; room
espalda (*f.*)   back
espantar   to scare, frighten
espantapájaros (*m.*)   scarecrow
esparcer   to scatter, spread
espejo (*m.*)   mirror
esperar   to hope, wait (for)
espía (*m./f.*)   spy
esposo/a (*m./f.*)   husband/wife; spouse
esquiar   to ski
esquina (*f.*)   corner; street corner
establecer   to establish
estación (de bomberos) (*f.*)   (fire) station
estacionar   to park
estado (*m.*)   state
Estados Unidos (*m.*)   United States
estampilla (*f.*)   stamp
estancia (*f.*)   stay; habitation
estante (*m.*)   shelf
estaño (*m.*)   tin
estar   to be

estar a dieta to be on a diet
estómago *(m.)* stomach
estornudar to sneeze
estos días these days
estrella (de cine) *(f.)* (movie) star
estudiante *(m./f.)* student
estudiar to study
estudios *(m.)* studies
estupendo great
examen *(m.)* test; examination
exigir to demand
existir to exist
exposición *(f.)* exposition; exhibit
expresarse to express oneself
extinguir to extinguish

f

falsificar to falsify, forge (one's signature)
faltar to be lacking to, be missing to
faltar a su palabra to break one's promise
fantasía *(f.)* fantasy
fantasma *(m.)* ghost; phantasm
farmacia *(f.)* pharmacy
fascinar to fascinate
favor *(m.)* favor
felicidad *(f.)* happiness
feliz happy
fiesta *(f.)* party
fin de semana *(m.)* weekend
financiero financial
fingir to pretend
firma *(f.)* signature
firmar to sign (one's name)
flor *(f.)* flower
florista *(m./f.)* florist
flotar to float
fluir to flow
folleto *(m.)* pamphlet
fondo *(m.)* bottom; back; background
fontanero *(m.)* plumber
foto *(f.)* photo

frase *(f.)* sentence; phrase
(con) frecuencia (with) frecuency; often
frecuentemente frequently; often
fregar (e → ie) to scrub, wash dishes
freír (e → i) to fry
fresco cool
frío cold
frontera *(f.)* border
fumar to smoke
funcionar to work, run (machine)
fútbol *(m.)* soccer
fútbol americano *(m.)* football

g

gabinete *(m.)* cabinet
gafas de sol *(f.)* sunglasses
galleta *(f.)* cracker
galletita *(f.)* cookie
ganador *(m.)* winner
ganar to win, earn
ganas (tener _____ de) to feel like doing (something), looking forward to
gasolina *(f.)* gasoline
gastar to spend (money)
gemir (e → i) to moan, groan, whine
gente *(f.)* people
gigante *(m.)* giant
gimnasio *(m.)* gym; gymnasium
girar to turn
gozar de to enjoy
gran great; grand
Gran Cañón *(m.)* Grand Canyon
grande (gran) big; large
granja *(f.)* farm
granjero *(m.)* farmer
grave serious
gravedad *(f.)* gravity
grifo *(m.)* faucet; tap
guante *(m.)* glove
guapo handsome
guardar un secreto to keep a secret

guerra *(f.)* war
guerrero *(m.)* warrior
guitarra *(f.)* guitar
gustar to be pleasing to, like
gusto *(m.)* taste

h

haber to have (auxiliary)
habitación *(f.)* room; hotel room
hablar to speak
hacer to make, do
hacer ejercicio to exercise
hacer una pregunta to ask a question
hacerse to become
hamburguesa *(f.)* hamburger
hambre *(f.)* hunger
hasta until
hay there is; there are
hecho *(m.)* fact
helado *(m.)* ice cream
hermano *(m.)* brother
hermanastra *(f.)* stepsister
hervir (e → ie) to boil
hielo *(m.)* ice
hipoteca *(f.)* mortgage
hogar *(m.)* home
hoja *(f.)* leaf
hombre *(m.)* man
homicidio *(m.)* homicide
honrado honest
horno *(m.)* oven; furnace
hotel *(m.)* hotel
hoy today
hueso *(m.)* bone
huevo *(m.)* egg
huir to flee, run away
humano *(m.)* human
húmedo humid
humor *(m.)* humor; mood
huracán *(m.)* hurricane

i

idioma *(m.)* language (particular)
iglesia *(f.)* church

ignorar to be ignorant of, ignore
igual(es) equal; (the) same
imaginarse to imagine
impedir (e → i) to impede, hinder
imponer to enforce
importar to be important to
impuestos (*m.*) taxes
incendio (*m.*) fire
incluir to include
incluso including
inducir to induce, lead
influir (en) to influence
información (*f.*) information
Inglaterra (*f.*) England
inglés (*m.*) English
inocente innocent
insistir (en) to insist (on)
instituir to institute
intentar to try
interés (*m.*) interest
interesar to interest
introducir to introduce
intruso (*m.*) intruder
invertir (e → ie) to invest
investigar to investigate
invitación (*f.*) invitation
invitado (*m.*) guest
invitar to invite
invierno (*m.*) winter
ir (al cine) to go (to the movies)
irse to go away, leave
ir de compras to go shopping
(a la) izquierda (to the) left

j

jardín (*m.*) garden
jardín de casa (*m.*) backyard
jardinero (*m.*) gardener
jefe (*m.*) boss; employer
jirafa (*f.*) giraffe
joya (*f.*) jewel
juego (*m.*) game
jugar (o → ue) to play (a game)
jugar a los naipes to play cards

juicio (*m.*) trial
juntos together
jurado (*m.*) jury
justificar to justify
justo fair; just

l

ladrar to bark
ladrillo (*m.*) brick
ladrón (*m.*) thief
lago (*m.*) lake
lágrima (*f.*) tear
langosta (*f.*) lobster
lanzador (*m.*) quarterback
largo long
lástima (*f.*) pity; shame
lavar(se) to wash (oneself)
lección (*f.*) lesson
leer to read
lenguaje (*m.*) language (in general)
león (*m.*) lion
levantarse to stand up, get up
ley (*f.*) law
libertad (*f.*) freedom; liberty
libra (*f.*) pound
librería (*f.*) bookstore
libro (*m.*) book
licencia (*f.*) license
líder (*m.*) leader
lienzo (*m.*) canvas
limonada (*f.*) lemonade
limpiar to clean, wash (windows)
limpio clean
listo ready
llamar(se) to call (oneself)
llave (*f.*) key
llegar to arrive
llenar to fill
llevar to wear, carry
llorar to cry
llover to rain
lloviznando drizzling
lluvia (*f.*) rain
lluvioso rainy; wet
lobo (*m.*) wolf
loco crazy; insane
lodo (*m.*) mud

lucir to light up, display
luego later
lugar (*m.*) place
luna (*f.*) moon
luna de miel (*f.*) honeymoon
luz (*f.*) light

m

madera (*f.*) wood
maduro mature; ripe
maestro/a (*m./f.*) teacher
mago (*m.*) wizard; magician
maldecir (e → i) to curse
maleta(s) (*f.*) suitcase (*pl.* luggage)
maletero (*m.*) trunk (of car)
malísimo wretched
malo bad; evil
manejar to drive, manage, run (a machine)
manga (*f.*) sleeve
mano (*f.*) hand
manopla (*f.*) mitten
manteca (*f.*) lard
mantequilla (*f.*) butter
mantener to maintain, keep
manzana (*f.*) apple; city block
mañana tomorrow
mañana (*f.*) morning
maratón (*m.*) marathon
maravilloso wonderful
mariposa (*f.*) butterfly
martes (*m.*) Tuesday
martillar to hammer
martillo (*m.*) hammer
más tarde later
mayor older
mecánico (*m.*) mechanic
medianoche (*f.*) midnight
medicina (*f.*) medicine
(en) medio (*m.*) (in the) middle
mediodía (*m.*) noon; midday
medir (e → i) to measure, be long
mejor best
menor younger
menos less
mentir (e → ie) to lie, tell a lie

mentira *(f.)* lie
mentiroso *(m.)* liar
merecer to deserve
mes *(m.)* month
mesero *(m.)* waiter
meter (en) to put (into)
meterse (en) to put oneself
   (through)
método *(m.)* method
mientras (que) while
mil thousand
milagro *(m.)* miracle
milla *(f.)* mile
mirar to watch, look at
(lo) mismo (the) same (thing)
misterio *(m.)* mystery
(buenos) modales *(m.)*
   (good) manners
modelo *(m./f.)* model
mohoso moldy
mojado wet
molestar to bother, be both-
   ersome to
moneda *(f.)* coin
mono *(m.)* monkey
monstruo *(m.)* monster
montar (en bicicleta) to
   wind, ride (a bike)
monumento *(m.)* monument
morder (o → ue) to bite, chew
morir (o → ue) to die
mosca *(f.)* fly
mosquito *(m.)* mosquito
mostrador *(m.)* counter
mostrar (o → ue) to show
mover(se) (o → ue) to move
   (oneself)
muchas veces many times
mucho a lot; much
(por) mucho tiempo (for) a
   long time
muchos many
mudarse to move, change
   residence
mueble *(m.)* piece of furniture
muebles *(m.)* furniture
muerte *(f.)* death
muerto dead
mujer *(m.)* woman
multa *(f.)* traffic ticket; fine
multitud *(f.)* crowd

mundo *(m.)* world
muñeca *(f.)* wrist
muro *(m.)* wall (exterior)
música *(f.)* music
muy very

N

nacer to be born
nada nothing; not anything
nada menos "all of it"
nadar to swim
nadie nobody; no one
naipes *(m.)* playing cards
nariz *(f.)* nose
navaja *(f.)* razor
Navidad *(f.)* Christmas
necesitar to need
negar (e → ie) to deny
nervioso nervous
nevada *(f.)* snowstorm; blizzard
nevar (e → ie) to snow
niebla *(f.)* fog
nieto *(m.)* grandson; grandchild
nieve *(f.)* snow
ningún; ninguno not any; not
   a single (one)
noche *(f.)* night
nombre *(m.)* name
nota *(f.)* note
(buenas/malas) notas *(f.)*
   (good/bad) grades
noticias *(f.)* news
novia girlfriend; fiancée;
   bride
novio boyfriend; fiancé;
   groom
nublado cloudy
nudo *(m.)* knot
número (de teléfono) *(m.)*
   (telephone) number
nunca (más) never (ever)

O

o . . . o . . . either . . . or . . .
obedecer to obey
obtener to obtain, get

océano *(m.)* ocean
ocupado busy
odiar to hate
odio *(m.)* hatred
oficina (de correos) *(f.)*
   (post) office
ofrecer to offer
oír to hear
ojalá I hope so!, God willing,
   if only he (it, they, etc.)
   would
ojo *(m.)* eye
oler (bien; mal) (o → ue) to
   smell (good; bad)
olimpiadas *(f.)* Olympics
olvidar to forget
oponer to oppose
ordenado neat
organizar to organize
oro *(m.)* gold
oso *(m.)* bear
otoño *(m.)* fall; autumn
otra vez again; another time

P

padrino(s) *(m.)* godfather
   (godparents)
pagar to pay (for)
página *(f.)* page
pájaro *(m.)* bird
palabra *(f.)* word
palacio *(m.)* palace
pan *(m.)* bread
panadería *(f.)* bakery
panadero *(m.)* baker
pantalones *(m.)* pants;
   slacks
Papa *(m.)* (the) Pope
papa *(f.)* potato
papá *(m.)* father
papel *(m.)* paper
paquete *(m.)* package
(un) par de (a) couple of
para (que) for (so that)
para siempre forever
parecer to seem, appear
parecerse a to look like,
   resemble physically
pared *(f.)* wall (interior)
parque *(m.)* park

parte *(f.)* part
participante *(m./f.)* participant; contestant
partido *(m.)* game
partir to leave, depart
pasa *(f.)* raisin
pasta de dientes *(f.)* toothpaste
patata *(f.)* potato
patinar to skate
pato *(m.)* duck
pavo *(m.)* turkey
payaso *(m.)* clown
paz *(f.)* peace
pedazo *(m.)* piece
pedir (e → i) to ask for, request
peinarse to comb one's hair
peldaño *(m.)* step; stair
película *(f.)* movie; film
pelo *(m.)* hair
pensar (en) (e → ie) to think (about)
pequeño small; little
perder (e → ie) to lose
perder (e → ie) el tiempo to waste time
perezoso lazy; slothful
periódico *(m.)* newspaper
perla *(f.)* pearl
perlita *(f.)* little pearl
permitir to permit, allow
perseguir (e → i) to pursue, persecute
persona *(f.)* person *(pl.* people)
personaje *(m.)* character
pertenecer to belong
pesadilla *(f.)* nightmare
pesar to weigh
pescado *(m.)* fish (prepared)
peso *(m.)* weight
pez *(m.)* fish (living)
pie *(m.)* foot
pierna *(f.)* leg
pijama *(m.)* pajamas
pintor *(m.)* painter
pintura *(f.)* picture; painting; paint
piscina *(f.)* swimming pool
pistola *(f.)* pistol; gun
placer to please, gratify

plancha *(f.)* iron
planchar to iron
planear to plan
planeta *(m.)* planet
planta *(f.)* plant
plata *(f.)* silver
plato *(m.)* plate; dish
playa *(f.)* beach
pobreza *(f.)* poverty
poder (o → ue) to be able to
policía *(m.)* policeman
policía *(f.)* policewoman; police force
política *(f.)* politics
político *(m.)* politician
Polo Sur *(m.)* South Pole
pollo *(m.)* chicken
poner to put, place
ponerse to become, put on (clothing), set (sun)
ponerse a dieta to go on a diet
por casualidad by accident; by chance
por ninguna parte not anywhere
por primera vez for the first time
¿Por qué? Why?
por separado separately
por supuesto of course
por un rato for a while
porque because
poseer to possess
practicar to practice
preferir (e → ie) to prefer
premio *(m.)* prize
preparar to prepare
preocuparse (por) to worry (about)
presentación *(f.)* presentation; introduction
prestar to loan, lend
primavera *(f.)* spring
(por) primera vez (for) the first time
primero first
primo *(m.)* cousin
probar (o → ue) to prove, test, sample, taste
probarse (o → ue) to try on (clothing)

problema *(m.)* problem
producir to produce
profesional *(m./f.)* professional; pro
programa *(m.)* program
progreso *(m.)* progress
prohibido prohibited
promesa *(f.)* promise
prometer to promise
pronunciación *(f.)* pronunciation
proteger to protect
proveer to provide
próximo next
prueba *(f.)* quiz
público *(m.)* public; audience
pudrir to rot, spoil
puerta (principal) *(f.)* door (front)
pues well
pulgada *(f.)* inch
pulgar *(m.)* thumb
pulsera *(f.)* bracelet
punto de vista *(m.)* point of view
puré *(m.)* purée
puré de patatas mashed potatoes

q

que that; than
¿Qué? What?
quedarse to stay, remain
quejarse (de) to complain (about)
querer (e → ie) to want
queso *(m.)* cheese
quien; ¿Quién? who; Who(m)?
(de) quita y pon detachable
quitar (la nieve) to remove (shovel snow)
quitarse to take off, remove (clothing)

r

rabia *(f.)* rage
radio *(m./f.)* radio (apparatus)

radio *(f.)* radio (station)
raer to scrape, rub off
rama *(f.)* branch
ramo (de flores) *(m.)* bouquet (of flowers)
rana *(f.)* frog
rápidamente fast; quickly; rapidly
rápido fast; rapid
rebaja *(f.)* sale
rebajar de peso to lose weight
recepción *(f.)* reception
recibir to receive
recoger to pick up, gather
reconocer to recognize
recordar (o → ue) to remember, recall
reducir to reduce, cut down
referir (e → ie) to refer
refrigerador *(m.)* refrigerator
regalo *(m.)* gift; present
regar (e → ie) to water (a plant)
regla *(f.)* rule
rehacer to redo, remake
reina *(f.)* queen
reír (se) (e → i) to laugh
relajarse to relax
releer to reread
reloj *(m.)* watch; clock
remontar (una cometa) to fly (a kite)
renunciar a to quit (a job, etc.)
repetir (e → i) to repeat
reportaje *(m.)* report
reprobar (o → ue) to fail
resfriado *(m.)* cold
resolver (o → ue) to solve, resolve
respuesta *(f.)* answer
restaurante *(m.)* restaurant
retraer to bring back, dissuade
reunión *(f.)* meeting
revista *(f.)* magazine
rey *(m.)* king
rezar to pray
rico rich
ridículo ridiculous
río *(m.)* river

riqueza *(f.)* richness; wealth
robar to rob, steal
robo *(m.)* robbery
rodilla (de rodillas) knee (kneeling)
rogar (o → ue) to pray, beg
rollo de película *(m.)* film (for a camera)
romper to break
ropa *(f.)* clothing; clothes
roto broken
rubí *(m.)* ruby
rubio blonde
rueda *(f.)* wheel
ruido *(m.)* noise
ruso *(m.)* Russian

S

saber (de) to know information (about)
sacar to take out
sacar una foto to take a picture
sacerdote *(m.)* priest
sala *(f.)* living room
sala de juntas *(f.)* boardroom
salchicha *(f.)* sausage
salir (de) to leave (from)
saltar to jump
sangre *(f.)* blood
secar(se) to dry (oneself)
seco dry
secreto *(m.)* secret
sed *(f.)* thirst
segar (e → ie) to mow (grass, etc.)
seguir (e → i) to follow, continue
sello *(m.)* stamp (postage)
selva *(f.)* jungle
selva tropical *(f.)* rain forest
semana *(f.)* week
semilla *(f.)* seed
sentado sitting; seated
sentarse (e → ie) to sit down, be seated
sentir (e → ie) to regret
sentirse (e → ie) to feel
ser to be

Serie Mundial *(f.)* World Series
servilleta *(f.)* napkin
servir (e → i) to serve
siempre always
siesta *(f.)* nap
siglo *(m.)* century
siguiente next; following
silla *(f.)* chair
simbolizar to symbolize
sin (que) without
sirvienta *(f.)* servant; maid
sobrar to be in surplus, be left over
sobre *(m.)* envelope
sociedad *(f.)* society
sofá *(m.)* sofa; couch
sol *(m.)* sun
solamente only
soldado *(m.)* soldier
solo alone
sólo only; just
sombra *(f.)* shade; shadow
sombrero *(m.)* hat
sonar (a) (o → ue) to ring, resound, sound (like)
sonreír (e → i) to smile
sonrisa *(f.)* smile
soñar (con) (o → ue) to dream (of)
sopa *(f.)* soup
sostener to sustain, support, uphold
sótano *(m.)* basement
subir to climb, go up
sucio dirty
suegro/a *(m./f.)* father/mother-in-law
suelo *(m.)* floor
sueño *(m.)* dream
suéter *(m.)* sweater
suficiente enough
sufrir to suffer
sugerir (e → ie) to suggest
sumergir to submerge, immerse
supersticioso *(m.)* superstitious (person)
suponer to suppose, assume
sur *(m.)* south
surgir to surge, spurt

suspender   to fail (a test)
sustituir   to substitute
sustraer   to remove, take away

t

tabloide (m.)   tabloid
tacón (alto) (m.)   (high) heel
tal cosa   such a thing
talla (f.)   size
tamaño (m.)   size
también   also; too
tampoco   not either
tan   so
tan pronto como   as soon as
tanque (de gasolina) (m.)   (gas) tank
tanto/a (como)   so much; as much (as)
tantos/as   so many
tardar (en)   to take time
tarde   late
tarde (f.)   afternoon
tarea (f.)   assignment; task; chore
tarjeta (de crédito) (f.)   (credit) card
taza (f.)   coffee cup; mug
té (m.)   tea
teatro (m.)   theater
tela (f.)   canvas (painting)
teléfono (m.)   telephone
telegrama (m.)   telegram
televisión (f.), **televisor** (m.)   television (system); television (set)
temblar (e → ie)   to tremble
temer   to fear, suspect, dread
temor (m.)   fear
temprano   early
tenedor (m.)   fork
tener   to have
tener calor   to be warm
tener frío   to be cold
tener hambre   to be hungry
tener miedo   to be afraid
tener prisa   to be in hurry
tener que + inf.   to have to do something

tener que ver con   to have something/anything to do with
tener razón   to be right
tener sed   to be thirsty
tener sueño   to be tired
tener suerte   to be lucky
tenis (m.)   tennis
teoría (f.)   theory
terminar   to finish
terremoto (m.)   earthquake
tesoro (m.)   treasure
tiempo (m.)   time; weather
tienda (f.)   store
tierra (f.)   land; earth; world
toalla (f.)   towel
tocar   to touch, play (an instrument)
(en) todas partes   everywhere
todavía   still; yet
todo (m.)   all; everything
todo el día (año)   all day (year) long
todo el mundo   everybody
todos (m.)   everybody; all
tolerar   to tolerate
tomar   to take
tomar una decisión   to make a decision
tomate (m.)   tomato
tonto   silly; ridiculous
tormenta (f.)   storm
torta (f.)   cake
tostar (o → ue)   to toast
trabajar   to work
trabajo (m.)   work; academic paper
traducir   to translate
traer   to bring
tragar   to swallow
trágico   tragic
traje (de baño) (m.)   (bathing) suit
tratar de + inf.   to try to do something
trazar   to trace
triste   sad
tristeza (f.)   sadness
trombón (m.)   trombone
tropezar con (e → ie)   to bump into

u

último   last; ultimate
único   only; one and only; unique
uniforme (m.)   uniform
unir   to unite
universidad (f.)   university
unos cuantos   a few
uña (f.)   fingernail
uva (f.)   grape

v

vaciar   to empty, clean out
vacaciones (f.)   vacation
vagar   to wander, roam
valer   to be worth
vampiro (m.)   vampire
variedad (f.)   variety
varios   several; various
vaso (m.)   drinking glass; vase
vecindad (f.)   neighborhood; vicinity
vecino (m.)   neighbor
vehículo (m.)   vehicle
vela (f.)   candle
vencer   to conquer
vendedor (m.)   salesman
vender   to sell
venir   to come
ventana (f.)   window
ver(se)   to see (oneself)
verano (m.)   summer
verdad (f.)   truth
verdadero   true; real
vestido (m.)   dress
vestir(se) (e → i)   to dress (oneself)
vez (veces) (f.)   time; instance
(de) vez en cuando   from time to time; once in a while
viajar   to travel
viaje (m.)   trip
vida (f.)   life
vidrio (m.)   glass
viejo   old
viento (m.)   wind
viga (f.)   support beam
vigilar   to watch over
vino (m.)   wine

violín *(m.)*   violin
vista *(f.)*   view
vitamina *(f.)*   vitamin
vivir   to live
volante   flying
**volar (o → ue) (de un lado a
   otro)**   to fly (around)
voleibol *(m.)*   volleyball
voltear los pulgares   to twiddle one's thumbs

volver (o → ue)   to return
vomitar   to vomit
votar   to vote
voz *(f.)*   voice

y

ya   already
yacer   to lie down

z

zapatear   to tap-dance
zapatilla *(f.)*   slipper
zapato *(m.)*   shoe
zurcir   to mend, darn

Glossary: English-Spanish

a

a lot   mucho
about   acerca de
abstain (from doing something)   abstenerse de + inf.
accept   aceptar
accident; by _____   accidente *(m.);* por casualidad
acquire   adquirir (e → ie)
act   actuar; comportarse
address   dirección *(f.)*
admit   admitir
adult   adulto *(m.)*
advise   advertir (e → ie)
afraid   asustado
(to be) afraid (of)   tener miedo (de)
after; afterwards   después (de)
afternoon   tarde *(f.)*
again   otra vez
against   contra
agree to do something   convenir en + inf.
Aha!   ¡Ajá!
airline   aerolínea *(f.)*
airplane   avión *(m.)*
airport   aeropuerto *(m.)*
alas!   ¡ay!
all   todo; todos
all day (year) long   todo el día (año)
all of it   nada menos
alone   solo
already   ya
also   también
always   siempre
among   entre
and   y; e (preceding a word beginning with *i* or *hi*)
angry   enfadado; enojado
another   otro
answer   respuesta *(f.);* contestar; responder
any; anything   algo; cualquiera; cualquier cosa

(not) any   ningún
anyway   de cualquier forma
anywhere; not _____   en cualquier parte; en ninguna parte
apartment   apartamento *(m.)*
appear   aparecer
apple   manzana *(f.)*
appointment   cita *(f.)*
approve   aprobar (o → ue)
architect   arquitecto *(m.)*
area   área *(f.)*
army   ejército *(m.)*
around   alrededor (de)
arrange   arreglar
arrest   detener
arrive   llegar
article   artículo *(m.)*
as a child   de niño/a
as much (as)   tanto (como)
as soon as   tan pronto como
ask (for)   pedir (e → i)
ask (a question)   preguntar
assignment   tarea *(f.)*
astronaut   astronauta *(m./f.)*
at first   al principio
at this rate   a este paso
at times   a veces
athlete   atleta *(m./f.)*
attend   asistir (a)
attic   desván *(m.)*
attitude   actitud *(f.)*
attract   atraer
authorize   autorizar
autumn   otoño *(m.)*

b

baby   bebé *(m./f.)*
back; background   espalda *(f.);* fondo *(m.)*
backyard   jardín de casa *(m.)*
bad   malo
bad mood   mal humor *(m.)*
bag   bolsa *(f.)*
baker   panadero *(m.)*
bakery   panadería *(f.)*

band   banda *(f.)*
bank   banco *(m.)*
baptize   bautizar
bark   ladrar
baseball   béisbol *(m.)*
basement   sótano *(m.)*
basketball   baloncesto *(m.)*
bath; bathroom   baño *(m.)*
bathe (oneself)   bañar(se)
bathing suit   traje de baño *(m.)*
be (location; short-term)   estar
be (enduring)   ser
be able to ("can")   poder (o → ue)
be born   nacer
be ready   estar listo
be thankful   agradecer
beach   playa *(f.)*
beam (support)   viga *(f.)*
bear   oso *(m.)*
because   porque
become   ponerse; hacerse
bed   cama *(f.)*
beer   cerveza *(f.)*
before; beforehand   antes (de)
beg   rogar (o → ue)
begin   comenzar; empezar (e → ie)
behave   comportarse
behind   atrás (de); detrás (de)
believe   creer
belong   pertenecer
best; better   mejor
between   entre
bicycle   bicicleta *(f.)*
big   grande; gran
bilingual   bilingüe
bill   cuenta *(f.)*
billiards   billar *(m.)*
billion   billón *(m.)*
bird   ave *(f.);* pájaro *(m.)*
birthday   cumpleaños *(m.)*
bite   morder (o → ue)
bless   bendecir (e → i)
blizzard   nevada *(f.);* tormenta de nieve *(f.)*
block (city)   manzana; cuadra *(f.)*

blonde rubio

blood sangre *(f.)*

boardroom sala de juntas *(f.)*

boat barco *(m.)*

boil hervir (e → ie)

bomb bomba *(f.)*

bone hueso *(m.)*

book libro *(m.)*

bookstore librería *(f.)*

border frontera *(f.)*

bored; boring aburrido

born (to be) nacer

boss jefe *(m.)*

bother molestar

bottom fondo *(m.)*

bouquet (of flowers) ramo (de flores) *(m.)*

box caja *(f.)*

boyfriend novio *(m.)*

bracelet pulsera *(f.)*

brain cerebro *(m.)*

branch rama *(f.)*

brave bravo; valiente

bread pan *(m.)*

break romper; quebrar

break one's promise faltar a su palabra

breakfast desayuno *(m.)*

brick ladrillo *(m.)*

bride novia *(f.)*

bring traer

bring back retraer; devolver (o → ue)

broken roto; dañado

brother hermano *(m.)*

brown café; marrón

brush (oneself) cepillar(se)

bubble burbuja *(f.)*

build construir

building edificio *(m.)*

bump into tropezar(se) con (e → ie)

bury enterrar (e → ie)

bus autobús *(m.)*

busy ocupado

butter mantequilla *(f.)*

butterfly mariposa *(f.)*

button botón *(m.)*

buy comprar

by (accident; chance) por (casualidad)

C

cabinet alacena *(f.)*; armario *(m.)*

cafeteria cafetería *(f.)*

caffeine cafeína *(f.)*

cake torta *(f.)*

call (oneself) llamar(se)

calorie caloría *(f.)*

camera cámara *(f.)*

camp campamento *(m.)*

candidate candidato *(m.)*

candle vela *(f.)*

candy dulces; caramelos *(m.)*

canvas (painting) tela *(f.)*; lienzo *(m.)*

capital (city) capital *(f.)*

capital (wealth) capital *(m.)*

card tarjeta; carta *(f.)*

cards (playing) naipes *(m.)*

care cuidado *(m.)*

care for (an animal or thing) cuidar de

care for (oneself) cuidarse

care for (a person) cuidar a

career carrera *(f.)*

case caso *(m.)*

(in) cash (al) contado

castle castillo *(m.)*

catalogue catálogo *(m.)*

catch coger

caterer abastecedor *(m.)*

celebrate celebrar

center centro *(m.)*

centerpiece centro de mesa *(m.)*

century siglo *(m.)*

ceremony ceremonia *(f.)*

chair silla *(f.)*

change cambio *(m.)*; cambiar

chapter capítulo *(m.)*

character personaje; carácter *(m.)*

cheat engañar

check cheque *(m.)*

checkbook talonario de cheques *(m.)*

checkers damas *(f.)*

cheese queso *(m.)*

chef cocinero *(m.)*

chess ajedrez *(m.)*

chicken pollo *(m.)*

chimney chimenea *(f.)*

choice elección *(f.)*

choose elegir (e → i)

chore tarea *(f.)*

Christmas Navidad *(f.)*

church iglesia *(f.)*

cigar cigarro; puro *(m.)*

Cinderella Cenicienta *(f.)*

clarify clarificar

class clase *(f.)*

classify clasificar

clean limpio; limpiar

clean out vaciar

clerk dependiente *(m.)*

client cliente *(m./f.)*

climb subir

clock reloj *(m.)*

close cerrar (e → ie)

closed cerrado

closet armario *(m.)*

clothes; clothing ropa *(f.)*

cloudy nublado

clown payaso *(m.)*

club club *(m.)*

cockroach cucaracha *(f.)*

coffee café *(m.)*

coffee cup taza *(f.)*

coffee shop cafetería *(f.)*

coin moneda *(f.)*

cold resfriado *(m.)*; frío

(to be) cold tener frío

colleague compañero *(m.)*

comb (one's) hair peinar(se)

come venir

commence comenzar (c → ic)

commission comisión *(f.)*

companion compañero *(m.)*

company compañía *(f.)*

compete competir (e → i)

complain (about) quejarse (de)

complete cumplir

compliment cumplido *(m.)*

compose componer

concert concierto *(m.)*

conclude concluir

conduct conducir

confess confesar (e → ie)

conjugate conjugar

conquer conquistar; vencer

consent consentir (e → ie)

constitute constituir
construct construir
contain contener
contamination contami-
    nación *(f.)*
contest concurso *(m.)*
contestant participante
    (m./f.)
continue continuar; seguir
    (e → i)
contract contratar; contraer
contribute contribuir
convert (into) convertir (en)
    (e → ie)
convince convencer
cook cocinar
cookie galletita *(f.)*
corner (exterior) esquina *(f.)*
corner (interior) rincón *(m.)*
correct corregir (e → i)
couch sofá *(m.)*
counter mostrador *(m.)*
(a) couple of (un) par de
coupon cupón *(m.)*
courteous cortés
cost costar (o → ue)
count contar (o → ue)
cousin primo *(m.)*
cover cubrir
cover up encubrir
cracker galleta *(f.)*
credit card tarjeta de crédito
    (f.)
crime crimen *(m.)*
crowd multitud *(f.)*
cry llorar
crystal cristal *(m.)*
cup taza *(f.)*
curse maldecir (e → i)
curtain cortina *(f.)*
cut cortar

d

dance baile *(m.)*; bailar
darn zurcir
date fecha; cita *(f.)*
day día *(m.)*
daydream soñar en (o → ue)
dead muerto
death muerte *(f.)*

deceive engañar
decide decidir
deduce deducir; colegir
    (e → i)
defeat vencer
defective defectuoso
defend defender (e → ie)
defendant acusado *(m.)*
deliver entregar
demand exigir
demonstrate demostrar
    (o → ue)
deny negar(se) (e → ie)
depart partir
depend (on) depender (de)
deposit depositar
depressed deprimido
describe describir
desert desierto *(m.)*
deserve merecer
desire deseo *(m.)*
desk escritorio *(m.)*
dessert postre *(m.)*
destroy destruir
detachable de quita y pon
detain detener
diamond diamante *(m.)*
diary diario *(m.)*
die morir (o → ue)
diet dieta *(f.)*; ponerse a
    dieta
(be on a) diet estar a dieta;
    ponerse a dieta
different diferente; distinto
difficult difícil
difficulty dificultad *(f.)*
dine cenar
dining room comedor *(m.)*
dinner cena *(f.)*
diploma diploma *(m.)*
direct dirigir
dirty sucio
disappear desaparecer
disaster desastre *(m.)*
discover descubrir
discuss discutir
dish plato *(m.)*
display lucir
dissolve disolver (o → ue)
dissuade retraer
distance distancia *(f.)*
distinct distinto

distinguish distinguir
do hacer
document documento *(m.)*
dollar dólar *(m.)*
door (front _____) puerta
    (f.) (principal)
doubt duda *(f.)*; dudar
down abajo
downtown centro *(m.)*
dozen docena *(f.)*
drain desagüe *(m.)*
dread temer
dream (of) sueño *(m.)*; soñar
    (con) (o → ue)
dress vestido *(m.)*
dress (oneself) vestir(se)
    (e → i)
drink bebida *(f.)*; beber;
    tomar
drinking glass vaso *(m.)*
drive conducir; manejar
drizzling lloviznando
drunk borracho
dry seco
dry (oneself) secar(se)
duck pato *(m.)*
during durante

e

each cada
early temprano
earn ganar
earring arete; pendiente *(m.)*
earth tierra *(f.)*
earthquake terremoto *(m.)*
eat comer
eat breakfast desayunar
eat dinner cenar
eat lunch almorzar (o → ue)
education educación *(f.)*
egg huevo *(m.)*
egoistic egoísta
either . . . or . . . o . . . o . . .
(not) either tampoco
elect elegir (e → i)
election elección *(f.)*
element elemento *(m.)*
elevator ascensor *(m.)*
embarrassed avergonzado
employee empleado *(m.)*

employer   jefe; empleador *(m.)*
empty   vacío; vaciar
(be) enchanting to   encantarle a alguien
enemy   enemigo *(m.)*
energy   energía *(f.)*
enforce   imponer
England   Inglaterra *(f.)*
English   inglés *(m.)*
enigma   enigma *(m.)*
enjoy   gozar de
enough   bastante; suficiente
enter (into)   entrar (en)
entire   entero
entomologist   entomólogo *(m.)*
envelope   sobre *(m.)*
equal   igual
equipment   equipaje *(m.)*
erect   erguir
error   error *(m.)*
essay   ensayo *(m.)*
establish   establecer
ethic   credo *(m.)*
every   cada
everybody; everyone   todos *(m.);* todo el mundo
everything   todo *(m.)*
everywhere   en todas partes; por todas partes
examination; exam   examen *(m.)*
exercise   hacer ejercicio; ejercer
exert   ejercer
exhibit   exposición *(f.)*
exist   existir
express oneself   expresarse
extinguish   extinguir
eye   ojo *(m.)*

f

fail (a test)   suspender; reprobar (o → ue)
fair   justo
fairy tale   cuento de hadas *(m.)*
fall   otoño *(m.)*
fall (down)   caer (se)
fall asleep   dormirse (o → ue)

(be) familiar with   conocer
fantasy   fantasía *(f.)*
farm   granja *(f.)*
farmer   granjero *(m.)*
(be) fascinating to   fascinarle a alguien
fast   rápido
father   padre; papá *(m.)*
father-in-law   suegro *(m.)*
faucet   grifo *(m.)*
favor   favor *(m.)*
fear   temor *(m.);* temer; tener miedo de
feel   sentirse (e → ie)
feel like doing something   tener ganas de + inf.
feel sorry   sentir (e → ie)
(a) few   (unos) cuantos
fiancé; fiancée   novio/a; prometido/a *(m./f.)*
fill   llenar
film (camera)   (rollo de) película *(f.)*
financial   financiero
find   encontrar (o → ue)
find out   averiguar
fine   bien; multa *(f.)*
fingernail   uña *(f.)*
finish   terminar
fire   fuego; incendio *(m.);* despedir (e → i)
fire station   estación de bomberos *(f.)*
firefighter   bombero *(m.)*
fireplace   chimenea *(f.)*
first   primero
fish (living)   pez *(m.)*
fish (prepared)   pescado *(m.)*
fix   arreglar
fit   caber
flag   bandera *(f.)*
flee   huir
float   flotar
floor   suelo; piso *(m.)*
florist   florista *(m./f.)*
flow   fluir
flower   flor *(f.)*
fluently   con soltura
fly   mosca *(f.);* volar (o → ue)
fly a kite   remontar una cometa
flying   volante

fog   niebla *(f.)*
follow   seguir (e → i)
following   siguiente
food   comida *(f.)*
fool   engañar
foot   pie *(m.)*
football   fútbol americano *(m.)*
for (that)   para (que); por
for a while   por un rato
for the first time   por primera vez
forest   bosque *(m.)*
forever   para siempre
forge (a signature)   falsificar
forget   olvidar
fork   tenedor *(m.)*
freedom   libertad *(f.)*
French   francés *(m.)*
frequently   frecuentemente; con frecuencia
friendly   amistoso
frighten   espantar
frog   rana *(f.)*
from time to time   de vez en cuando
from top to bottom   de cabo a rabo
fry   freír (e → i)
fun   diversión *(f.)*
funny   cómico
furniture   mueble; muebles *(m.)*

g

gain   ganar
gain weight   engordar
game   juego; partido *(m.)*
game show   concurso *(m.)*
garbage   basura *(f.)*
garden   jardín *(m.)*
gardener   jardinero *(m.)*
gas tank   tanque de gasolina *(m.)*
gasoline   gasolina *(f.)*
genuine   genuino
get   obtener; adquirir (e → ie); conseguir (e → i)
get mad, angry   enojarse
get sick   enfermarse
get up   levantarse

get used to   acostumbrarse
ghost   fantasma *(m.)*
giant   gigante *(m.)*
gift   regalo *(m.)*
giraffe   jirafa *(f.)*
girlfriend   novia *(f.)*
give   dar
glass (material)   vidrio; cristal *(m.)*
glass (drinking)   vaso *(m.)*
glove   guante *(m.)*
go (away)   ir(se)
go to bed   acostarse (o → ue)
go to the movies   ir al cine
God; god   Dios; dios
God willing   ojalá
godfather; godparents   padrino; padrinos *(m.)*
gold   oro *(m.)*
good   bueno
good mood   buen humor *(m.)*
grab   coger
grades (good/bad _____)   notas *(f.)* (buenas/malas _____)
grand   gran; grande
Grand Canyon   Gran Cañon *(m.)*
grandfather   abuelo *(m.)*
grandchild; grandson   nieto *(m.)*
grant   conceder
grape   uva *(f.)*
gratify   placer
gravity   gravedad *(f.)*
great   estupendo; gran; grande
groan   gemir (e → i)
groom   novio *(m.)*
grow   crecer; cultivar (plantas)
guest   invitado *(m.)*
guitar   guitarra *(f.)*
gym; gymnasium   gimnasio *(m.)*

h

hair   pelo *(m.)*
hallway   pasillo *(m.)*
hamburger   hamburguesa *(f.)*
hammer   martillo *(m.)*; martillar

hand   mano *(f.)*
(on the other) hand   en cambio
handsome   guapo
hang (up)   colgar (o → ue)
happiness   felicidad *(f.)*
happy   feliz
hard   duro; difícil
hat   sombrero *(m.)*
hate   odiar
hatred   odio *(m.)*
haunted   embrujado
have   tener; haber (auxiliary)
have to do something   tener que + inf.
have something to do with   tener que ver con
head   cabeza *(f.)*
hear   oír
heart   corazón *(m.)*
heel (high _____)   tacón (alto) *(m.)*
help   ayuda *(f.)*; ayudar
here   aquí
hide   esconder
highway   carretera; autopista *(f.)*
hinder   impedir (e → i)
hire   contratar; emplear
hold   contener
home   hogar *(m.)*
homicide   homicidio *(m.)*
honest   honrado
honeymoon   luna de miel *(f.)*
hope (for)   esperar
horse   caballo *(m.)*
host   anfitrión *(m.)*
hotel   hotel *(m.)*
How?   ¿Cómo?
How many?   ¿Cuántos?
How much?   ¿Cuánto?
human   humano *(m.)*
humid   húmedo
humor   humor *(m.)*
hunger   hambre *(f.)*
(to be) hungry   tener hambre
hunt   cazar
hurricane   huracán *(m.)*
(to be in a) hurry   tener prisa
husband   esposo *(m.)*

i

ice   hielo *(m.)*
ice cream   helado *(m.)*
(be) ignorant of   ignorar
imagine   imaginarse
immerse   sumergir
impede   impedir (e → i)
(be) important to   importarle a alguien
in case (of)   en caso de que
in front (of)   enfrente (de)
in the beginning   al principio
inch   pulgada *(f.)*
include   incluir
increase   aumentar
induce   inducir
influence   influir (en)
information   información *(f.)*
innocent   inocente
insane   loco
insert   introducir
inside   adentro; dentro (de)
insist (on)   insistir (en)
instead (of)   en vez (de)
institute   instituir
item   artículo *(m.)*
interest   interés *(m.)*
(be) interesting to   interesarle a alguien
introduce   introducir; presentar
introduction   presentación *(f.)*
intruder   intruso *(m.)*
invest   invertir (e → ie)
investigate   investigar
invitation   invitación *(f.)*
invite   invitar
iron   plancha *(f.)*; planchar

j

jail   cárcel *(f.)*
January   enero
jewel   joya *(f.)*
joke   broma *(f.)*
jump   saltar
jungle   selva *(f.)*
jury   jurado *(m.)*
just   justo; sólo
justify   justificar

k

keep a secret   guardar un
  secreto
key   llave (f.)
kindle   encender (e → ie)
king   rey (m.)
knee   rodilla (f.)
kneel   estar de rodillas
knife   cuchillo (m.)
knot   nudo (m.)
know a person   conocer
know information (about)
  saber (de)

l

(be) lacking to   faltarle a
  alguien
ladder   escalera (f.)
lake   lago (m.)
lamb   cordero (m.)
land   tierra (f.)
language (particular)   idioma
  (m.)
language (general)   lenguaje
  (m.)
lard   manteca (f.)
large   grande
last   último; durar
last night   anoche
late   tarde
later   más tarde; luego
laugh   reír(se) (e → i)
law   ley (f.)
lawn   césped (m.)
lawnmower   cortacéspedes (m.)
lawyer   abogado (m.)
lazy   perezoso
lead   conducir
leader   líder (m.)
leaf   hoja (f.)
learn   aprender
leave (from)   salir (de); irse;
  partir
leave behind   dejar
left (to the)   (a la) izquierda
(be) left over to   sobrarle a
  alguien
leg   pierna (f.)

lemonade   limonada (f.)
lend   prestar
less   menos
lesson   lección (f.)
Let's see . . .   A ver . . .
letter   carta (f.)
liar   mentiroso (m.)
liberty   libertad (f.)
library   biblioteca (f.)
license   licencia (f.)
lie; (tell a) lie   mentira (f.);
  mentir (e → ie)
lie down   yacer; acostarse
  (o → ue)
life   vida (f.)
light   luz (f.); encender
  (e → ie)
light up   lucir
lightbulb   bombilla (f.)
line   cola; línea (f.)
lion   león (m.)
listen (to)   escuchar
little   pequeño; poco
Little Red Riding Hood
  Caperucita Roja (f.)
live   vivir
living room   sala; sala de estar
  (f.)
loaf (of bread)   barra (de
  pan) (f.)
loan   préstamo (m.);
  prestar
lobster   langosta (f.)
long   largo
(be) long   medir (e → i)
long time   mucho tiempo
  (m.)
look (at)   mirar
look for   buscar
look like (someone)   parecerse a (alguien)
lose   perder (e → ie)
lose weight   adelgazar; rebajar de peso
(a) lot (of)   mucho
love   amor (m.); amar
(to be) lucky   tener suerte
luggage   equipaje (m.); maletas (f.)
lunch   almuerzo (m.);
  almorzar (o → ue)

m

mad   enojado
magazine   revista (f.)
magician   mago (m.)
maid   criada; sirvienta (f.)
mail   correo (m.); echar al
  correo
maintain   mantener
make   hacer
make a decision   tomar una
  decisión
make a mistake   cometer un
  error
mall   centro comercial (m.)
man   hombre (m.)
manage   manejar
manners (good)   (buenos)
  modales (m.)
many   muchos
marathon   maratón (m.)
married   casado
marry (someone)   casarse
  (con alguien)
mashed   puré (m.)
mature   maduro
meal   comida (f.)
measure   medir (e → i)
meat   carne (f.)
mechanic   mecánico (m.)
medicine   medicina (f.)
meet   conocer
meet (with)   concontrarse
  (o → ue) (con)
meeting   reunión (f.)
mend   zurcir
merit   merecer
messy   desordenado
method   método (m.)
midday   mediodía (m.)
(in the) middle   (en) medio
  (m.)
midnight   medianoche (f.)
mile   milla (f.)
miracle   milagro (m.)
mirror   espejo (m.)
(be) missing to   faltarle a
  alguien
mistake   error (m.)
mitten   manopla (f.)
moan   gemir (e → i)

model   modelo *(m./f.)*
moldy   mohoso
money   dinero *(m.)*
monkey   mono *(m.)*
mood   humor *(m.)*
monster   monstruo *(m.)*
month   mes *(m.)*
monument   monumento *(m.)*
moon   luna *(f.)*
morning   mañana *(f.)*
mortgage   hipoteca *(f.)*
mosquito   mosquito *(m.)*
mother   mamá; madre *(f.)*
mother-in-law   suegra *(f.)*
mouth   boca *(f.)*
move (oneself)   mover(se)
  (o → ue)
move (change residence)
  mudarse
movie   película *(f.)*
must (conjecture)   deber de +
  inf.
movie theater   cine *(m.)*
(to the) movies   (al) cine
mow (grass, etc.)   cortar;
  segar (e → ie)
much   mucho
mud   lodo *(m.)*
music   música *(f.)*
mystery   misterio *(m.)*

N

name   nombre *(m.)*; nombrar;
  llamar
nap   siesta *(f.)*
napkin   servilleta *(f.)*
neat   ordenado
necklace   collar *(m.)*
necktie   corbata *(f.)*
need   necesitar
neighbor   vecino *(m.)*
neighborhood   vecindad *(f.)*
nervous   nervioso
never (ever)   nunca (más)
news   noticias *(f.)*
newspaper   periódico *(m.)*
next   próximo; siguiente
next (door) to   al lado de
nice   amable; simpático
night   noche *(f.)*

nightmare   pesadilla *(f.)*
nobody; no one   nadie
noise   ruido *(m.)*
noon   mediodía *(m.)*
nose   nariz *(f.)*
not any; not a single one
  ningún; ninguno
not anything   nada
note   nota *(f.)*
nothing   nada
now   ahora
nowhere   en ninguna parte
number (telephone _____)
  número *(m.)* (_____ de
  teléfono)

O

obey   obedecer
obtain   obtener; conseguir
  (e → i)
ocean   océano *(m.)*
of; (of course)   de (por
  supuesto)
office (post office)   oficina
  (f.) (oficina de correos)
offer   ofrecer
often   a menudo; frecuentemente
oil   aceite *(m.)*
old   viejo
older   mayor
Olympics   olimpiadas *(f.)*
on time   a su hora; a tiempo
once   una vez
once in a while   de vez en
  cuando
only   sólo; solamente; único
open   abrir
oppose   oponer
or   o
organize   organizar
otherwise   de lo contrario
ought   deber
out of tune   desafinadamente
outside   afuera
oven   horno *(m.)*
owe   deber
own   poseer; tener
owner   dueño *(m.)*

P

pack   empacar
package   paquete *(m.)*
page   página *(f.)*
pail   balde *(m.)*
(be) painful to   dolerle a
  alguien (o → ue)
paint   pintura *(f.)*; pintar
painter   pintor *(m.)*
painting   pintura *(f.)*; cuadro
  (m.)
pajamas   pijama *(m.)*
palace   palacio *(m.)*
pamphlet   folleto *(m.)*
pants   pantalones *(m.)*
paper   papel; trabajo *(m.)*
parade   desfile *(m.)*
pardon oneself   disculparse
park   parque *(m.)*; aparcar;
  estacionar
parking space   aparcamiento
  (m.)
part   parte *(f.)*
participant   participante
  (m./f.)
party   fiesta *(f.)*
pay (for)   pagar
peace   paz *(f.)*
pearl (little _____)   perla
  (f.) (perlita)
pen; fountain pen   bolígrafo
  (m.); pluma *(f.)*
people   gente; personas *(f.)*
performance (job)
  desempeño *(m.)*
permit   permitir
persecute   perseguir (e → i)
person   persona *(f.)*
persuade   persuadir; inducir;
  convencer
pet   animal doméstico *(m.)*
pharmacy   farmacia *(f.)*
photo   foto; fotografía *(f.)*
pick up   recoger
picture   pintura *(f.)*; cuadro
  (m.)
piece   pedazo *(m.)*
pig   cerdo *(m.)*
pillow   almohada *(f.)*
pistol   pistola *(f.)*
pity   lástima *(f.)*

place lugar *(m.);* poner
plan plan *(m.);* planear
planet planeta *(m.)*
plant planta *(f.);* sembrar (e → ie)
plate plato *(m.)*
play drama *(m.)*
play a game jugar (u → ue)
play (an instrument) tocar (un instrumento)
please por favor; placer
(be) pleasing to gustarle a alguien
plumber fontanero *(m.)*
pocket bolsillo *(m.)*
point (of view) punto *(m.)* (de vista)
point-blank categóricamente
police (force); policewoman policía *(f.)*
policeman policía *(m.)*
polite cortés; educado
politician político *(m.)*
politics política *(f.)*
pollution contaminación
pool piscina; alberca *(f.);* billar *(m.)*
(the) Pope Papa *(m.)*
possess poseer
potato patata; papa *(f.)*
pound libra *(f.)*
pour echar
poverty pobreza *(f.)*
practice practicar
pray rezar; rogar (o → ue)
prefer preferir (e → ie)
pregnant embarazada
prepare preparar
present regalo *(m.)*
pretend fingir
priest sacerdote *(m.)*
prison prisión; cárcel *(f.)*
prize premio *(m.)*
problem problema *(m.)*
produce producir
professional; pro profesional *(m.)*
program programa *(m.)*
progress progreso *(m.)*
prohibited prohibido
promise promesa *(f.);* prometer

pronunciation pronunciación *(f.)*
protect proteger
prove probar (o → ue)
provide proveer
provided that con tal que
pump bomba *(f.)*
pumpkin calabaza *(f.)*
purchase compra *(f.);* comprar
purse bolsa *(f.)*
pursue perseguir (e → i)
put (on oneself) poner(se)
put into meter en
put oneself through meterse en
puzzle enigma *(m.)*

q

quarterback lanzador *(m.)*
queen reina *(f.)*
question pregunta; cuestión *(f.)*
quick rápido
quickly rápidamente
(be) quiet callarse
quit (a job, etc.) renunciar a
quiz prueba *(f.)*

r

rabbit conejo *(m.)*
radio radio *(m./f.)*
rage rabia *(f.)*
rain lluvia *(f.);* llover
rain forest selva tropical *(f.)*
rainy lluvioso
raise aumento *(m.)*
raise (children, animals, etc.) criar
raisin pasa *(f.)*
razor navaja *(f.)*
reach (a goal) alcanzar (un objetivo)
read leer
ready listo
real verdadero
reality realidad *(f.)*

really realmente; verdaderamente
reception recepción *(f.)*
recibir to receive
recognize reconocer
record disco *(m.)*
redo rehacer
reduce reducir
refer referir (e → ie)
refrigerator refrigerador *(m.)*
regret sentir (e → i)
regulation reglamento *(m.)*
relax relajarse
rely (on) depender (de)
remain quedarse
remake rehacer
remember recordar
remove remover (o → ue); sustraer
remove (clothing) quitar(se)
repeat repetir (e → i)
report reportaje *(m.)*
(be) repugnant to disgustarle a alguien
request pedir (e → i)
require exigir
reread releer
resolve resolver (o → ue)
rest descansar
restaurant restaurante *(m.)*
return (an object) regresar; (de)volver (o → ue)
ribbon cinta *(f.)*
rice arroz *(m.)*
rich rico
richness riqueza *(f.)*
ride (a bike) montar (en bicicleta)
ridiculous ridículo; tonto
right derecho *(m.)*
right now ahora mismo; ahorita (Mexico)
(to be) right tener razón
(to the) right (a la) derecha
ring anillo *(m.);* sonar (o → ue)
ripe maduro
river río *(m.)*
road camino *(m.)*
roam vagar
rob robar
robbery robo *(m.)*

room   cuarto; espacio *(m.);* habitación *(f.)*
roommate   compañero *(m.)*
rot   pudrir
rotten   podrido
rub off   raer
ruby   rubí *(m.)*
rule   regla *(f.)*
run   correr; funcionar; manejar (máquina)
run away   huir
Russian   ruso *(m.)*

§

sad   triste
sadness   tristeza *(f.)*
salad   ensalada *(f.)*
sale   rebaja *(f.)*
salesman   vendedor *(m.)*
(the) same   (lo) mismo; igual(es)
sample   muestra *(f.);* probar (o → ue)
sand   arena *(f.)*
sausage   salchicha *(f.)*
save (money)   ahorrar
save (a life)   salvar
say   decir (e → i)
say goodbye (to someone)   despedirse (de alguien) (e → i)
scare   espantar
scarecrow   espantapájaros *(m.)*
scatter   esparcir
scene   escena *(f.)*
(high) school   escuela (secundaria) *(f.)*
scrape   raer
scratch   arañar
scrub   fregar (e → ie)
search   busca; búsqueda *(f.);* buscar
seated; sitting down   sentado
secret   secreto *(m.)*
see (oneself)   ver(se)
seed   semilla *(f.)*
seem   parecer
seize   coger
select   escoger

selfish   egoísta
sell   vender
sentence   frase *(f.)*
separately   por separado
servant   sirviente *(m.);* criada *(f.)*
serve   servir (e → i)
set (sun)   poner(se)
several   varios
shade; shadow   sombra *(f.)*
shame   lástima *(f.)*
shave (oneself)   afeitar(se)
shelf   estante *(m.)*
shoe   zapato *(m.)*
shop   ir de compras
shopping mall   centro comercial *(m.)*
shovel snow   quitar la nieve
show   mostrar (o → ue)
shower   ducha *(f.);* ducharse
shut   cerrar (e → ie)
sick; get sick   enfermo; enfermarse
sign   letrero *(m.)*
sign (one's name)   firmar
signature   firma *(f.)*
silly   tonto
silver   plata *(f.)*
sing   cantar
sister   hermana *(f.)*
sit down   sentarse (e → ie)
size   talla *(f.);* tamaño *(m.)*
skate   patín *(m.);* patinar
ski   esquiar
sleep   dormir (o → ue)
Sleeping Beauty   Bella Durmiente *(f.)*
(to be) sleepy   tener sueño
sleeve   manga *(f.)*
slim   delgado
slipper   zapatilla *(f.)*
slob   cochino *(m.)*
small   pequeño
smell   oler
smile   sonrisa *(f.);* sonreír (e → i)
smoke   humo *(m.);* fumar
snake   culebra *(f.)*
sneeze   estornudar
snow   nieve *(f.);* nevar
snowstorm   nevada *(f.);* tormenta de nieve *(f.)*

so   tan
so many   tantos
so much   tanto
so that   para que
soccer   fútbol *(m.)*
society   sociedad *(f.)*
socks   calcetines *(m.)*
sofa   sofá *(m.)*
soldier   soldado *(m.)*
solve   resolver (o → ue)
somebody; someone   alguien
something   algo
sometimes   a veces
song   canción *(f.)*
sound (like)   sonar (a) (o → ue)
soup   sopa *(f.)*
south   sur *(m.)*
South Pole   Polo Sur *(m.)*
space   espacio *(m.)*
speak   hablar
speech   discurso *(m.)*
spend (money)   gastar
spider   araña *(f.)*
spoil   pudrir; deslucir
spread   esparcir
spring   primavera *(f.)*
spoon   cuchara *(f.)*
spouse   esposo/a *(m./f.)*
spurt   surgir
spy   espía *(m./f.)*
square   cuadro *(m.)*
stair   peldaño *(m.)*
stairway   escalera *(f.)*
stamp (postage)   sello *(m.);* estampilla *(f.)*
stand out   destacar
stand up   levantarse
star (movie _____)   estrella (de cine) *(f.)*
start (a car)   arrancar (un coche)
state   estado *(m.)*
stay   estancia *(f.);* quedarse
steal   robar; hurtar
step   peldaño *(m.)*
stepsister   hermanastra *(f.)*
still   todavía
stomach   estómago *(m.)*
stop doing something   dejar de + inf.
store   tienda *(f.)*

storm   tormenta *(f.)*
story   cuento *(m.)*
street   calle *(f.)*
student   estudiante *(m./f.)*
studies   estudios *(m.)*
study   estudiar
stumble   tropezar (e → ie)
submerge   sumergir
substitute   sustituir
subtract   sustraer
suburbs   afueras *(f.)*
such (a thing)   tal (cosa)
suggest   sugerir (e → ie)
suit   traje *(m.)*
suitcase   maleta *(f.)*
suffer   sufrir
suffice   bastar
sugar   azúcar *(m.)*
suggest   sugerir (e → ie)
summer   verano *(m.)*
sun   sol *(m.)*
sunglasses   gafas de sol *(f.)*
superstitious (person)   supersticioso *(m.)*
support; sustain   sorportar
suppose   suponer
(be in) surplus   sobrarle a alguien
swallow   tragar
sweater   suéter *(m.)*
sweep   barrer
sweet   dulce
swim   nadar
swimming pool   piscina *(f.)*
symbolize   simbolizar

t

T-shirt   camiseta *(f.)*
tabloid   tabloide *(m.)*
take   tomar
take a picture   sacar una foto
take a walk   dar un paseo
take off (clothing)   quitarse (ropa)
take out   sacar
take time   durar; tardar (en)
tale   cuento *(m.)*
talk   hablar
tank (gas _____)   tanque (de gasolina) *(m.)*

tap dance   zapatear
tape   cinta *(f.)*
tarnish   deslucir
task   tarea *(f.)*
taste   gusto *(m.); probar (o → ue)*
taxes   impuestos *(m.)*
tea   té *(m.)*
teach   enseñar
teacher   maestro/a *(m./f.)*
tear   lágrima *(f.)*
teenager   adolescente *(m./f.)*
telegram   telegrama *(m.)*
telephone   teléfono *(m.)*
television   televisión *(f.); televisor (m.)*
tell   decir (e → i)
tennis   tenis *(m.)*
test   examen *(m.); probar (o → ue)*
thank-you letter   carta de agradecimiento
That's it!   ¡Ajá!
theater   teatro *(m.)*
then   entonces
theory   teoría *(f.)*
there is; there are   hay
thief   ladrón *(m.)*
thin   delgado; flaco
thing   cosa *(f.)*
think (about)   pensar (en) (e → ie)
thirst   sed *(f.)*
(to be) thirsty   tener sed
thousand   mil
thumb   pulgar *(m.)*
ticket (traffic)   boleto *(m.); multa (f.)*
time   tiempo *(m.); vez (f.)*
(for the first) time   por primera vez
(from) time to time   (de) vez en cuando
tin   estaño *(m.)*
tired   cansado
(to be) tired   tener sueño; estar cansado
to the movies   al cine
toast   tostada *(f.); tostar (o → ue)*
today   hoy

together   juntos
tolerate   tolerar
tomato   tomate *(m.)*
tomorrow   mañana
tonight   esta noche
tooth   diente *(m.)*
toothpaste   pasta de dientes *(f.)*
touch   tocar
towel   toalla *(f.)*
trace   trazar
tragic   trágico
train   tren *(m.); entrenar*
translate   traducir
trash   basura *(f.)*
travel   viajar
travel agent   agente de viajes *(m./f.)*
treasure   tesoro *(m.)*
tree   árbol *(m.)*
tremble   temblar (e → ie)
trial   juicio *(m.)*
trick   engañar
trip   viaje *(m.)*
trombone   trombón *(m.)*
truck   camión *(m.)*
true   verdadero; cierto
truth   verdad *(f.)*
trunk   maletero; baúl *(m.)*
try (on clothing)   probar (se) (o → ue)
try to do something   tratar de + inf.; intentar
Tuesday   martes *(m.)*
turkey   pavo *(m.)*
turn   girar
turn off   apagar
twiddle one's thumbs   voltear los pulgares

u

ultimate   último
under; underneath   debajo (de)
understand   comprender; entender (e → ie)
undo   deshacer
undress (oneself)   desvestir(se) (e → i)
uniform   uniforme *(m.)*
unique   único

unite unir
United States Estados Unidos *(m.)*
university universidad *(f.)*
unless a menos que
until hasta

V

vacation vacaciones *(f.)*
valentine tarjeta *(f.)* para el Día de los Enamorados
vampire vampiro *(m.)*
van camioneta *(f.)*
variety variedad *(f.)*
various varios
vase vaso *(m.)*
vehicle vehículo *(m.)*
very muy
vicinity vecindad *(f.)*
view vista *(f.)*
vitamin vitamina *(f.)*
voice voz *(f.)*
volleyball voleibol *(m.)*
vomit vómito *(m.); vomitar
vote votar

W

wait (for) esperar
waiter mesero *(m.)*
wake up despertarse (e → ie)
walk andar; caminar
walk away alejarse
wall (exterior) muro *(m.)*
wall (interior) pared *(f.)*
wander vagar
want querer (e → ie)

war guerra *(f.)*
(to be) warm tener calor
warmth calor *(m.)*
warn advertir (e → ie)
warrior guerrero *(m.)*
wash (oneself) lavar(se)
wash dishes fregar (e → ie)
waste (time) malgastar (perder [e → ie] el tiempo)
watch reloj *(m.); mirar
watch over vigilar
water agua *(f.); regar (e → ie)
wealth riqueza *(f.)*
wear llevar; usar
wedding boda *(f.)*
week semana *(f.)*
weekend fin de semana *(m.)*
weigh pesar
weight peso *(m.)*
well bien; pues
wet mojado
What? ¿Qué?
wheel rueda *(f.)*
when; When? cuando; ¿Cuándo?
where?; to _____? ¿Dónde?; ¿Adónde?
Which? ¿Cuál(es)?
while mientras (que)
whitewash encubrir
who; Who? quien; ¿Quién?
Why? ¿Por qué?
wife esposa *(f.)*
win ganar
wind viento *(m.)*
wind (a watch) dar cuerda a
window ventana *(f.)*
wine vino *(m.)*

winner ganador *(m.)*
winter invierno *(m.)*
wish deseo *(m.); desear; querer (e → ie)
witch bruja *(f.)*
with con
with me; with you conmigo; contigo
without sin
wizard mago *(m.)*
wolf lobo *(m.)*
woman mujer *(f.)*
wonderful maravilloso
wood madera *(f.)*
woods bosque *(m.)*
word palabra *(f.)*
work trabajo; empleo *(m.);* trabajar; funcionar
world mundo *(m.)*
World Series Serie Mundial *(f.)*
worry (about) preocuparse (por)
(be) worth valer
wrap (up) envolver (o → ue)
wretched malísimo
wrist muñeca *(f.)*
write escribir
(to be) wrong no tener razón

Y

year año *(m.)*
yellow amarillo
yesterday ayer
yet todavía
young joven
younger menor

Answer Key

Unit 1: Conjugation of Regular Verbs

ejercicio 1-1-1

1. Yo canto.
2. Tú cantas.
3. Él canta.
4. Nosotros cantamos.
5. Ellos cantan.
6. Yo pago.
7. Yo pago la casa.
8. Tú pagas.
9. Ellas pagan.
10. Ella estudia.
11. Él estudia.
12. Yo estudio.
13. Estudiamos.
14. Tú andas (caminas).
15. Nosotros andamos (caminamos).
16. Yo trabajo.
17. Él trabaja.
18. Ellos trabajan.
19. Trabajamos.
20. Él baila.
21. Yo amo.
22. Tú amas.
23. Ella ama.
24. Nosotros amamos.
25. Ellos aman.
26. Yo practico.
27. Él practica.
28. Ellos entran.
29. Yo miro la casa.
30. Yo miro el jardín.
31. Ellos miran el coche.
32. Ella escucha.
33. Ellas escuchan.
34. Yo escucho.
35. Él compra el coche.
36. Yo compro el perro.
37. Tú compras la casa.
38. Yo hablo con Miguel.
39. Ella paga los libros.
40. Estudiamos español.

ejercicio 1-1-2

1. Yo aprendo.
2. Yo bebo.
3. Él bebe.
4. Tú comes.
5. Comemos.
6. Yo comprendo.
7. Yo no comprendo.
8. Ellos comprenden.
9. Tú comprendes.
10. Tú no comprendes.
11. Yo corro.
12. Tú corres.
13. Ella corre.
14. Ellos no corren.
15. Corremos.
16. Yo creo.
17. Yo no creo.
18. Él cree.
19. Debemos.
20. Yo leo.
21. Tú lees.
22. Tú no lees.
23. Él lee.
24. Ella lee.
25. Leemos.
26. Cometo un error.
27. Yo meto.
28. Tú metes.
29. Él mete.
30. Metemos.
31. Ellos meten.
32. Ellas meten.
33. Rompemos.
34. Ellas rompen.
35. Yo rompo.
36. Tú vendes.
37. Vendemos.
38. Yo no vendo.
39. Ella no vende.
40. Aprendemos.

ejercicio 1-1-3

1. Abro las ventanas.
2. Ella sufre mucho.
3. Vivimos en los Estados Unidos.
4. Escribes muchas cartas.
5. El niño admite todo.
6. Juan sube la escalera.
7. Descubro un gato en la casa.
8. Muchas personas sufren.
9. Decidimos.
10. Los unicornios no existen.
11. Ustedes escriben bien.
12. María describe las arañas.
13. Escribimos muchas cartas.
14. Ellos no asisten a la escuela.
15. María y Juan discuten el libro.
16. Unes las dos partes.
17. Los chicos describen todo.
18. Cubrís las mesas.
19. Juan no asiste a la reunión.
20. Recibo regalos para mi cumpleaños.

raducción   1-2-4

Cuando estoy feliz yo canto, pero hoy estoy de mal humor. Mi gato está enfermo, mi televisor está roto, y esta mañana mi café está terrible. Hoy es lunes. Trabajo en una librería. Dos personas están en la tienda ahora, un hombre y una mujer. El hombre es alto y busca libros que no existen. ¿Por qué está aquí? La mujer es baja y muy delgada. Ella compra el periódico aquí cada día. A veces ella lee cinco o seis revistas antes. Siempre lleva gafas del sol y un sombrero grande. Ella es muy misteriosa. Creo que ella es espía. ¿Quién es y por qué está aquí?

Unit 3: *Hay*

ejercicio   1-3-1

1. Hay un perro en el carro.
2. Hay tres tenedores en la mesa.
3. ¿Hay un baño en este edificio?
4. ¿Hay sillas en la sala?
5. No hay agua en el vaso.

Unit 4: *Tener*

ejercicio   1-4-1

1. Tengo diez dólares.
2. Tienes mis libros.
3. Ella tiene un diamante.
4. Él tiene los cuchillos y las cucharas.
5. Tenemos una nueva casa.
6. Tenéis muchos amigos.
7. Ellos tienen muchos primos.
8. No tengo el dinero.
9. ¿Quién tiene mis llaves?
10. ¿Por qué tienes un pájaro en tu carro?

ejercicio   1-4-2

1. Tengo _____ años.
2. Tienes quince años.
3. María tiene cuarenta años.
4. Mi coche tiene cuatro años.
5. ¿Cuántos años tienes?

6. ¿Cuántos años tiene el Presidente?
7. Esos chicos tienen quince años.
8. Su gato tiene ocho años.
9. Nuestra casa tiene cien años.
10. ¿Cuántos años tienen ellos?

ejercicio   **1-4-3**

1. Tengo hambre.
2. Tienes sed.
3. Él tiene frío.
4. Tenemos suerte.
5. Ellos tienen prisa.

6. Tengo mucha hambre.
7. Tienes mucha sed.
8. Él tiene calor.
9. Tengo mucha suerte.
10. Tenéis mucha prisa.

ejercicio   **1-4-4**

1. Tengo mucha hambre.
2. Él tiene sed.
3. Ella tiene mucha suerte.
4. Tengo frío.
5. Él no tiene razón.
6. Ella tiene mucha prisa.
7. Tengo mucho calor.
8. Tengo mucho miedo.
9. Tengo razón.
10. Ellas tienen sueño.

ejercicio   **1-4-5**

1. Tengo que leer este libro.
2. Tienes que mirar este programa.
3. Fred y Ginger tienen que bailar.
4. Él tiene que abrir la tienda cada mañana.
5. Tenemos que decidir ahora.
6. Tenéis que escribir cartas de agradecimiento.
7. Ellos tienen que vender su coche.
8. No tengo que comer esta sopa.
9. Tienes que tomar la medicina.
10. Tenemos que comprar vino para la fiesta.

¡Te toca a ti!
Make sure all statements start with "Tengo que."

traducción   **1-4-6**

Mi nombre es Paco y hoy es mi cumpleaños. Tengo siete años. Todos mis amigos están en mi casa porque cada año tengo una gran fiesta. Ellos tienen hambre y sed. Tengo hambre y sed, también. Tenemos torta, helado y leche. Pero primero ellos tienen que cantar "Feliz Cumpleaños". Después comemos. Luego abro mis regalos porque hay muchos regalos para mí.

Unit 5: The Personal *a*

The following sentences require the personal **a:** 1; 3; 5; 8; 10.

1. Romeo ama a Julieta.
2. Veo a Juan.
3. No creo a María.
4. Escuchamos a Jorge.
5. Buscas a Andrés.
6. Ellos descubren a un ladrón en la casa.
7. ¿A quién amas?
8. ¿Ves a la chica?
9. ¿Crees al Presidente?
10. Esperamos a Silvia.
11. Miro a Felipe y a Teresa.
12. Timoteo ama a Lassie.

Unit 6: A Dozen Highly Useful Irregular Verbs

ejercicio   1-6-1

1. Doy.	7. Hago.	13. Pones.	19. Salgo.
2. Digo.	8. Veis.	14. Pongo.	20. Dices.
3. Ellos oyen.	9. Damos.	15. Vemos.	21. Oigo.
4. Él oye.	10. Ella va.	16. Veo.	22. Él quiere.
5. Haces.	11. Ellos vienen.	17. Ellos quieren.	23. Voy.
6. Juego.	12. Él dice.	18. Juegas.	24. Ellos juegan.

¡Te toca a ti!
1. Quiero . . .
2. Normalmente, lo pongo . . .
3. Típicamente, vengo a la escuela a las . . .
4. Desde la ventana de mi sala, veo . . .
5. Este año le doy . . .
6. Cuando estoy enojado(a), digo . . .
7. Más o menos, voy al cine . . .
8. Usualmente, voy a . . .
9. Generalmente, salgo de casa a las . . .
10. Cuando alguien me dice una mentira . . .

ejercicio   1-6-2

1. Puedo . . .
2. No puedo . . .
3. Quiero . . .
4. Debo . . .
5. No debo . . .
6. Puede cantar.
7. Puede tocar el violín.
8. Puede jugar al béisbol.
9. Puede cocinar.
10. Puede escribir.
11. Puede nadar.
12. Puede bailar.

ejercicio   1-6-3

1. Hace . . .
2. Hace . . . en diciembre.
3. Hace mucho frío; hace viento; hace mal tiempo.
4. Hace calor; hace sol; hace buen tiempo.
5. Hace . . .

ejercicio   1-6-4

1. Babe Ruth juega al béisbol
2. Wayne Gretzky juega al hockey.
3. Minnesota Fats juega al billar.
4. Pelé juega al fútbol.
5. Bobby Fischer y Boris Spasky juegan al ajedrez.
6. Chris Evert y Billie Jean King juegan al tenis.
7. Arnold Palmer juega al golf.
8. Kareem Abdul Jabar y Larry Bird juegan al baloncesto.
9. Joe Namath juega al fútbol americano.
10. Los niños juegan a las damas en una tabla roja y negra.

ejercicio   1-6-5

1. Voy a practicar.
2. Vas a trabajar.
3. Ella va a mirar la televisión.
4. Vamos a vender el coche.
5. Ellos van a beber la leche.
6. No voy a hacer nada.
7. ¿Qué vas a hacer?
8. ¿Vas a estudiar o mirar la televisión?
9. No vamos a comprar caramelos.
10. ¿Cuándo vais a jugar?

¡Te toca a ti!
Make sure that all responses start with "Voy a."

traducción   1-6-6

Mañana es el cumpleaños de mi mejor amigo. Voy a tener una fiesta para él. Puedo invitar a muchas personas porque mi casa es grande. Tengo muchas fiestas y siempre hago lo mismo. Voy a la panadería y compro una torta. Le digo al panadero que quiero muchas flores y el nombre de mi amigo en la torta. Pongo la torta en la mesa en el comedor donde todos pueden verla—oigo que un centro de mesa dramático es importante. Los invitados vienen a mi casa a las siete. Hablamos y comemos y bebemos—a veces bailamos o jugamos a un juego—y entonces le damos regalos al invitado de honor. Va a ser una fiesta maravillosa.

Unit 7: *Saber* and *Conocer*

ejercicio   1-7-1

1. Sé tu nombre.
2. Sabes la respuesta.
3. Ella sabe dónde vives.
4. No sabemos por qué él está enojado.
5. ¿Sabes quién tiene el dinero?
6. Ellos no saben nada de mí.
7. ¿Sabe él dónde está María?
8. Sabéis mucho.

ejercicio   1-7-2

1. Sé que Juan es alto.
2. Sabes que tengo hambre.
3. Ella sabe que tienes sed.
4. ¿Sabes que tengo veintinueve años?
5. Sabemos que él tiene prisa.
6. Ellos no saben que estoy aquí.
7. ¿Sabéis que hay culebras en el jardín?
8. Él no sabe que estás en el jardín.

ejercicio   1-7-3

1. Sé cantar.
2. Sabes hablar español.
3. Ella sabe cocinar muy bien.
4. Él no sabe hablar francés.
5. Fred y Ginger saben bailar.
6. Sabéis tocar el piano.
7. ¿Sabes esquiar?
8. ¿Quién sabe abrir esta puerta?

traducción | **I-7-4**

Juan es mi mecánico. Él sabe mucho de carros y estoy feliz porque yo no sé nada de carros. No, no es completamente cierto. Yo sé dónde está el tanque de gasolina y sé llenarlo. Sé conducir y sé que no puedo aparcar enfrente de una estación de bomberos. Juan sabe que él tiene que saber de carros y de la gente, porque muchas personas saben muy poco de carros.

ejercicio | **I-7-5**

1. Conozco a Antonia.
2. Conoces a Isabel.
3. Él conoce a su suegro.
4. Te conocemos.
5. Conocéis a Juan.
6. Ella conoce a Juana y a Paco.
7. ¿Conoces a mis gatos Fifi y Fufu?
8. Él no me conoce.

9. La conozco.
10. La conoces.
11. Él lo conoce.
12. Nos conoces.
13. Lo conocéis.
14. Ella los conoce.
15. Sí, los conozco.
16. Nadie me conoce aquí.

ejercicio | **I-7-6**

1. Yo (no) conozco Chicago.
2. El Presidente conoce bien Washington, D.C.
3. El alcalde conoce bien la ciudad.
4. Dorotea conoce Oz.
5. Ellos no conocen París.
6. ¿Conoces Irlanda?
7. Jorge conoce la selva.
8. El pájaro conoce su árbol.

ejercicio | **I-7-7**

1. El médico conoce bien el cuerpo.
2. El sacerdote conoce bien la Biblia.
3. El peluquero conoce el pelo de sus clientes.
4. Bo conoce el baloncesto.
5. La manicurista conoce las uñas de sus clientes.
6. El cocinero conoce la comida de México.
7. El arquitecto conoce la arquitectura de Chicago.
8. El granjero conoce la tierra.

traducción | **I-7-8**

No sé por qué, pero creo que te conozco. ¿Conoces a mi primo, Enrique? ¿Sí? Pues, entonces tú sabes que su esposa sabe hablar ruso—pero no puede leerlo. Ella tiene muchas fiestas maravillosas porque conoce a todo el mundo y porque sabe cocinar como una cocinera profesional. Yo sé que quieres conocerla. Voy a arreglar la presentación.

Unit 8: Stem-Changing Verbs

ejercicio   1-8-1

1. Yo almuerzo.
2. Tú almuerzas.
3. El perro muerde.
4. Aprobamos.
5. Rogáis.
6. Ellos cuentan el dinero.
7. Muestras la casa.
8. Ella duerme.
9. Resolvemos el problema.
10. Ella envuelve el regalo.
11. Cuelgo el teléfono.
12. Devuelves la camisa.
13. Él muere.
14. El teléfono suena.
15. Encuentro el dinero.
16. Volvemos.
17. Dumbo vuela.
18. Juana tuesta el pan.
19. Rogamos por la paz.
20. Él sueña con un tigre.
21. No recuerdo nada.
22. El libro cuesta diez dólares.
23. Mueves las sillas.
24. Pruebo el café.

ejercicio   1-8-2

1. Cierro la puerta.
2. Aciertas.
3. Él friega los platos.
4. Te advertimos.
5. Ellos niegan todo.
6. Él lo siente mucho.
7. Empezáis.
8. Ella me defiende.
9. Hierves el agua.
10. Ellos me mienten.
11. Consentís.
12. Ella sugiere.
13. Temblamos.
14. Prefiero agua.
15. Él quiere un perro.
16. ¿Entiendes?
17. Él pierde la revista.
18. Ella tropieza con el sofá.
19. Ellos confiesan.
20. El programa comienza.
21. Pienso en la guerra.
22. Enciendes la vela.
23. Convertimos el dinero a dólares.
24. Refiero el caso al profesor.

ejercicio   1-8-3

1. Compito.
2. Corriges el examen.
3. Él pide ayuda.
4. Ella ríe mucho.
5. Él consigue trabajo.
6. Elegimos al ganador.
7. Freímos las papas.
8. Decís la verdad.
9. Despides al empleado.
10. Pedimos más dinero.
11. Ella gime.
12. Él impide el progreso.
13. Ellos nos dicen la verdad.
14. Te sigo.
15. Nos servís.
16. ¿Quién dice esto?
17. Ella mide cinco pies.
18. Ellos maldicen.
19. Él colige la verdad de los hechos.
20. Compites contra él.
21. Ellos ríen mucho porque están contentos.
22. Repiten la lección.
23. El sacerdote te bendice.
24. ¿Qué pides?

traducción   1-8-4

Hola. Soy Osvaldo. Vendo casas. Es difícil, pero alguien tiene que hacerlo. Las casas cuestan mucho estos días y por eso usualmente le muestro a cada cliente más o menos veinte casas. A menudo volvemos a la primera casa y el cliente me dice que quiere comprarla. Tiemblo con rabia (a veces maldigo o gimo) porque pienso en todo el tiempo que pierdo, pero entonces pienso en mi comisión y entiendo por qué vendo casas. No te miento cuando te confieso que quiero vender casas para siempre.

Unit 9: Noteworthy Infinitives

1. conozco   2. pertenezco   3. reconozco   4. ofrezco   5. merezco   6. parece   7. pertenecen   8. nacen   9. crece   10. aparece

Possible answers:

1. Conduzco un coche automático (de marchas).
2. Sí, produzco mucho trabajo.
3. Sí, traduzco muchas frases en este libro.
4. El panadero produce pan.
5. Sí, introduzco una moneda en el teléfono público.
6. No, normalmente los políticos no reducen los impuestos.

1. Esparzo semillas en el jardín.
2. Venzo al enemigo.
3. Zurzo los calcetines.
4. Ejerzo mucha energía en mis estudios.
5. Los guerreros vencen a sus enemigos.

ejercicio I-9-4

1. Protejo a mi familia.
2. Corrijo mis problemas.
3. El maestro corrige muchos trabajos.
4. A veces finjo estar feliz cuando estoy triste.
5. Escojo a mis amigos con mucho cuidado.
6. Cada cuatro años elegimos a un nuevo líder.
7. Recojo mis calcetines del suelo.
8. Cojo un taxi para el aeropuerto.
9. Exijo mucho de mis empleados.
10. Sumerjo el suéter en agua fría.

ejercicio I-9-5

1. traigo   2. rae   3. atrae   4. contrae   5. sustraen

ejercicio I-9-6

1. construyo   2. contribuyo   3. fluye   4. huye   5. influyen   6. destruye   7. concluyes   8. constituye   9. incluye   10. contribuyen

 **1-9-7**

1. distingo 2. sigue 3. extingo 4. consigo 5. irguen 6. persiguen 7. consigue 8. siguen 9. distinguen
10. sigo 11. consiguen 12. extinguen

Unit 10: Reflexive Verbs

 **1-10-1**

1. Me acuesto.
2. Te lavas el pelo.
3. Él se afeita cada mañana.
4. Ella se afeita las piernas.
5. Os despertáis.
6. Ellos se sientan.
7. Ella se va.
8. Me llamo Rex.

9. Te duchas.
10. Nos vestimos.
11. Os dormís.
12. Ella se baña.
13. Me preocupo por el futuro.
14. Uds. se despiertan.
15. Me desnudo en la noche.
16. Te llamas Alicia.

17. Se quita la camisa.
18. Uds. se ven en el espejo.
19. Me siento enfermo/a.
20. Te peinas (el pelo).
21. Nos cepillamos los dientes.
22. Ella se duerme.
23. ¿Te duchas?
24. Se llama Martín.

traducción **1-10-2**

Cada noche Marta se acuesta a las once y media. Se duerme rápidamente y nunca tiene pesadillas. Cada mañana se despierta a las seis y media, pero no se levanta hasta las siete. Ella entra en el baño donde se cepilla los dientes y se mira en el espejo. Algunos días se baña, pero usualmente se ducha porque es más rápido y porque Marta se siente más limpia. Después de la ducha (o del baño), Marta se peina y se seca el pelo. Se viste, anda a la cocina donde se sienta, toma el café y lee el periódico por quince minutos. Entonces se va al trabajo.

Unit 11: *Gustar* et al.

 **1-11-1**

1. Me importa la verdad.
2. No me gustan las arañas.
3. Me duele el estómago.
4. Me sobran los libros.
5. A ella le gusta el otoño.
6. Me parece ridículo.
7. ¡Me encanta tu vestido!
8. Nos sobran diez dólares.

9. Me disgusta tu actitud.
10. Me encanta el helado.
11. Te falta un botón.
12. Nos fascinan estas fotos.
13. A ellos les interesa la película.
14. ¿Qué te importa?
15. Me disgustan sus modales.
16. Me parece egoísta.

¡Te toca a ti!

1. Me gusta más . . .
2. Me encanta . . .
3. Me interesan . . .
4. Me interesa mucho . . .
5. Sí, (No) me falta dinero . . .
6. Me molesta mucho . . .
7. Me encanta . . .
8. Me fascina(n) . . .

traducción   **I-11-2**

Hoy es el cuatro de julio. Esta noche vamos a tener una fiesta y mañana por la mañana voy a dormir hasta muy tarde porque no tengo que trabajar. ¡Me encanta el verano! Me parece que junio, julio y agosto son los mejores meses del año. No tengo que ir a la escuela. Me acuesto tarde y me levanto tarde. Yo como cuando tengo hambre; bebo cuando tengo sed; y me duermo cuando tengo sueño. Nada me molesta en el verano. En cambio, me bastan tres meses de sol y calor, y para el primero de septiembre estoy listo/a para el otoño.

Unit 12: The Present Progressive

ejercicio   **I-12-1**

1. Estoy comprando un regalo para Juan.
2. Estás mirando la televisión.
3. Él está tocando el piano.
4. Estamos comiendo pizza y bebiendo limonada.
5. Estáis recibiendo muchos regalos.
6. Uds. están cubriendo los muebles.
7. Estamos almorzando.
8. Estoy pensando en mi mejor amigo/a.
9. ¿Qué estás haciendo?
10. ¿Qué está comiendo ella?

ejercicio   **I-12-2**

1. El río está fluyendo al sur.
2. El cliente no está creyendo al vendedor de coches.
3. No estamos leyendo nada.
4. El Presidente está influyendo a la gente.
5. El odio está destruyendo nuestra sociedad.
6. Romeo está huyendo con Julieta.
7. Ella no está oyendo nada en el sótano.
8. ¿Qué estás leyendo?
9. ¿Quién está trayendo vino a la fiesta?
10. ¿Por qué están construyendo una casa en las afueras?

ejercicio   1-12-3

1. durmiendo 2. mintiendo 3. hirviendo 4. sirviendo 5. riendo 6. compitiendo 7. diciendo 8. muriendo 9. siguiendo 10. pidiendo

ejercicio   1-12-4

1. Estoy estudiándolo.
2. Estás cantándonosla.
3. Él está escribiéndome una carta.
4. ¿Estás escribiéndoles?
5. ¿Por qué están Uds. diciéndome esto?
6. ¿Por qué estás diciéndomelo?
7. Ellos están sentándose.
8. Estamos leyéndolo.
9. Ella está mintiéndome.
10. ¿Qué estás dándome?
11. Ellos están siguiéndonos.
12. ¿Qué está leyéndote ella?

Part II   The Past, Future, and Conditional Tenses

Unit 1: The Preterite Tense

ejercicio   II-1-1

1. Yo compré una camisa ayer.
2. Tú estudiaste anoche.
3. Ella trabajó por dos horas.
4. Nosotros lavamos los platos.
5. Ellos cantaron cinco canciones.
6. Yo corrí a la esquina.
7. Escribiste una carta
8. Ella abrió la puerta.
9. No abrimos esas ventanas.
10. Ellos vendieron el carro.
11. Bailamos el tango anoche.
12. Ellos hablaron con el dueño.
13. Me duché esta mañana.
14. Te lavaste el pelo.
15. Ellos se acostaron a las once y media.

¡Te toca a ti! Possible answers:
1. Sí, hablé por teléfono anoche.
2. Compré la camisa en el centro comercial.
3. Comí paella.
4. Recibí flores y colonia.
5. No, hoy no escuché la radio.
6. Sí, tomé café ayer por la mañana.
7. No, no bailé el fin de semana pasado.
8. Sí, estudié español el año pasado.

ejercicio   II-1-2

1. Practiqué el piano por una hora.
2. Llegué a las dos.
3. Organicé la fiesta.
4. Empecé a bailar en la mesa.
5. Toqué la guitarra por dos horas en la recepción.
6. Jugué al tenis con el jugador profesional.
7. Saqué veinte fotos de mi gato.
8. Autoricé la compra.
9. Clasifiqué la información.
10. Me tropecé con el peldaño de tu casa.
11. Aparqué el carro en un espacio prohibido.
12. Nunca destaqué en inglés por mi pronunciación.
13. Tragué la medicina sin pensar.
14. Pagué la cuenta del gas.
15. Regué las plantas de mi amiga Lola.

ejercicio   II-1-3

1. Yo anduve a la tienda.
2. Él vino a mi fiesta.
3. Anoche no pude dormir.
4. Ellos tuvieron un accidente el martes pasado.
5. Hicimos las camas esta mañana.
6. ¿Cuándo supiste la respuesta?
7. Estuvisteis aquí (por) no más de diez minutos.
8. Puse la ropa en el armario.
9. ¿Qué hiciste anoche?
10. Ellos tuvieron que trabajar (por) diez horas ayer.
11. Me puse los zapatos.
12. Estuvimos allí (por) media hora.
13. ¿Quién hizo estas invitaciones?
14. Ella no vino a la reunión porque tuvo un accidente.
15. Estuve en la tienda (por) veinte minutos y entonces vine aquí.

¡Te toca a ti!
Make sure that all verbs are in the preterite, first person singular.

ejercicio   II-1-4

1. Yo fui al partido.
2. Yo fui presidente/a del club (por) un año.
3. Él fue a la tienda para comprar huevos.
4. ¿Por qué te fuiste?
5. Ellos no fueron ayer porque fueron la semana pasada.
6. No fuimos a la boda.
7. ¿Fuisteis a la escuela hoy?
8. ¿Quién fue el gran ganador ayer?
9. La fiesta fue terrible.

10. La reunión fue bien.
11. Anita y Pepe fueron novios por dos años pero nunca fueron a Venecia.
12. Él fue mi mejor amigo por diez años.
13. Fuimos por separado a la misma tienda.
14. ¿Adónde fueron Uds. anoche?
15. ¿Cómo fue la fiesta? ¡Fue un desastre!

ejercicio   II-1-5

1. Les dije a los niños mi nombre.
2. Me dijiste una mentira.
3. Él trajo vino a la fiesta.
4. Él dijo que habló con Carlos la semana pasada.
5. Dijimos que no comimos las galletas.
6. La televisión me distrajo.
7. ¿Qué dijeron Uds. a María?
8. ¿Qué le dijiste?
9. Sus modales me atrajeron.
10. ¿Qué dijo él cuando le dijiste que escribiste la carta?
11. No les dije nada.
12. ¿Qué nos trajiste?
13. Ellos no me dijeron la verdad.
14. ¿Te dijo lo que me dijo ayer?
15. El azúcar atrajo a las moscas.

ejercicio   II-1-6

1. Le di a Juan un paquete ayer.
2. Vi a Juan ayer.
3. Ella me dio un libro.
4. Ella nos vio en el cine.
5. ¿Qué le diste para su cumpleaños?
6. ¿Qué película visteis anoche?
7. Cuando me vieron, me dieron el dinero.
8. Ustedes no nos dieron nada.
9. ¿Viste el gato que Miguel me dio?
10. No vi el regalo que nos dieron.

traducción   II-1-7

Fui a Puerto Rico el enero pasado. ¡Fue maravilloso! Una amiga mía es agente de viajes y cuando me ofreció la oportunidad de ir al Caribe para una semana de sol y diversión—por muy poco dinero—le dije, "¿Cuándo vamos?" El día que salimos, nevó seis pulgadas aquí. Cuando llegamos a San Juan, el sol, el calor y la arena nos saludaron. Tomamos un taxi a nuestro hotel, saqué mi traje de baño de la maleta y fuimos a la playa. Al día siguiente fuimos a El Yunque, la selva tropical, donde anduvimos por horas y vimos muchos pájaros y árboles hermosos. No pude creerlo—¡fue tan hermoso! Al día siguiente fuimos a la Playa Luquillo y nadamos y leímos y nos relajamos. Hicimos esto cada día hasta que—¡ay!—tuvimos que volver a la realidad.

ejercicio   II-1-8

1. Ella durmió (por) diez horas.
2. Ellos me mintieron.
3. Él pidió más café.
4. Las cucarachas murieron.
5. Nuestro abogado nos advirtió del peligro.
6. En aquel momento ella prefirió no decir nada.
7. ¿Te advirtieron de tus derechos?
8. Dorothy siguió el camino amarillo de ladrillos.
9. Ellos repitieron la pregunta dos veces.
10. Él pidió un aumento.

ejercicio   II-1-9

1. Juan no me oyó.
2. Ellos leyeron mi libro dos veces.
3. Los árboles se cayeron durante la tormenta.
4. Romeo y Julieta huyeron.
5. Los abastecedores no proveyeron suficiente pan.
6. Los ladrones destruyeron nuestra casa.
7. ¿Leíste mi periódico?
8. Ellos contribuyeron ciento cincuenta dólares el año pasado.
9. El plato huyó con la cuchara.
10. Humpty Dumpty se cayó.
11. Las lágrimas fluyeron de mis ojos.
12. La rama se cayó del árbol.
13. Huyeron de la escena del crimen.
14. Construyeron una casa enorme.
15. ¿Por qué no nos incluyó?

respuestas   II-1-10

1. Produje una película el año pasado.
2. Tradujiste bien el documento.
3. Condujimos al teatro.
4. El mago produjo un conejo del sombrero.
5. Condujisteis veinte millas.
6. Traduje esta frase del inglés al español.
7. Condujimos a los chicos a la cafetería.
8. Nos condujeron a la boda.
9. ¿Cuántas páginas tradujiste?
10. ¿Hasta dónde condujiste?
11. Deduje la respuesta.
12. El Presidente no redujo los impuestos el año pasado.

 **traducción** **II-1-11**

H. L. Mencken fue un gran escritor. Nació en Baltimore en 1880, donde vivió toda su vida, y murió en 1956. Escribió muchos ensayos sobre la política y las cuestiones sociales, pero su interés principal, creo, fue el lenguaje, en particular, el inglés de los Estados Unidos. Uno de sus libros más conocidos es *El idioma americano,* en el cual Mencken discutió la riqueza de los Estados Unidos y cómo muchos otros idiomas influyeron en este idioma. También produjo una serie de autobiografías y diarios. Leyó toda clase de literatura y poseyó un estricto credo personal. Creyó que una persona debe trabajar duro, jugar duro y, sobre todo, pensar.

ejercicio **II-1-12**

1. Conocí a Felipe hace un año y medio.
2. Él no pudo ver mi punto de vista.
3. Ellos no lo supieron hasta ayer.
4. Mi hermana tuvo un niño (una niña) el mayo pasado.
5. ¿Por qué no quisisteis salir?
6. Él sintió ganar el dinero.
7. Ella quiso salir pero no pudo encontrar sus llaves.
8. Pude pagar las cuentas a tiempo este mes.
9. Nos conocimos en un ascensor.
10. Cuando supe que Juana pudo falsificar mi firma, no pude pensar.

Unit 2: The Imperfect Tense

ejercicio **II-2-1**

1. Yo estudiaba con Juan.
2. Él trabajaba en un banco.
3. Vivíamos en un apartamento.
4. Ellos escribían notas en clase.
5. Leías muchas revistas.
6. Abríais las ventanas en enero.
7. Yo hacía la cama cada mañana.
8. Mickey Mantle jugaba al béisbol para los Yankees.
9. Ellos nos llamaban cada noche.
10. ¿Dónde trabajabas?
11. ¿Dónde vivían ustedes?
12. Él nadaba en nuestra piscina.
13. Marcos era presidente de nuestro club.
14. Yo iba a Florida cada invierno.
15. Invitábamos a todos a nuestras fiestas.

ejercicio   II-2-2

1. Presidente   2. arquitecto   3. payaso   4. antropóloga   5. policías   6. escritor   7. pianista   8. filósofo   9. pintor
10. psiquiatra   11. bailarines   12. explorador

ejercicio   II-2-3

1. Mi padre era granjero.
2. María tenía un corderito.
3. Llevábamos uniformes a la escuela.
4. Yo estaba avergonzado/a.
5. La tienda no tenía la camisa que quería.
6. Las ventanas estaban abiertas pero la puerta estaba cerrada.
7. Susana estaba embarazada.
8. Llevabais sombreros ridículos.
9. Jorge era alto y guapo.
10. El gato estaba en el desván.
11. Mi pluma (bolígrafo) no funcionaba.
12. ¿Dónde estaba el dinero?
13. Yo tenía muchos amigos en el campamento.
14. El gato era blanco y negro.
15. El monstruo tenía dos cabezas.

ejercicio   II-2-4

1. Yo lavaba los platos.
2. Nadie escuchaba mientras el político hablaba.
3. Él andaba y yo corría.
4. Ellos escuchaban la radio mientras estudiaban.
5. Intentábamos dormir pero el bebé lloraba.
6. ¿Por qué mirabas la televisión mientras yo estudiaba?
7. Los niños jugaban en el jardín.
8. Vivíamos en una casa de cristal.
9. Vendíais camisetas en la esquina.
10. Yo sufría de un resfriado.
11. Las ranas saltaban cerca del lago.
12. Me duchaba mientras ellos se desayunaban.
13. Carmen preparaba la cena.
14. Pensábamos mucho en ti.
15. Mientras ella explicaba la teoría, todos se iban.

ejercicio   II-2-5

1. Yo sabía la respuesta.
2. Juana odiaba el color rojo.
3. ¿Lo conocías?
4. Ellos no me creían.
5. Mi familia me amaba mucho.
6. Estábamos muy tristes por mucho tiempo.

7. Él odiaba a su nuevo jefe.
8. Me gustaba la foto de tu familia.
9. Me gustaban las flores en su jardín.
10. Aunque él me molestaba, lo amaba.
11. Ella se preocupaba mucho por ti.
12. ¿Pensabas en mí?
13. ¿En qué pensabas?
14. ¿Cómo te sentías durante el juicio?
15. Él no se llevaba bien con su suegra.

 **II-2-6**

1. De niño, Juan veía (miraba) la televisión cada día después de la escuela.
2. Cuando vivíamos en Francia, tomábamos vino con cada comida.
3. El año pasado ellos no podían hablar español.
4. ¿Por qué no podías ir conmigo?
5. Cuando yo era joven, miraba debajo de la cama cada noche antes de apagar la luz.
6. Lou Gehrig podía jugar al béisbol mejor que Ty Cobb.
7. Cuando Juana trabajaba en el banco, tomaba quince tazas de café cada día.
8. Cuando usted era menor, podía recordar las capitales de cada estado.
9. Cuando Roberto trabajaba para la CIA, nunca decía a nadie su nombre verdadero.
10. Ellos no podían votar porque no tenían identificación.
11. Tú nunca estabas en casa. ¿Adónde ibas esas noches?
12. No podíamos llamarte porque el teléfono no funcionaba.
13. Para cada fiesta que teníamos, María traía papas fritas y yo traía salsa de tomate.
14. El pan estaba mohoso. No podía comerlo.
15. De niña, Victoria tenía que hacer la cama cada mañana antes de salir para la escuela.

 **II-2-7**

1. Siempre estudiaba antes de un examen.
2. Él frecuentemente me llamaba después de las diez de la noche.
3. Toda mi vida quería tener un piano.
4. Ellos siempre nos engañaban cuando jugábamos a los naipes.
5. Comías allí con frecuencia.
6. A menudo escribíais cartas largas.
7. De vez en cuando enviábamos (mandábamos) dinero a la organización.
8. A veces él no ganaba tanto dinero como su esposa.
9. Todo el tiempo que yo estaba allí, nunca decíais nada.
10. Él siempre enviaba una nota de agradecimiento después de recibir un regalo.
11. Ella nunca compraba nada sin cupón.
12. Él nos mentía con frecuencia, pero nunca le decíamos nada.
13. Siempre me preguntaba por qué ella se lavaba las manos tantas veces cada día.
14. Ella nunca estaba feliz. Se quejaba cada día, todo el día.
15. A veces leíamos y a veces escribíamos.

II-2-8

1. hablé   2. vivía   3. comió   4. comía   5. fuimos   6. compré   7. llegamos   8. llegó   9. estudiaba   10. estudió
11. comían   12. jugaron   13. era   14. eras   15. fueron

ejercicio II-2-9

1. Eran las dos y media cuando me llamaste.
2. María tenía veintidós años cuando compró su primer coche (carro).
3. Eran las cuatro y cuarto cuando encontré el dinero.
4. Ellos tenían dieciocho años cuando se graduaron de la escuela secundaria.
5. Eran las cinco menos cinco cuando el árbol se cayó.
6. Trabajábamos duro cuando teníamos quince años.
7. Cuando me levanté eran las seis y cuarto.
8. Aprendí a montar en bicicleta cuando tenía seis años.
9. Eran las cuatro menos cuarto cuando sonó el teléfono.
10. Ella tuvo un niño cuando tenía cuarenta años.
11. No sabíamos que eran las doce y media.
12. Eran las tres de la mañana cuando salieron.
13. ¿Dónde vivías cuando tenías catorce años?
14. ¿Qué hora era cuando terminaste el libro?
15. ¿Cuántos años tenía Juan cuando se casó?

¡Te toca a ti! Possible answers:

1. Eran las once cuando me acosté.
2. Eran las seis cuando me levanté.
3. Tenía cinco años cuando comencé la escuela.
4. Tenía diez años cuando aprendí a montar en bicicleta.
5. Eran las ocho cuando salí de casa.
6. Eran las seis y media cuando volví a casa.
7. Tenía veinte años cuando empecé a estudiar español.
8. Tenía cuatro años cuando aprendí a nadar.

ejercicio II-2-10

1. Había una araña debajo de mi cama esta mañana.
2. Había veinte personas en la fiesta.
3. Había una mosca en mi sopa.
4. Había cien preguntas en el examen.
5. Había mucho ruido durante la tormenta.
6. Había quinientas páginas en el libro.
7. No había gasolina en el tanque.
8. No había hojas en los árboles.
9. No había suficiente tiempo para preguntas.
10. Había más mujeres que hombres en la reunión.
11. Había basura en la mesa.
12. Había tanta niebla que no podía conducir (manejar).
13. En enero no había nadie afuera.
14. En el verano había mucha gente por las calles.
15. No había mujeres en ese restaurante.

traducción II-2-11

Cuando yo era joven, había una exposición de insectos en el zoológico cada verano. Mi familia y yo siempre íbamos. Había un edificio sólo para mariposas, y había diez clases de mariposas volando de un lado a otro. También había un edificio que tenía docenas de insectos. Yo nunca sabía que había tantos insectos. Había información en todas partes. Leí que por cada libra de ser humano, hay doce libras de insectos. También supe que la señorita Muffett verdaderamente existía. Su papá, Thomas Muffett, era un entomólogo que le daba a su hija puré de arañas cuando estaba enferma. ¡Esto era un remedio común para los resfriados hace doscientos años!

 **ejercicio** **11-2-12**

1. Yo iba a comer.
2. ¿Ibas a decirme algo?
3. Él iba a llevar su camisa blanca pero estaba sucia.
4. Íbamos a quitar la nieve.
5. Ellos iban a pasar el día en el campo pero hacía mal tiempo.
6. ¿Cuándo iban (ustedes) a sentarse?
7. Yo iba a acostarme a las diez y media pero había un buen programa en la televisión.
8. ¿Cómo ibas a hacer esto?
9. ¿Por qué iba ella a construir una casa en el bosque?
10. ¿Quién iba a arreglar este grifo?
11. Íbamos a cepillarnos los dientes pero no había pasta de dientes.
12. Yo iba a darle dinero para su cumpleaños.
13. ¿Adónde ibais a enviar este paquete?
14. ¿Cuándo ibas a traernos las flores?
15. ¿Por qué no iba él a llenar los vasos con agua?

ejercicio **11-2-13**

1. Yo estaba comiendo.
2. Estabas estudiando.
3. Dumbo estaba volando.
4. Ella estaba almorzando.
5. Estábamos bebiendo leche.
6. Estabais diciendo la verdad.
7. Ellos estaban acostándose.
8. Ustedes estaban cepillándose el pelo.
9. Yo estaba bañándome.
10. Juan estaba afeitándose.
11. María estaba tocando el piano.
12. María estaba jugando al tenis.

 **traducción** **11-2-14**

Miré "La Corte del Pueblo" esta tarde mientras almorzaba (estaba almorzando). Me encanta ese programa. Había una mujer—que no estaba feliz—que demandaba (estaba demandando) a los dueños de una tienda de animales domésticos porque ella compró un perrito, lo llevó a casa, no lo entrenó y después de unas cuantas semanas el perrito comenzó a morder los muebles y destruirlos. Esta mujer quería un reembolso por el costo del perro, su comida, inyecciones, ¡hasta por sus juguetes! Los dueños parecían normales. Esta mujer parecía estar desquiciada. El juez probablemente pensaba (estaba pensando) lo mismo porque ella perdió el caso. Después, ella le dijo al locutor que iba a matar al perro. Después de unos anuncios (comerciales), el locutor dijo a sus telespectadores fieles que él compró el perro y lo llamó C. P. (por la Corte del Pueblo).

Unit 3: The Future Tense

ejercicio   II-3-1

1. compraré   2. correrán   3. abriréis   4. serás   5. estará   6. jugaremos   7. llevará   8. me ducharé   9. llegarán
10. vomitará   11. nevará   12. se acostarán

ejercicio   II-3-2

1. Te hablaré (Hablaré contigo) mañana.
2. Ella comprará un carro nuevo el año que viene.
3. Él dormirá hasta mañana por la tarde.
4. Llegaremos a las diez mañana por la noche.
5. ¿A qué hora te acostarás?
6. ¿Cuánto dinero necesitaréis?
7. Ellos se quedarán en un hotel el mes que viene.
8. Nunca nevará en Panamá.
9. ¿Dónde estarás esta noche a las once y media?
10. ¿A qué hora comenzará el programa?
11. No quiero darle el dinero porque sé que él lo perderá.
12. No me quitaré este suéter hasta el verano que viene.
13. Asistiremos a la universidad el otoño que viene.
14. No firmaré esta carta porque no es verdad.
15. Si yo compro este traje en lugar de ése (aquéllo), ahorraré cincuenta dólares.

¡Te toca a ti! Possible answers:
1. Comeré arroz con pollo.
2. ¡Yo seré el próximo Presidente!
3. Iré a México.
4. Sí, hablaré español mañana.
5. Estaré en mi oficina.
6. Me acostaré a las diez.
7. Llevaré mis vaqueros.
8. No miraré ningún programa esta semana.
9. España ganará la Copa Mundial.
10. Sí, la colgaré antes de acostarme.
11. Mañana me levantaré a las siete.
12. Estudiaré español (por) dos horas.

traducción   II-3-3

Mañana es el primero de enero, y por eso, trataré de hacer todas las cosas que escribí en mi lista de resoluciones para el año que viene. El año pasado hice diez resoluciones, y por un rato las cumplí, pero una por una falté a mi palabra. Este año, sin embargo, adelgazaré—el año pasado engordé diez libras. Trabajaré más duro—perdí mucho tiempo el año pasado. Leeré más—leí sólo dos libros este año pasado. Iré al gimnasio más a menudo—pertenezco a un club, pero nunca voy. Gastaré menos dinero—iba de compras dos o tres veces cada semana. Andaré o montaré en bicicleta en vez de conducir (manejar) (ayer conduje [manejé] tres manzanas [cuadras] para comprar un periódico—¡qué ridículo!). Me quejaré menos—no fui un angelito este año. Finalmente, estudiaré español más. Seré perfecto/a—exactamente como el año pasado.

   **II-3-4**

1. haremos   2. pondrán   3. tendrá   4. cabrá   5. sabrá   6. querrá   7. podrán   8. diremos   9. vendréis   10. saldrán   11. valdrá   12. Habrá

ejercicio   **II-3-5**

1. Querré ver tus fotos.
2. ¿Dónde pondrás el sofá? Lo pondré en la sala.
3. María hará el vestido de novia.
4. ¿A qué hora vendrán?
5. No podrán ver el barco desde allí.
6. Habrá trescientas tiendas en el nuevo centro comercial.
7. Juan sabrá la respuesta.
8. ¿Cuánto valdrá el coche (carro) el año que viene?
9. No habrá ruido durante el programa.
10. ¿Habrá tiempo para hacer preguntas?
11. ¿Podrás llamarme hoy más tarde?
12. Estos martillos nunca cabrán en esa caja.
13. Esta casa valdrá más de dos millones de dólares en cinco años.
14. No le diré tu secreto a nadie.
15. Ellos harán su cheque por quinientos dólares.

ejercicio   **II-3-6**

1. Me pondré el sombrero.
2. Él deshará este nudo.
3. ¿Te opondrás al Presidente?
4. Os abstendréis de fumar por dos semanas.
5. ¿Quién compondrá la música?
6. Nos atendremos a ti.
7. ¿Contendrá este balde toda la pintura?
8. Él rehará su cama más tarde.
9. Supondré que sabes la respuesta.
10. El policía te detendrá si conduces (manejas) borracho.
11. Ella mantendrá buenas notas en la universidad.
12. ¿Dónde obtendrás bastante dinero para comprar los muebles nuevos?
13. ¿Convendrán en quedarse conmigo por un rato?
14. Estas vigas no sostendrán una casa.
15. Mañana me abstendré de comer.

traducción   **II-3-7**

En un par de semanas, renunciaré a este trabajo y comenzaré una nueva vida. Vendí mi casa y compré una camioneta. Anoche puse comida, ropa, mi cámara y una almohada—todo lo que necesitaré—en la camioneta. ¡No puedo creerlo! Dentro de poco ese vehículo será mi hogar. Durante los últimos cinco años ahorré bastante dinero para vivir por diez años. No podré ir a restaurantes elegantes, ni comprar trajes de Armani, pero podré viajar. Visitaré nuevos lugares y conoceré a nuevas personas. Siempre soñaba con hacer esto. No seré rico/a, pero seré feliz. Por primera vez en mi vida, mi realidad y mis sueños serán iguales.

ejercicio   II-3-8

1. Juan llegará a las diez.
2. ¿Dónde pondrás el cortacéspedes?
3. Comeremos las pasas de la caja.
4. ¿Cuándo averiguarás si tienes el empleo?
5. Ellos no se acostarán hasta la medianoche.
6. Nunca sabré tocar el violín.
7. De vez en cuando, te visitaré en la cárcel.
8. ¿Cuánto valdrá este anillo en veinte años?
9. ¿Obedecerá usted las leyes de esta ciudad?
10. Nunca nevará en Panamá y nunca lloverá en el desierto.
11. Ellos nos dirán mentiras pero no creeremos nada.
12. ¿Tendrás que viajar mucho? ¿Podrás viajar mucho?
13. Mi coche no cabrá en el garaje. Tendré que dejarlo en la calle.
14. Enterraré el tesoro esta noche; de lo contrario, no estará aquí mañana.
15. El tesoro entero no cabrá en este baúl; tendré que meter los diamantes en mi bolsillo.

Unit 4: The Conditional Tense

ejercicio   II-4-1

1. Yo comería las galletitas pero estoy a dieta.
2. ¿Se casaría con Juan?
3. ¿Adónde irías?
4. Ellos no vivirían en esa casa porque está embrujada.
5. ¿Entregarían los periódicos a nuestra casa?
6. Si enseño esta clase, seríais mis alumnos.
7. No voy a darles el dinero porque lo perderían.
8. Cambiaríamos las palabras de la canción, pero sería demasiado difícil.
9. Me levantaría pero me duele la pierna.
10. Sé que te darían el dinero que necesitas.
11. ¿Comprarías un carro usado de este hombre?
12. ¿Quién pensaría tal cosa?
13. ¿Por qué no se afeitaría él con esa navaja?
14. ¿Por qué leería alguien esto?
15. Yo no tocaría el piano enfrente de una multitud.

ejercicio   II-4-2

1. pondría   2. podrías   3. tendría   4. valdría   5. haría   6. cabrían   7. vendríamos   8. Habría   9. dirías   10. diría

ejercicio   II-4-3

1. Yo vendría a tu fiesta, pero estoy enfermo/a.
2. ¿Dónde pondrías estas sillas?

3. Esta pulsera valdría más, pero está rota.

4. ¿Qué diríais a ese hombre?

5. Tendríamos la recepción en nuestra casa, pero no hay suficiente espacio.

6. ¿Crees que Roberto sabría la respuesta?

7. ¿Quién podría hacer tal cosa?

8. Yo querría el carro, pero no es mi elección.

9. Habría dos docenas de huevos en el refrigerador, pero comimos cuatro para el desayuno.

10. ¿Cabrían estos platos en la alacena?

11. ¿Qué harías durante un huracán?

12. Yo no le diría porque él no puede guardar un secreto.

13. Haríamos el cheque, pero no hay suficiente dinero en el banco.

14. No voy a dar estos zapatos a Marcos porque sé que él no podría usarlos (llevarlos).

15. Yo pondría las flores enfrente de la casa, no atrás.

traducción   II-4-4

Cuando yo era joven, me encantaba leer los cuentos de hadas. Uno de mis personajes favoritos era Aladino porque siempre le concedía a la gente sus fantasías en la forma de tres deseos. ¿Qué haría yo? Primero le pediría un millón de deseos, pero sé que él no haría eso. Por eso, estos son mis tres deseos: 1. Mi gata podría hablar y ella y yo tendríamos conversaciones largas. 2. Nunca tendría que preocuparme por mi peso. 3. Y el deseo más importante es que nadie en el mundo sufriría otro minuto: no habría guerra; no habría hambre; no habría pobreza; no habría tristeza.

Unit 5: The Present Perfect Tense

ejercicio   II-5-1

1. He trabajado.

2. Tú has escuchado.

3. Ella ha bebido la leche.

4. Hemos comprendido.

5. Ellos han recibido un regalo.

6. Hemos vendido la casa.

7. ¿Has mirado la televisión hoy?

8. ¿Dónde han vivido?

9. Me he duchado.

10. Él ha estado conmigo.

11. Usted ha aprendido mucho.

12. ¿Te has cepillado los dientes?

13. Él me ha llamado seis veces.

14. He corrido tres millas.

15. Ella no se ha lavado el pelo.

ejercicio   II-5-2

1. He leído veinte páginas.

2. Ella ha abierto el libro.

3. ¿Dónde has puesto los platos?

4. El conejo ha muerto.

5. ¿Le has dicho la verdad?

6. ¿Qué has visto?

7. El cocinero ha frito todos los huevos.

8. ¿Qué has hecho hoy?

9. La tienda nos ha provisto de ropa.

10. Ella se ha roto otra uña.

11. ¿Ha resuelto él sus problemas?

12. No hemos dicho nada.

13. El político no ha dicho la verdad.

14. ¿Por qué no han vuelto?

15. ¿Qué has hecho para nosotros?

ejercicio   **II-5-3**

1. He tenido el dinero por más de veinte años.

2. Ella ha abierto la ventana y yo he cerrado la puerta.

3. El perro de mi vecino ha ladrado toda la noche, y no he podido dormir.

4. ¿Dónde has puesto tu maleta?

5. ¿Cuántas veces te has cepillado los dientes hoy?

6. ¿Por qué no te has afeitado hoy?

7. ¿Por cuántos años has conocido a Carlos?

8. Has llegado tarde cada día (todos los días) esta semana.

9. ¿La han visto (ustedes)?

10. Los ladrones han robado nuestras joyas y han roto todos mis discos.

11. ¿Han vuelto los recién casados de su luna de miel?

12. Tus modales me han atraído.

13. Ellos han demostrado su amor por la música de Beethoven.

14. Si ella es tan rica como dices, entonces, ¿por qué ha robado el banco?

15. El teléfono ha sonado veinte veces. ¿Por qué no lo has contestado?

traducción   **II-5-4**

Quiero ir de compras porque no he salido de esta casa en más de una semana. Necesito comprar un par de zapatos tenis. Creo que he perdido mi otro par. He buscado en todas partes: debajo de la cama, en el armario, en el sótano, hasta en el maletero (baúl) de mi coche, pero no he podido encontrarlos en ninguna parte. Mi hermana los ha pedido prestados de vez en cuando en el pasado, pero ella siempre devuelve las cosas. Por eso, he llegado a la conclusión de que los he perdido para siempre y si quiero jugar al tenis otra vez, tengo que comprar un nuevo par.

Unit 6: The Past Perfect Tense

 **ejercicio**   **II-6-1**

1. Yo había pagado.
2. Ella había vivido en Texas.
3. Ellos habían perdido todas las cartas.
4. No habíamos recibido una invitación.
5. ¿Habías llevado esos zapatos antes de la boda?
6. Yo había comido todos los dulces antes de descubrir el premio.
7. Habíamos practicado (por) cuatro horas antes del concierto.
8. ¿Por cuánto tiempo habías fumado antes de dejarlo?
9. Ella había vivido en St. Louis antes de mudarse a St. Paul.
10. Habíamos salido por tres años antes de casarnos.
11. Los soldados habían sufrido mucho antes del fin de la guerra.
12. Antes de la fiesta, yo había limpiado la casa de cabo a rabo.
13. Él no se había lavado el pelo en tres semanas.
14. Yo nunca había disfrutado con el (del) teatro tanto como él.
15. Antes de acostaros, ¿habíais apagado las luces?

 **ejercicio**   **II-6-2**

1. Yo no había abierto las ventanas hasta mayo de ese año.
2. Ellos no habían hecho nada.
3. Ella no había visto la película antes del sábado.
4. Todos los árboles habían muerto.
5. No habíamos resuelto los problemas antes de la reunión.
6. Los ladrones habían roto las sillas y las ventanas.
7. ¿Habían cubierto las mesas antes de la tormenta?
8. ¿Dónde habías puesto el dinero?
9. Yo había escrito cincuenta cartas antes de recibir una respuesta.
10. ¿Te habían provisto de bastante información?
11. La comida se había podrido en el refrigerador.
12. Habíamos frito suficientes papas para un ejército.
13. ¿Qué habías hecho para ayudarlos?
14. El perro no había descubierto los huesos debajo de la cama.
15. Los libros se habían caído del estante.

¡Te toca a ti!
Make sure that all verbs are in the past perfect, first person singular.

 **traducción**   **II-6-3**

Nunca habíamos estado en Europa antes. Habíamos viajado mucho por Sudamérica y, por supuesto, por los Estados Unidos, pero nunca por ninguna parte de Europa. Mi esposo había ganado el viaje en un concurso (siempre le había gustado "Su Lugar o el Mío", pero nunca había soñado con ser un participante). De cualquier forma, antes de ganar dos millones de dólares (él ha ganado más dinero que nadie en el mundo en televisión), Fenton ya había decidido en Europa—nada menos. Antes de salir, habíamos comprado maletas nuevas, gafas de sol y, por supuesto, muchos rollos de película para la nueva cámara. Todavía no me he acostumbrado a esa cámara. Debe de ser defectuosa. Ahora que hemos ido a Europa, queremos conquistar el Polo Sur.

Part III | **The Imperative, Subjunctive, and Compound Tenses, and the Passive Voice**

Unit 1: The Imperative

ejercicio   III-1-1

1. ¡Estudia!	5. ¡Lee!	8. ¡Baila!	12. ¡Paga!	16. ¡Comienza! *or*	19. ¡Sigue! *or*
2. ¡Trabaja!	6. ¡Corre!	9. ¡Escribe!	13. ¡Sufre!	¡Empieza!	¡Continúa!
3. ¡Mira!	7. ¡Anda! *or*	10. ¡Decide!	14. ¡Cuenta!	17. ¡Piensa!	20. ¡Confiesa!
4. ¡Escucha!	¡Camina!	11. ¡Vende!	15. ¡Vuela!	18. ¡Duerme!	

ejercicio   III-1-2

1. ¡No mires!   2. ¡No cantes!   3. ¡No estudies!   4. ¡No corras!   5. ¡No pienses!   6. ¡No bebas el agua!   7. ¡No llegues tarde!
8. ¡No practiques ahora!   9. ¡No pagues la cuenta!   10. ¡No organices los papeles!   11. ¡No leas mi diario!
12. ¡No bailes en la mesa!   13. ¡No abras las ventanas!   14. ¡No admitas nada!   15. ¡No creas nada!

ejercicio   III-1-3

1. ¡Pon el libro aquí!	9. ¡No pongas los zapatos en la mesa!
2. ¡Di la verdad!	10. ¡No digas nada!
3. ¡Haz la cama!	11. ¡No hagas las camas!
4. ¡Sal de la casa!	12. ¡No salgas ahora!
5. ¡Ven a la cocina!	13. ¡No vengas mañana!
6. ¡Sé amable!	14. ¡No seas egoísta!
7. ¡Ve a la sala!	15. ¡No vayas de compras hoy!
8. ¡Ten el dinero para mañana!	16. ¡No tengas animales en la casa!

ejercicio   III-1-4

1. ¡Cómpralo!	6. ¡Dime un cuento!	11. ¡Dínoslo!
2. ¡Véndela!	7. ¡Ponlo aquí!	12. ¡Escríbemela!
3. ¡Siéntate!	8. ¡Vete!	13. ¡Cántasela!
4. ¡Acuéstate!	9. ¡Ponlas allí!	14. ¡Cómpramelo!
5. ¡Báñate!	10. ¡Déjanos en paz!	15. ¡Háztelo!

ejercicio   III-1-5

1. ¡No lo leas!	6. ¡No te vayas!	11. ¡No se la des!
2. ¡No la bebas!	7. ¡No te levantes!	12. ¡No se lo digas!
3. ¡No lo beses!	8. ¡No te duches!	13. ¡No nos lo vendas!
4. ¡No me digas mentiras!	9. ¡No te acuestes!	14. ¡No me lo leas!
5. ¡No me mientas!	10. ¡No me odies!	15. ¡No se la cantes!

ejercicio   III-1-6

1. ¡Cante!
2. ¡Venda!
3. ¡Cuente!
4. ¡Pague!
5. ¡Corra!

6. ¡Hágalo!
7. ¡Toque el piano!
8. ¡Léalo!
9. ¡Tráigalo aquí!
10. ¡Levántese!

11. ¡Démelo!
12. ¡Dígamelo!
13. ¡No me diga una mentira!
14. ¡No nos espere!
15. ¡No robe el banco!

16. ¡Deme el dinero!
17. ¡Siéntese!
18. ¡Póngalo allí!
19. ¡No lo haga!
20. ¡Dígale un cuento!

ejercicio   III-1-7

1. ¡Váyase!
2. ¡Sépalo!
3. ¡Sea bueno!
4. ¡No se vaya!

5. ¡No sea malo!
6. ¡No vaya a la fiesta!
7. ¡Sepa todo para mañana!
8. ¡Vaya al frente de la sala!

ejercicio   III-1-8

1. ¡Trabajen!
2. ¡Piensen!
3. ¡No hagan eso!
4. ¡No salgan!
5. ¡Siéntense!

6. ¡Pónganlos aquí!
7. ¡No me digan nada!
8. ¡Toquen el piano!
9. ¡Jueguen al béisbol!
10. ¡Tráiganme la comida!

11. ¡Díganle el secreto!
12. ¡No se vayan enojadas!
13. ¡Acuéstense!
14. ¡Lávense las manos!
15. ¡Cepíllense los dientes!

ejercicio   III-1-9

1. ¡Volad!
2. ¡Volved!
3. ¡Venid!
4. ¡Paraos!

5. ¡Corred!
6. ¡Hervid el agua!
7. ¡Dormid!
8. ¡Leedlo!

9. ¡Id a la tienda!
10. ¡Ponedla en la casa!
11. ¡Hacednos un favor!
12. ¡Llegad a las diez!

ejercicio   III-1-10

1. ¡No comáis!
2. ¡No habléis!
3. ¡No juguéis aquí!
4. ¡No cantéis!

5. ¡No durmáis en el parque!
6. ¡No hirváis el agua!
7. ¡No os durmáis!
8. ¡No salgáis!

9. ¡No toméis el dinero!
10. ¡No me sigáis!
11. ¡No os acostéis!
12. ¡No os vayáis!

ejercicio   III-1-11

1. ¡Estudiemos!
2. ¡Caminemos!
3. ¡No estudiemos!
4. ¡No comamos!
5. ¡Vendamos el coche!

6. ¡Hagamos algo!
7. ¡No hagamos nada!
8. ¡Almorcemos!
9. ¡Pongamos el perro afuera!
10. ¡Cantémosles!

11. ¡No mintamos!
12. ¡No comencemos ahora!
13. ¡Digamos la verdad!
14. ¡No digamos nada!
15. ¡Comprémoslo!

 **III-1-12**

1. ¡Sepamos todo!	5. ¡No seamos cobardes!
2. ¡Seamos amables!	6. ¡Vamos al cine mañana!
3. ¡No vayamos a la fiesta!	7. ¡Seamos personas honradas!
4. ¡Vámonos esta noche!	8. ¡No nos vayamos esta tarde!

Unit 2: The Present Subjunctive

 **III-2-1**

1. Espero que ella hable conmigo mañana.
2. Quiero que comas el pan.
3. Él quiere que yo escriba una carta.
4. Rogamos que estés bien.
5. Ellos quieren que lo hagamos.
6. Ella espera que puedas venir a la fiesta.
7. Ellos sugieren que tú lo hagas.
8. Insisto en que trabajéis.
9. Él pide que estemos aquí a las nueve.
10. ¿Por qué pides que yo lo haga?
11. Prefiero que no salgamos de la casa hasta las cinco.
12. Ella espera que la conozcas.
13. Insistimos en que comas con nosotros.
14. ¿Quieres que yo cuente el dinero?
15. Ellos sugieren que pongamos los papeles en el gabinete.

traducción **III-2-2**

Mañana es el primer día de mi nuevo trabajo. Espero que todo me vaya bien. Mi jefa parece muy amable, pero prefiero que ella sea más justa que amable. Quiero que entienda que si yo cometo un error (y estoy segura de que cometeré muchos), quiero que ella me lo diga directamente. Antes de que termine la primera semana, voy a pedirle que me diga lo que piensa de mi desempeño. Si ella sugiere que yo cambie algún aspecto de mi trabajo, será más fácil hacerlo entonces que después de trabajar allí por unos cuantos meses.

ejercicio **III-2-3**

1. Dudo que ella coma en ese restaurante.
2. No supongo que me digas su nombre.
3. Ellos no creen que él toque el piano.
4. Ella no está segura que el café esté listo.
5. No pensamos que los Vikings ganen el partido.
6. Él no está convencido de que yo necesite tanto dinero.
7. ¿Por qué no crees que lo conozcamos?

8. No estamos convencidos de que la luna sea de queso verde.

9. Él duda que ellos sepan la respuesta.

10. Ella no está segura de que siempre digamos la verdad.

11. ¿Por qué no estás convencido/a de que yo siempre tenga razón?

12. No parece que él quiera estar aquí.

13. No estoy seguro/a de que puedas leer esto.

14. Él no cree que yo sea su primo/a.

15. No me imagino que creas mi historia.

---

traducción   III-2-4

Dudo que Juan sepa que planeamos una fiesta para él. No parece posible que él sea el nuevo presidente de esta compañía y no me imagino que él lo crea tampoco. Dudo que le guste esta nueva posición. No estoy convencido/a de que él esté listo para tan gran responsabilidad; en cambio, no supongo que nadie pueda hacerse un gran líder de la noche a la mañana. Quiero que todo le salga bien.

---

ejercicio   III-2-5

1. Es mejor que comamos en la cocina.

2. Es necesario que les llames mañana.

3. Es preferible que compres los huevos por docenas.

4. Es improbable que estén listos para las cinco.

5. Conviene que tenga un abogado con usted.

6. Es importante que nadie sepa ese secreto.

7. Puede ser que Alicia ya no trabaje aquí.

8. Es ridículo que tantos políticos no digan la verdad.

9. Es imposible que yo esté en dos lugares al mismo tiempo.

10. Es increíble que él hable doce idiomas.

11. Es una lástima que el helado tenga tantas calorías.

12. Ojalá que Juana no cante en la boda.

13. Es fantástico que no tengamos que sentarnos al lado de ellos.

14. Puede ser que Esteban no sea lo que dice que es.

15. Es imposible que me quede en este cuarto por un minuto más.

---

traducción   III-2-6

Anoche leí por primera vez las reglas y los reglamentos de la compañía donde he trabajado por seis años. Es posible que sea la única persona que ha leído este folleto. Hay tantas reglas absurdas. Por ejemplo, es ridículo que debamos mantener ordenados nuestros escritorios todo el tiempo. Es mejor que una persona tenga la libertad de ser cochino si eso es lo que necesita para trabajar bien. También, es increíble que tengamos que asistir a todas las reuniones, incluso las que no tienen nada que ver con nuestro propio trabajo (nadie asiste a estas reuniones). Es mejor que trabajemos en un escritorio desordenado que asistir a una reunión en una sala de juntas ordenada y volteemos los pulgares. ¡Ojalá que nadie imponga estas reglas!

---

ejercicio   III-2-7

1. No comeré hasta que tenga hambre.

2. Te escribiré una nota para que recuerdes comprar leche.

3. Te sentirás mejor después (de) que tomes esta medicina.

4. Él no se casará con una mujer a menos que sea rica.

5. No podéis cazar a menos que tengáis una licencia.

6. Secaré los platos mientras que los laves.

7. El sacerdote no puede bautizar al bebé antes (de) que lleguen los padrinos.

8. El juego no se acaba hasta que se acabe.

9. Lo creeré cuando lo vea.

10. Él va a leer este libro otra vez en caso de que tengamos una prueba.

11. Él no comerá nada a menos que tenga una servilleta en el regazo.

12. Cada semana ahorro veinticinco dólares para que tenga suficiente dinero para mis vacaciones.

13. Ella nunca estará feliz hasta que sepa conjugar los verbos.

14. Debes cepillarte los dientes antes (de) que salgamos para la consulta del dentista.

15. No podré llevar estos pantalones hasta que pierda diez libras.

 **traducción   III-2-8**

"Te escribiré tan pronto como llegue." Éstas fueron las últimas palabras famosas de Marco. Lo que él debería haber dicho fue, "Te escribiré a menos que me divierta (esté divirtiéndome)" o "Te mandaré una carta cuando no haya nada más que hacer" o, más simple, "Te contaré todo acerca de mi viaje después de que llegue a casa". El día que yo reciba una carta de Marco será el día que los milagros ocurran en todas partes. A menos que alguien le ponga una pistola en la cabeza, Marco no escribirá nunca una carta a nadie.

 **ejercicio   III-2-9**

1. Buscamos una casa que tenga tres dormitorios.

2. Ella quiere un perro que no ladre.

3. ¿Hay alguien aquí que pueda tocar la guitarra?

4. Necesito una criada que limpie las ventanas.

5. ¿Hay alguien en el mundo que sepa expresarse claramente?

6. Busco un gato que no arañe los muebles.

7. ¿Dónde puedo comprar una camisa que no sea de poliéster?

8. No hay nadie aquí que pueda ayudarte.

9. Para su cumpleaños este año él quiere un loro que hable tres idiomas.

10. Quiero vivir en una ciudad donde no haya crimen.

traducción   III-2-10

Fui de compras con Giralda esta mañana. Nunca más me meteré en esa tortura otra vez. ¡Giralda es imposible! Primero, ella quiere un aparcamiento que no esté a más de diez pies de la puerta principal del centro comercial. En esto tardó media hora. Entonces, quiere un vestido que tenga mangas de quita y pon para que pueda llevarlo todo el año. También quiere un collar que parezca algo que llevaría una reina, pero también quiere que este collar cueste menos de diez dólares. Quiere zapatos que tengan joyas en los tacones y quiere guantes que tengan perlitas en las muñecas. En cada tienda le decía a la dependienta exactamente lo que quería y cada dependienta le decía a Giralda que no hay ninguna tienda en ese centro comercial, ni en ningún centro comercial en este planeta, que venda tales artículos. Giralda estaba furiosa y me dijo que no hay nadie en este mundo que entienda su gusto fabuloso.

ejercicio   III-2-11

1. Quizá/Tal vez/Acaso él tenga el dinero.
2. Quizá/Tal vez/Acaso podamos ir.
3. Quizá/Tal vez/Acaso ellos vivan aquí.
4. Quizá/Tal vez/Acaso lo conozcas.
5. Quizá/Tal vez/Acaso ellos compren la casa hoy.
6. Quizá/Tal vez/Acaso estemos perdidos.
7. Quizá/Tal vez/Acaso él no sea la persona más inteligente en el mundo.
8. Quizá/Tal vez/Acaso no debáis beber esta leche.
9. Quizá/Tal vez/Acaso el político no diga la verdad.
10. Quizá/Tal vez/Acaso el gato tenga sólo ocho vidas.

traducción   III-2-12

A ver. No tengo que trabajar hoy. ¿Qué debo hacer? Tal vez (yo) lea un libro. Tal vez (yo) compre un libro. Tal vez (yo) vaya al cine. Tal vez (yo) estudie español. Tal vez (yo) remonte una cometa. Tal vez (yo) corte el césped. Tal vez (yo) coma un huevo. Tal vez (yo) dé un paseo. Tal vez (yo) saque la basura. Tal vez (yo) no haga nada. ¡Ajá! ¡No haré nada!

ejercicio   III-2-13

1. Aunque Juana cocine, no me quedaré.
2. Aunque quieran mirar la televisión, no los dejaremos.
3. Aunque me grites, no cambiaré mi idea.
4. Aunque él piense que es un genio, todo el mundo sabe que no lo es.
5. Aunque le ofrezcas mil dólares al policía, todavía te dará una multa.
6. Aunque ignoremos los candidatos, todavía tenemos el derecho de votar.
7. Aunque pongas el gato en el sótano, Bárbara todavía estornudará.
8. Aunque os sintáis enfermos, todavía tenéis que tomar el examen.
9. Aunque des cuerda al reloj cincuenta veces, nunca funcionará.
10. Aunque él sonría todo el tiempo, en su interior es malo.
11. Aunque (yo) sepa la respuesta, no te la diré.
12. Aunque piensen que estoy loco/a, sé que tengo razón.

traducción   III-2-14

¡Ay! Alguien llama a la puerta. Estoy mirando por la ventana. No se parece a nadie que (yo) conozca. Es posible que sea un político, pero es más probable que sea un vendedor. O tal vez sea UPS. No—ellos siempre llevan paquetes. Tal vez sea el florista con un ramo de flores para mí. No—ellos siempre tienen flores. No sé quien pueda ser esta persona. Tal vez sea Publishers' Clearing House porque he ganado diez millones de dólares. No—ellos siempre tienen ese cheque gigante. No voy a abrir la puerta. Ojalá que el intruso se vaya.

traducción   III-2-15

No hay nadie que pueda cocinar tan bien como mi amiga Catarina. Es fantástico que ella tenga una fiesta este fin de semana porque no he comido una buena comida en mucho tiempo (es decir, desde la última vez que comí en su casa). Espero que ella haga su famosa tarta de manzana otra vez, pero dudo que ella la haga este fin de semana porque la sirvió hace menos de un año y rara vez se repite. Aunque prepare esta delicia, no será lo mismo porque siempre cambia (mejora) cada receta un poco cada vez que la usa. Temo que nunca pruebe esa misma tarta otra vez. Quizá le ruegue para que ella me prepare la tarta para mi cumpleaños. Sé que cuando pruebe esa tarta otra vez o estaré en el cielo o en el comedor de Catarina.

Unit 3: The Imperfect Subjunctive

1. Yo quería que Juan comprara las toallas.
2. Fue una lástima que tuvieras que trabajar el domingo pasado.
3. No había nadie en la clase que hablara francés.
4. Dudábamos que Humpty Dumpty se cayera del muro.
5. Nadie creía que María tuviera un corderito.
6. El señor Clean pidió que nos quitáramos los zapatos antes de entrar en su palacio.
7. ¿Fue necesario que me llamarais en medio de la noche?
8. No estaban seguros de que yo pudiera cuidarme.
9. Ella preparó la cena para que no nos muriéramos de hambre.
10. Limpiamos la casa antes de que llegaran.
11. Ella estudió en caso de que hubiera un examen el día siguiente.
12. Él me rogó que (yo) no pidiera la langosta.
13. No creímos/pensamos que nadie nos oyera.
14. ¿Había alguien allí que supiera todas las capitales de los estados?
15. Pedimos que continuaran sin nosotros.

1. Ellos no creen que yo hiciera estas galletas.
2. Es improbable que Francis Bacon escribiera estos dramas.
3. No estamos convencidos de que la señorita Muffet tuviera miedo a la araña.
4. Siento que estuvieras enfermo/a y que no pudieras venir a nuestra fiesta.
5. No supongo que supieras que ella era la ladrona.
6. No parece que la sirvienta limpiara la casa esta mañana.
7. Ojalá que pagaras las cuentas a tiempo este mes.
8. Puede ser que nadie oyera tu discurso.
9. Él se porta como si tuviera tres años.
10. No creo que él estudiara anoche.
11. Él espera que te lavaras las manos antes de comer.
12. Puede ser que ella no quisiera sacar nuestra foto.
13. Es un milagro que la aerolínea no perdiera tu equipaje.
14. ¿Es posible que dejaras tus llaves en el carro?
15. Es increíble que nacieras el mismo día que yo.

ejercicio   III-3-3

1. Si yo tuviera un martillo, martillaría en la mañana.
2. Ella no se casaría con él si fuera el último hombre en la Tierra.
3. ¿Qué harías si yo cantara desafinadamente?
4. ¿Si supieras la respuesta, nos la dirías?
5. Si las jirafas no tuvieran cuellos largos, no podrían comer las hojas.
6. Si no fuera por la gravedad, flotaríamos como burbujas.
7. Los osos no comerían tu comida si la colgaras de un árbol.
8. Si Pinocho no mintiera tanto, la gente lo creería de vez en cuando.
9. Si no hubiera carros, no habría tanta contaminación.
10. Si él no fuera tan perezoso, yo lo contrataría.
11. Si no lloviera, podríamos dar un paseo por el parque.
12. Si no hiciera tanto frío, iría en bicicleta al trabajo.
13. Este anillo valdría mucho más dinero si el diamante fuera genuino.
14. Si mi coche (carro) arrancara en este tiempo, sería un milagro.
15. Si los cerdos pudieran volar, ¿adónde irían?

ejercicio   III-3-4

1. Él habla como si fuera el mismo Daniel Webster.
2. En tu situación, yo actuaría como si no supiera nada.
3. Ella habla como si fuera la dueña de esta compañía.
4. Bailamos como si fuéramos Fred Astaire y Ginger Rogers.
5. Él gasta dinero como si no hubiera un mañana.
6. Te ves como si vieras un fantasma.
7. Él se ve como si perdiera a su mejor amigo.
8. El crítico se ve como si le gustara el drama.
9. Cantas como si tragaras un pájaro (un ave).
10. Fue como si no pudiera recordar nada.
11. Él se sintió como si ya la conociera.
12. Ella vivía cada día como si fuera el último.
13. Él me habló como si yo no tuviera cerebro.
14. Ella se veía como si perdiera mucho peso.
15. Fumabas como si fueras una chimenea.

ejercicio   III-3-5

1. Yo quisiera una limonada fría, por favor.
2. ¿Qué quisieras hacer esta noche?
3. ¿Si pudieras, echarías al correo estas cartas para mí?
4. ¿Si pudieras, me harías un favor?
5. Quisiéramos una habitación con una vista al río.
6. ¿Si pudieras, te moverías un poco a la derecha?
7. ¿Adónde quisieras ir para tu luna de miel?
8. ¿Dónde quisierais cenar mañana por la noche?
9. La Reina quisiera hablar.
10. ¿Si pudieras, te callarías, por favor?
11. ¿Qué quisieran hacer esta tarde?
12. Quisiéramos patinar sobre ruedas en el centro comercial.

13. ¿Si pudiera, me prepararía una taza de café?
14. ¿Si pudiera, me llevaría a su líder?
15. ¿Quisieras comer estas moscas cubiertas con chocolate?

1. (Yo) quisiera que no estuvieras tan nervioso/a.
2. Quisiéramos que estuvieras aquí.
3. (Yo) quisiera que hubiera una máquina que pudiera lavar y secar la ropa al mismo tiempo.
4. (Yo) quisiera que no tuvieras que oír esto.
5. Juana quisiera que su esposo no mirara tanta televisión.
6. Los niños siempre quisieran ser mayores y los adultos menores.
7. (Yo) quisiera hablar español con soltura.
8. Él quisiera poder manejar.
9. Él quisiera poder ver a través de las paredes.
10. (Yo) quisiera que no estuviéramos detrás de los caballos en el desfile.
11. (Yo) quisiera ganar más dinero.
12. (Yo) quisiera que nevara.
13. Quisiéramos que se fueran a su casa.
14. (Yo) quisiera que no hubiera calorías en el helado.
15. Luisa quisiera no tener que pagar impuestos.

En "El Mago de Oz", todo el mundo quisiera que su vida fuera diferente. El Espantapájaros quisiera tener cerebro. El Hombre de Estaño quisiera tener corazón. El León quisiera ser valiente. Toto quisiera que los monos volantes desaparecieran. El árbol quisiera que la gente no comiera sus manzanas. El mago quisiera ser mago y la bruja quisiera dos cosas: tener los zapatos de Dorotea y poder tolerar mejor el agua. Sobre todo, Dorotea quisiera estar en Kansas.

Unit 4: The Future Perfect

ejercicio   III-4-1

1. En dos semanas, habré vivido aquí (por) cuatro años.
2. Para el año que viene, McDonald's habrá vendido otro billón de hamburguesas.
3. Ella no habrá preparado la cena para las cinco y media.
4. ¿Cuándo habrán terminado el trabajo?
5. Nos habremos conocido por doce años este agosto.
6. ¿Habréis planchado vuestros vestidos para esta tarde?
7. ¿Habrás lavado toda esta ropa para esta noche?
8. Él no habrá abierto la farmacia para entonces.
9. Tenemos que ir ahora; si vamos más tarde, ellos ya se habrán ido.
10. Si das toda la comida al perro, la habrá comido toda para mañana.
11. No necesitas preocuparte: Estoy seguro/a que para este momento se lo habrán dicho todo.
12. Supongo que todos se habrán acostado para la medianoche.

13. A este paso, habrás frito más patatas (papas) que McDonald's para el fin de la semana.

14. Si pierdes esta elección, habrás perdido más elecciones que nadie.

15. Si ganas esta elección, habrás probado que es posible engañar a toda la gente todo el tiempo.

ejercicio   III-4-2

1. Fernando me habrá enviado estas flores.
2. Él habrá pagado nuestra cuenta. ¡Qué amable!
3. Fido habrá robado estas zapatillas.
4. ¿Adónde se habrá ido mi perrito?
5. Abdul parece bien enfadado (enojado); Farrah le habrá dicho todo.
6. ¡La cocina huele muy mal! Dorotea habrá preparado la cena otra vez.
7. ¡Eso es una mentira! Lo habrás oído de Roque.
8. ¿Cómo sabe él estas cosas? Él habrá leído mi diario.
9. ¿Cuándo habrá ocurrido esto?
10. Arturo habrá sabido que María quemó todas sus cartas de amor.
11. Habrás sabido que él estaba casado.
12. Habré estado loco/a para comprar vitaminas por teléfono.
13. Los osos habrán comido nuestra comida.
14. Habrá sido terrible descubrir que las cucarachas eran los dueños verdaderos de tu casa.
15. Ella te habrá dado un falso número de teléfono.

traducción   III-4-3

¡No puedo creerlo! Para finales de mes habré pagado esta casa completamente. Nunca pensaba que esto ocurriría. Creía que o me mudaría o me moriría antes de hacer ese último cheque miserable. Cuando haga ese último cheque, tomando en consideración todo el interés que he pagado, habré comprado esta casa casi tres veces. De ahora en un año, supongo que habré olvidado que el banco tenía más de esta casa que yo por muchos años y el banco habrá olvidado que yo existí una vez. Habré estado loco/a para creer que una hipoteca de cuarenta años me haría sentir como si fuera un adulto/a maduro/a. Sólo me hacía sentir pobre. En dos años, habré ahorrado miles de dólares y tomado por lo menos dos largas vacaciones. Quisiera estar en Tahití ahora mismo.

Unit 5: The Conditional Perfect

ejercicio   III-5-1

1. Te habría llamado, pero mi teléfono no funciona.
2. Él habría ido al cine con nosotros, pero le dolía la cabeza.
3. ¿Me habrías dicho la respuesta si la supieras?
4. Te habríamos dado un pedazo más grande de pastel si no estuvieras a dieta.
5. Sherlock Holmes es la única persona que habría sabido quién robó los diamantes.
6. Él me habría contratado si hablara español.
7. ¿Habríais ido a la playa si no lloviera?
8. Habríamos invitado a los Jones, pero la última vez que estuvieron aquí se enfermaron.
9. ¿Qué habrías hecho si no tuvieras tu tarjeta de crédito?

10. Yo habría comprado el vestido si fuera una talla más pequeña.

11. Si ella no fuera tan egoísta, te habría ayudado.

12. Me habría puesto a dieta, pero no tengo voluntad.

13. Yo habría hecho la cena, pero estaba de mal humor.

14. Él habría cambiado la bombilla, pero no había nadie para girar la escalera.

15. Él habría entregado su tarea, pero su perro la comió.

 **ejercicio   III-5-2**

1. (Yo) habría llevado el anillo solamente dos o tres veces antes del robo.

2. ¿Dónde habría escondido ella el dinero?

3. Habría sido la una de la mañana cuando sonó el teléfono.

4. Habría sido julio o agosto cuando te conocí porque hacía mucho calor.

5. Nunca habrían conocido a nadie como tú.

6. Habría sido noviembre cuando compré esto porque recuerdo que había pavos en todas partes.

7. ¿Nos habrían mentido?

8. Habría sido un martes cuando nos conocimos porque ese día todo el mundo estaba votando.

9. Habría sido febrero cuando recibí esta carta porque había una tarjeta para el Día de los Enamorados dentro del sobre.

10. No habrían estudiado mucho.

11. Habrían sido las cuatro de la mañana cuando Barbarita regresó de su cita con Ken.

12. Habría sido el cuatro de julio porque yo tenía puesta una camiseta roja, blanca y azul.

13. Habría sido un día de fiesta porque la oficina de correos estaba cerrada.

14. ¿Quién habría dejado esos zapatos en la carretera?

15. ¿Por qué habría puesto Pedro a su esposa dentro de una calabaza?

traducción   III-5-3

Ayer, mientras caminaba (estaba caminando) por el parque, encontré una caja llena de dinero. Al principio, estuve feliz, porque, pues, ¿quién no estaría feliz en esta situación? Pero después de un rato empecé (comencé) a preocuparme, y decidí llevar la caja a la estación de policía. Anoche les pregunté a algunos de mis amigos lo que habrían hecho ellos. John me dijo que habría comprado un coche (carro) nuevo—había por lo menos diez mil dólares. Ana me dijo que ella habría donado el dinero a la caridad. Roberto me dijo que él habría dejado sola la caja y habría salido del parque inmediatamente. ¿Qué habrías hecho tú?

Unit 6: The Present Perfect Subjunctive

 **ejercicio   III-6-1**

1. Espero que el gato no haya comido mi carpa dorada.

2. Es improbable que nadie aquí haya conducido (manejado) un Rolls Royce.

3. No creo que esas personas en Michigan hayan visto a Elvis.

4. No has vivido hasta que hayas visto el Gran Cañón.

5. ¿Conoces a alguien que haya leído todos los dramas de Shakespeare?

6. El jurado duda que el acusado haya dicho la verdad.

7. Es increíble que nadie haya encontrado el dinero que enterramos (habíamos enterrado) en el jardín de casa.

8. Podéis bailar después de que la banda haya comenzado a tocar.

9. Es un milagro que el banco le haya prestado dinero.

10. Puede ser que ellos nunca hayan aprendido a leer.

11. Es ridículo que yo haya tenido que esperar en esta cola por más de una hora.

12. No podemos ir hasta que todos hayan votado.

13. Esperamos que usted haya gozado de su estancia aquí.

14. ¿Hay alguien en el mundo que no haya leído *The Cat in the Hat?*

15. Busco un estudiante que nunca haya suspendido (reprobado) un examen.

ejercicio   III-6-2

1. No contrataré a nadie que haya conseguido su diploma del fondo de un tabloide.

2. ¿Qué harás después que hayas vencido todos tus temores?

3. Después (de) que hayamos contado nuestro dinero, lo depositaremos en el banco.

4. El programa comenzará cuando hayan llegado.

5. Él no te dirá nada hasta que le hayas pagado.

6. Tan pronto como hayas puesto la mesa, cenaremos.

7. Traeré una ensalada a la fiesta en caso de que el anfitrión no haya preparado bastante comida.

8. Él no se acostará hasta que se haya cepillado los dientes.

9. Nunca conocerás la verdadera felicidad hasta que hayas aparecido en el *Programa de Oprah Winfrey.*

10. Él nunca podrá correr una milla en cuatro minutos hasta que haya dejado de fumar.

11. ¿Qué haremos después (de) que hayamos gastado todo nuestro dinero?

12. No beberé leche que haya estado en el mostrador todo el día.

13. No tomaremos ninguna decisión financiera hasta que hayamos pagado los impuestos de este año.

14. El Capitán Kirk irá a donde ningún hombre haya ido antes.

15. Tan pronto como él haya tomado esta medicina, se sentirá mejor.

traducción   III-6-3

"Es estupendo que hayas ahorrado tanto dinero con todas estas semillas pero, ¿qué harás el año que viene cuando no haya crecido nada?" Esto es lo que quisiera decirle a mi vecino que frecuentemente "pasa sobre un dólar para recoger diez centavos". El año pasado invirtió tres mil dólares en una pequeña compañía absurda que hace acondicionadores para casas de perros. Puedo oírle ahora: "En dos años, cuando este país por fin se haya dado cuenta de que los perros también tienen calor en (el) verano, habré ganado muchos miles de dólares con esta inversión." Eso fue lo último que oí de esa empresa. Continúo rezando para que él haya escarmentado, pero temo que siempre sea así.

Unit 7: The Pluperfect Subjunctive

ejercicio   III-7-1

1. (Yo) no estaba seguro/a de que ellos me hubieran oído.

2. Juan esperaba que los estudiantes hubieran estudiado la lección.

3. Fue una lástima que el fontanero no hubiera arreglado el desagüe.

4. Les escribimos una carta en caso de que no nos hubieran entendido.

5. ¿Fue posible que ellos nunca hubieran oído de Leo Tolstoy?

6. Actuaban como si nunca se hubieran conocido antes.
7. Él no creyó que yo hubiera dicho tal cosa.
8. Fue improbable que ella hubiera pagado el coche (carro) al contado.
9. No había nadie en la fiesta que hubiera viajado alrededor del mundo.
10. (Yo) no creía nunca que ella hubiera sido Miss América.
11. Él se negó a hablar hasta que hubiéramos cerrado las puertas.
12. Le envié un telegrama en caso de que él todavía no hubiera oído las buenas noticias.
13. Fue trágico que el jardinero—no el criado—lo hubiera hecho.
14. Ella siempre dudaba que él hubiera sido honrado con ella.
15. No había nadie en la casa que se hubiera levantado antes de las diez y media.

ejercicio III-7-2

1. Si (yo) hubiera leído este libro antes, no habría hecho (cometido) tantos errores en mi vida.
2. Si Bárbara hubiera sabido la verdad acerca de Ken, ¿se habría casado con él?
3. Si nos hubieras advertido de los terremotos, no habríamos construido nuestra casa en este área.
4. Habría sido bueno si hubieras incluido una foto con este artículo.
5. Si me hubieras llamado diez minutos antes, (yo) no habría estado en casa.
6. No sé dónde estaría si no te hubiera conocido.
7. Si hubiera habido una onza de verdad en tu discurso, alguien te habría creído.
8. Si hubieras nacido dos días antes, habríamos tenido el mismo cumpleaños.
9. Si no hubiera habido una nevada ayer, habría habido una hoy.
10. Si hubiéramos sabido que tenías dificultades, te habríamos ofrecido ayuda.
11. Si no me hubieras dado estas manoplas, creo que me habría muerto de frío.
12. Si no hubieras puesto otro sello en esa carta, la oficina de correos no la habría aceptado.
13. Si alguien me hubiera dicho eso, no lo habría creído.
14. Si no hubieras dado a tu carpa dorada tanta comida, no se habría muerto.
15. ¿Cómo se habrían sentido si no hubieras recibido una invitación?

ejercicio III-7-3

1. Yo quisiera que él hubiera estudiado más en la escuela secundaria.
2. ¿Quisieras que él hubiera cumplido su palabra?
3. Él quisiera que no hubiera comido tanto.
4. Quisiéramos que nos hubieras dicho que esto sería una fiesta formal.
5. Yo quisiera que no hubiéramos almorzado aquí.
6. Él quisiera que hubiera ahorrado más dinero.
7. Yo quisiera que me hubiera probado estos pantalones antes de comprarlos.
8. Yo quisiera que no hubieras frito estas salchichas en manteca.
9. ¿Quisierais que hubiera habido más variedad en el programa?
10. Yo quisiera que no hubiera llovido en mi desfile.
11. ¿A veces quisieras que hubieras nacido en otro siglo?
12. Yo quisiera que hubiera apagado las luces hace tres horas.
13. Yo quisiera que no hubiera hecho tanto frío.
14. Quisiéramos que nos hubieran dicho algo acerca de las cucarachas en este hotel.
15. Yo quisiera que no hubieras puesto tanta canela en este té.

traducción | **III-7-4**

Si yo hubiera tenido más cuidado, no estaría en esta oficina disputando esta multa de aparcamiento. Yo pensé que era extraño que hubiera un aparcamiento directamente enfrente del teatro cinco minutos antes de que comenzara el drama pero, ¿quién soy yo para cuestionar tan buena suerte? De hecho, había un letrero que decía "Prohibido Estacionar" a dos pies de mi coche, pero un hombre muy alto estaba de pie enfrente, bloqueando la vista, no—nadie creería eso. Había una mujer vendiendo globos y no pude ver el letrero por los globos, por eso, si alguien va a tener que pagar esta multa, ella debe pagarla—nadie creerá eso tampoco. La verdad es que me doy cuenta de que si yo le hubiera dicho a alguien alguna de estas historias absurdas, tendría que pagar más de lo que probablemente debo ahora. ¿Dónde está la oficina del cajero?

Unit 8: The Passive Voice

ejercicio | **III-8-1**

1. vende   2. venden   3. juega   4. juegan   5. mira   6. cultiva   7. cultivan   8. construyen   9. debe   10. puede

ejercicio | **III-8-2**

1. Se habla francés.
2. Se habla japonés.
3. Se habla alemán.
4. Se habla portugués.
5. Se hablan suizo, italiano, alemán y francés.
6. Se habla ruso.
7. Se hablan inglés y francés.
8. Se habla inglés.

ejercicio | **III-8-3**

1. No se puede comprar un buen puro hoy en día por menos de dos dólares.
2. Se toma vino blanco con el pollo y el pescado.
3. Se dice que el café colombiano es el mejor.
4. Se necesita tener cuidado cuando se maneja en una tormenta de nieve.
5. ¿Cómo se dice "perro" en francés?
6. Se habla portugués en Brasil. (En Brasil se habla portugués.)
7. ¿Dónde se escribe que el Presidente tiene que ser un hombre?
8. Si se maneja como un loco, te darán una multa.
9. Se dice que el cerdo es más inteligente que el caballo.
10. Siempre se pierde mucho tiempo en estas reuniones.
11. Si se mantiene correctamente, un carro durará veinte años.
12. Nunca se llevan zapatos blancos después del primero de septiembre.
13. Si se hace ejercicio y se come menos, se adelgazará.

14. ¿Adónde se va en esta ciudad para una buena hamburguesa?
15. Si se puede poner un hombre en la luna, ¿por qué no se puede fabricar un carro que dure más de cinco años?

ejercicio   III-8-4

1. ¿Cuándo se sacaron estas fotos?
2. ¿Dónde se hizo tu sofá?
3. Se vendía el pan por cinco centavos la barra.
4. Se pintó la casa el año pasado.
5. Había tanto ruido en el restaurante que no se podía pensar.
6. Quería que se entregaran las flores para las cuatro y media.
7. No se podía oír nada; todos hablaban al mismo tiempo.
8. La fiesta fue un desastre. No se había arreglado la sala.
9. Se podía fumar en todas partes; ahora se puede fumar solamente fuera del edificio.
10. Se publicará el libro el año que viene.
11. Se descubrió el elemento por casualidad.
12. No se había pintado la casa durante cincuenta años.
13. Se cerrarán las puertas a las once y media.
14. Si se haya visto un castillo, se han visto todos.
15. No se ha vivido hasta que se haya oído a Van Morrison cantar "Gloria".

ejercicio   III-8-5

1. El drama *Romeo y Julieta* fue escrito por William Shakespeare.
2. Muchas casas nuevas fueron construidas después de la Segunda Guerra Mundial.
3. Los folletos serán repartidos por voluntarios mañana.
4. Estas galletitas fueron hechas por duendes.
5. El niño consentido fue dado demasiados juguetes por sus padres.
6. Los neumáticos fueron acuchillados por vándalos.
7. La televisión será puesta cuando Juan entre en esta casa.
8. Esta colcha fue cosida completamente a mano.
9. Las puertas serán abiertas y cerradas por guardias armados.
10. La hierba fue sembrada por Martín.
11. Estas cuentas habrían sido pagadas por Juan, pero él perdió el talonario de cheques.
12. Cuando yo era joven, mis clases siempre eran enseñadas por excelentes profesores.
13. Espero que mi casa sea comprada por una persona agradable.
14. Espero que este lío no fuera hecho por ratones.
15. El himno nacional fue cantado por mi vecino antes del partido.

traducción   III-8-6

Después del Super Bowl, el lanzador ganador fue entrevistado por un reportero para ver cómo se sentía. Esto es lo que él dijo: "Pues, se trabaja duro todo el año y se entrena cada día. Claro que se espera algo como esto, pero se sabe que es sólo un sueño, y entonces se ganan muchos partidos, pero sólo porque se tienen estupendos compañeros, y se está verdaderamente feliz. Pero no se está preparado para un día como éste. Se despierta y se sabe que éste es el día más importante de la vida y se piensa que se tiene la oportunidad de ganar, pero no se puede estar demasiado seguro. Por eso, se reza. Y se juega lo mejor posible y se espera que se gane. Y cuando se gana, es lo más maravilloso que se ha sentido en la vida, y cuando se pregunta categóricamente cómo se siente, se encubre completamente toda la situación y se habla en la voz pasiva."

LANGUAGE AND REFERENCE BOOKS

Dictionaries and References
VOX Spanish and English Dictionaries
Cervantes-Walls Spanish and English Dictionary
Klett German and English Dictionary
Klett Super-Mini German & English Dictionary
The New Schöffler-Weis German & English Dictionary
NTC's New College French & English Dictionary
NTC's New College Greek & English Dictionary
Zanichelli New College Italian & English Dictionary
Zanichelli Super-Mini Italian & English Dictionary
NTC's Beginner's Dictionaries (Spanish and English,
    French and English, Italian and English)
NTC's Dictionary of Spanish False Cognates
Teach Yourself Dictionaries (Dutch, Esperanto, Swahili,
    Welsh)
NTC's Dictionary of German False Cognates
NTC's Dictionary of Faux Amis
NTC's Dictionary of French Faux Pas
NTC's American Idioms Dictionary
NTC's Dictionary of American Slang and Colloquial
    Expressions
Forbidden American English
Essential American Idioms
Contemporary American Slang
Everyday American English Dictionary
Everyday American Phrases in Content
Beginner's Dictionary of American English Usage
NTC's Dictionary of Grammar Terminology
Robin Hyman's Dictionary of Quotations
Guide to Better English Spelling
303 Dumb Spelling Mistakes
NTC's Dictionary of Literary Terms
The Writer's Handbook
Diccionario Inglés
El Diccionario Básico Norteamericano
British/American Language Dictionary
The French-Speaking World
The Spanish-Speaking World
Guide to Spanish Idioms
Guide to German Idioms
Guide to French Idioms
Au courant
Al corriente
Guide to Correspondence in Spanish
Guide to Correspondence in French
Guide to Correspondence in German
Español para los Hispanos
Business Russian
Yes! You Can Learn a Foreign Language
Japanese in Plain English
Korean in Plain English
Easy Chinese Phrasebook and Dictionary
Easy Russian Phrase Book and Dictionary
Japan Today!
Everything Japanese
Easy Hiragana
Easy Katakana
Easy Kana Workbook
NTC's New Japanese-English Character Dictionary
The Wiedza Powszechna Compact Polish & English
    Dictionary
NTC's Bulgarian and English Dictionary

Picture Dictionaries
English; French; Spanish; German
Let's Learn...Picture Dictionaries
English, Spanish, French, German, Italian

Verb References
Complete Handbook of Spanish Verbs
Complete Handbook of Italian Verbs
Complete Handbook of Russian Verbs
Spanish Verb Drills
French Verb Drills
German Verb Drills
Italian Verb Drills

Grammar References
Spanish Verbs and Essentials of Grammar
Nice 'n Easy Spanish Grammar
Nueva Gramática Comunicativa
French Verbs and Essentials of Grammar
French Reference Grammar
Nice 'n Easy French Grammar
German Verbs and Essentials of Grammar
Nice 'n Easy German Grammar
Italian Verbs and Essentials of Grammar
Essentials of Russian Grammar
Portuguese Verbs and Essentials of Grammar
Japanese Verbs and Essentials of Grammar
Hungarian Verbs and Essentials of Grammar
Essentials of English Grammar
Roots of the Russian Language
Reading and Translating Contemporary Russian
Essentials of Latin Grammar
Swedish Verbs and Essentials of Grammar
Teach Yourself Grammars (French, German, Italian,
    Spanish)

Welcome to...Books
Spain, France, Ancient Greece, Ancient Rome

"By Association" Series
Spanish, French, German, Italian

Language Programs: Audio and Video
Just Listen 'n Learn: Spanish, French, Italian, German,
    Greek
Just Listen 'n Learn PLUS: Spanish, French, German
Speak French
Speak Spanish
Speak German
Practice & Improve Your...Spanish, French, Italian,
    German
Practice & Improve Your...Spanish PLUS, French
    PLUS, Italian PLUS, German PLUS
Improve Your...Spanish, French, Italian, German: The
    P & I Method
Conversational...in 7 Days: Spanish, French, German,
    Italian, Portuguese, Greek, Russian, Japanese, Thai,
    Arabic
Teach Yourself Language Courses (Over 40 languages)
Everyday Japanese
Japanese for Children
Nissan's Business Japanese
Contemporary Business Japanese
Basic French Conversation
Basic Spanish Conversation
Everyday Hebrew
VideoPassport in French and Spanish
The French Experience
Italianissimo
How to Pronounce Russian Correctly
How to Pronounce Spanish Correctly
How to Pronounce French Correctly

How to Pronounce Italian Correctly
How to Pronounce Japanese Correctly
L'Express: Aujourd'hui la France
Der Spiegel: Aktuelle Themen in der Bundesrepublik
    Deutschland
Listen and Say It Right in English
Once Upon a Time in Spanish, French, German
Let's Sing & Learn in French & Spanish
I Can Sing ¡en español!
I Can Sing en français!

"Just Enough" Phrase Books
Chinese, Dutch, French, German, Greek, Hebrew,
    Hungarian, Italian, Japanese, Portuguese, Russian,
    Scandinavian, Serbo-Croat, Spanish
Business French, Business German, Business Spanish

BBC Phrase Books
Spanish, French, Italian, German, Arabic, Turkish

Destination Phrase Books
Spanish, French, German, Italian

Language Game and Humor Books
Easy French Vocabulary Games
Easy French Crossword Puzzles
Easy French Word Games and Puzzles
Easy French Grammar Puzzles
Easy Spanish Word Power Games
Easy Spanish Crossword Puzzles
Easy Spanish Vocabulary Puzzles
Easy French Word Games and Puzzles
Easy French Culture Games
Easy German Crossword Puzzles
Easy Italian Crossword Puzzles
Let's Learn about Series: Italy, France, Germany, Spain,
    America
Let's Learn Coloring Books in Spanish, French,
    German, Italian, English
Let's Learn...Spanish, French, German, Italian, English
    Coloring Book-Audiocassette Package
My World in...Coloring Books: Spanish, French,
    German, Italian
French Culture Coloring Book
German à la Cartoon
Spanish à la Cartoon
French à la Cartoon
Italian à la Cartoon
101 American English Idioms
101 French Idioms
101 Spanish Idioms
101 Japanese Idioms
El alfabeto
L'alphabet

Getting Started Books
Introductory language books in Spanish, French,
    German, Italian

Ticket to...Series
France, Germany, Spain, Italy (Guide and audiocas-
    sette)

Getting to Know...Series
France, Germany, Spain, Italy, Mexico, United States

PASSPORT BOOKS
a division of *NTC Publishing Group*
Lincolnwood, Illinois USA